AF521849

Painting with Metro

Painting with METRO

How a Crippled Racehorse Rescued Himself (and Me) with a Paintbrush

Ron Krajewski
with Susy Flory

NEW HORIZON PRESS
Far Hills, New Jersey

Requests for permission should be addressed to:
New Horizon Press
P. O. Box 669
Far Hills, NJ 07931

Ron Krajewski with Susy Flory
Painting with Metro:
How a Crippled Racehorse Rescued Himself (and Me) with a Paintbrush

Cover photo: Wendy Wooley, PeepsandPaws.com
Cover design: Charley Nasta
Interior design: Scribe Inc.

Library of Congress Control Number: 2015913635

ISBN-13 (hc): 978–0-88282–512–0
ISBN-13 (eBook): 978–0-88282–513–7

New Horizon Press

Manufactured in the U.S.A.

20 19 18 17 16 1 2 3 4 5

Authors' Note

In order to protect the privacy of various individuals,
some names and identifying details
have been changed.

Dedication

For Wendy:
Thanks for taking this journey with me.

Table of Contents

Acknowledgments

Thanks to my family, Darrell and Kathy Krajewski, Randi Mahler, Troy Krajewski, Ava and Peyton Mahler. I am grateful to Kim Brokaw for giving me more years with Metro and to Ed O'Neill and Kate Kershner for providing good homes for our Metro and Pork Chop. Esther Bell is the best lawyer a horse ever had. Kudos to Metro's supporters in the media, Susan Salk, Jason Bristol, Jill Rappaport and the WJLA News team. I thank Susy Flory for turning Metro's story into something special. I want to acknowledge Wendell and Jane Martin, Gallery 30, Sandy Zeigler, Susan Kerestes and Adams County Winery. I appreciate Dot Morgan and New Vocations Racehorse Adoption Program for all you do for horses. Special thanks to Wendy for being the best partner a guy could ever have. And thanks, Metro, for the ride.

—Ron Krajewski

My thanks to Wendy Krajewski for reading *Thunder Dog* and convincing Ron to look me up so I could meet you, Ron, Pork Chop and Metro. Thanks to Ron for the privilege of helping you tell your story and for making Teddy and me feel at home (and for letting Teddy paint with Metro, a once-in-a-lifetime experience). Thanks to Chip for connecting us with New Horizon Press and to Joan Dunphy and Charley Nasta for helping us share Metro's story with the world. A big thank you to our faithful readers group: Joe Elliott, Susan Pratt, Lori Harvest, Leanne Bush, Holly Rich, Maureta Ott, Renea Govekar, Esther Bell, Kelly Jo Gardner, Mary Perry, Eileen Grafton, Anne Campbell and Tina Hopkins. I so appreciate the kindness of Metro's friends who agreed to interviews: Linda Rice, Dave Engel, Rick Benas, Gus Schoenborn, Dave Lupo, Kim Brokaw, Dot Morgan and Glenn Thompson. Finally, a special and grateful thank you to my writers group and my family. I couldn't have done it without you!

—*Susy Flory*

Foreword

Ron and Metro's relationship embodies the very reason why I founded New Vocations Racehorse Adoption Program in 1992. Retired racehorses were being randomly discarded by the thousands, yet I knew from my experience as a trainer's wife and an equestrian that these horses had so much to offer. They are intelligent, capable athletes with an abundance of training. However, these facts were obscured by the perception that racehorses are crazy and runaways. With no one to represent them, to herald their versatility, beauty and courage, vast numbers were dumped in junk sales to an often tragic fate.

Ron saw the potential in Metro and came to his aid. Metro likewise came to Ron's aid. That's usually the way it is with these wise war horses. They may not speak our language, but they know us inside and out. Genuine time and devotion yielded rich rewards for both Ron and Metro.

Metro's story raises the question: What exactly is the future for a retired racehorse with no apparent useful skill to offer? In the beginning, each Thoroughbred or Standardbred foal is a potential star in its owner's eyes. The young horse goes into training and eventually starts racing. Dreams and visions of glory abound! But the day comes when the horse is no longer competitive, the vision fades and the dream dies. The former "star" leaves the track, often injured and thin. Without a safety net, many are still subject to being slaughtered.

In the compelling pages ahead, you will learn how Metro avoided that fate and, through the guidance of his devoted human, is helping hundreds of retired racehorses get the rehabilitation and skills needed to lead purposeful lives beyond the track. Beginning with the sale of Metro's very first painting, Ron Krajewski has dedicated and faithfully given 50 percent of the proceeds to New Vocations for its racehorse adoption efforts. Through this funding and the support of so many others, New Vocations is rehabilitating fractured knees and ankles, torn tendons and ligaments, and stressed-out minds and bodies. It is providing crucial vocational training to help ensure success in new careers and is finding qualified, loving homes where each horse can be a star once again.

New Vocations has placed over 6,000 retired racehorses, each with a unique story. The proceeds from Metro Meteor's work go primarily toward injured racehorses, those that would be cost-prohibitive to rehabilitate were it not for Ron's generous donations. One such horse is the sweet young mare Fast Double G, who arrived in

November of 2013 with a fractured knee. X-rays revealed a good prognosis if the injury was surgically repaired. However, surgery with the subsequent rehabilitation and healing time is a daunting expense for a charity. Dr. Patty Hogan generously donated her services, and then Metro Meteor's art proceeds covered the entire rehabilitation, including nine months of board.

Now, Fast Double G is enjoying life without limitations. Adopted by Susan Marshall, the former racehorse resides at a luxurious dressage facility where schooling is overseen by an Olympic competitor. "I'm absolutely in love with this mare," Marshall said. "She's incredibly balanced and correct, yet so very gentle. She follows us around like a puppy and lets the children climb all over her."

Fast Double G and so many others like her have directly benefited from Ron and Metro's ongoing donations. Each painting and associated item sold contributes to the healing, training and placement of these noble warriors. Every horse that finds a home makes room for another to get a home and then another. Enjoy Ron and Metro's journey, knowing that they are truly providing a gift that keeps on giving.

—Dot Morgan

Executive Director, New Vocations Racehorse Adoption Program
Harness Tracks of America Distinguished Service Award, 2005
Thoroughbred Charities of America Industry Service Award, 2008
United States Trotting Association President's Award, 2010
United States Harness Writers Unsung Hero Award, 2012
www.NewVocations.org, a 501 (c) (3) public charity

Introduction

Always Metro

The first time I saw Metro Meteor, I noticed his eyes. While the other horses had big, soft brown eyes, Metro's had a ring of white. His eyes were intense, like he was here for a purpose. If I were a betting man, I'd have left immediately to go place some money on Metro, but I didn't want to leave. I couldn't. I wanted to stand there and watch him put on his show.

He was dancing in the paddock, something the big, athletic Thoroughbreds do when they know they're moments away from the track. Racehorses are bred to compete, with trainers taking advantage of their natural fight-or-flight response and turning it into a drive to be out in front of the herd. When it's race time, somehow racehorses get taller and lighter on their feet, tail and head lifted high. The good ones do, anyway.

Then I noticed Metro's color. I didn't know what color *bay* was, but the artist in me saw colors I was familiar with. Metro was Burnt Umber, accented by Burnt Sienna on the parts of his body warmed by the sun. He had three Titanium White legs, with the fourth leg Ebony Black. His glossy mane matched the long black tail that seemed to rise like a flag every time he snorted. A white blaze made up of two separate patches of white was held together by a pencil-thin strip. The lower part of his blaze almost looked like a white necktie, dropping down to a point between his flared nostrils and just above his upper lip.

But that was five years ago in a different time. Metro Meteor's time. Today he's just Metro, and it's time to paint. At home, I had picked through my old acrylic paints and found a tube of Bronze Yellow I had purchased long before Metro ever picked up a paintbrush. It's the perfect color for the piece Metro and I started yesterday. I'm excited to get to it.

"Metro," I call out as I walk into the barn.

This has always been my favorite part of life with Metro—calling his name, only to have him answer back in his best Scooby Doo-style nicker.

He never fails to respond. Metro makes me feel special every time I enter the barn. If he didn't have a second career as a painter, he'd have made a top notch Walmart greeter. But, for some reason, today he's not answering.

I walk past Tommy's stall, then Pork Chop's, before rounding the corner toward Metro's. The overhead lights are out but the afternoon sun floods the barn. Metro's stall is dark and he isn't inside.

Silhouetted against the light is a much older horse, maybe twenty-five or thirty.

Who is this?

This horse is almost pure black; I can't see any color. But what I do notice is how the horse is standing: The poor old guy is backed into the corner, using the walls on either side of his rear end to hold himself upright. He is leaning on the walls with front legs extended. His left front leg is angled slightly outward, while the right is pushed up and out, the tip of the front hoof touching the wood shavings on the floor.

What horse is this in Metro's stall? Where is Metro? I stand looking at the strange horse for a few seconds while my eyes adjust. Then the darkness rolls back slightly and the horse's markings come into focus. I see the familiar titanium white socks and double blaze.

"Metro?" Still no answer. "Metro?!"

Nothing. I stand there not knowing what to do. This old horse must be Metro. I know it now, although he looks much older than his twelve years. A wave of panic begins to engulf me. Metro hasn't answered and he hasn't moved. But he *is* standing, albeit supported by two walls.

Maybe he's not moving because he can't *move.*

What should I do? Run to the lower barn for help? Call the vet? I'm gripped by the fear that the day I've been dreading has finally arrived. If it is, it's been weighing on my mind for the past few years. Metro is immobile and there's nothing I can do for him. I'd always been afraid of finding Metro lying in the pasture, unable to get to his feet. But I never thought I would find him upright, supported by the walls and unable to move.

Metro has been in a battle with his history since the day that he limped off the track. He should have been retired from racing long before that day. Now his history is rearing up and trampling the hell out of him.

I unlatch the stall guard that stretches across the front doorway and walk in. There is still no movement from my horse.

"Metro," I say again softly.

Suddenly, the horse's head comes up and his ears twitch. He's awake! He must have been in a very deep sleep. He sees me standing there and nickers.

His greeting, usually the highlight of my day, gives me no comfort now. I still need to see if he can walk.

I stand back and wait for him. *Will he limp? Or take a step and fall down?* I've never seen him like this and I don't know what to expect. But he snaps back to life and seems to grow a foot in height as he angles his butt away from the corner, then pulls his front legs back and gathers himself underneath, squaring up. He moves toward me and pushes his nose down toward my hands. I wipe the goop from the corner of his left eye. Horses get sleepy eyes, too.

My breath leaves in a whoosh of relief. I see the horse I know and love, not the thirty-year-old shell of a horse I saw in the darkness just a few moments before. I stand there feeling his breath on my hands and everything seems fine again. Metro is part of the fabric of my life—the last thing I think about before I go to bed and the first thing I think about when I wake up.

"Want to throw some paint around?" I ask my buddy.

I walk out the front of his stall and begin preparing his studio for today's painting session, all while keeping one eye on him. Nothing has changed. It's business as usual with Metro standing at the doorway of his stall, throwing his head up and down. He wants to be let out so he can get a brush in his mouth. I hurry and get him set up in front of the canvas.

As happy and excited as he is, I'm having a hard time feeling the joy. Instead, I'm scared. *Is Metro really happy with his life?* Seeing him backed into a corner, trying to find a position that offers him the most comfort for his arthritic knees, has shaken me. I wonder whether it's worth it to keep him going, this horse whose body is cobbled together by duct tape and pharmaceuticals. *Is he really happy?*

One thing I do know is that painting brings him happiness. I can see it in his eyes as he walks over and stands expectantly in front of his painting, no lead rope needed. He strokes Bronze Yellow across the canvas, reaching up from the field of grass at the bottom to a brilliant blue sky. I begin to feel a little more settled. Metro loves life. I just know it, even if he can't tell me in words. He tells me with his eyes.

Even though he's retired, Metro Meteor is still a racehorse. It's written on his bones and in his heart. He has lived his life fast and on fire. Some days he seems like more jackass than horse. But there are other days, the days when he stands in front of his easel, picks up a paintbrush dipped in bright colors and strokes it across a canvas to make something beautiful. That's when he seems like something more.

Somehow, Metro has stumbled into a second chance career and I've discovered he has the same complicated temperament as some of the great artists. He can be stubborn, opinionated and sometimes just plain cranky. But I gave up trying to change him a long time ago.

He's just Metro.

Chapter 1

He's a Lovely Smelling Boy

"If you've never been crazy about Thoroughbreds,
it's because you've never been around where they are...
and don't know any better. They're beautiful.
There isn't anything as lovely and clean and full of spunk
and honest and everything as some racehorses."
—*Sherwood Anderson, "I Want To Know Why"*

Racehorses are in my blood. Decades before I ever grasped a lead rope or untangled a mane, I loved watching horses with my grandmother from a seat in the grandstands.

I grew up in Seattle. My father worked at Boeing, but I didn't fall in love with airplanes. My grandfather and my uncles spent their summers commercial salmon fishing in Alaska. I didn't fall in love with that, either, although I joined my grandfather on his boat when I was old enough. But before that, I spent summer weekends with my grandmother and that meant going to the racetrack. She was an avid and successful handicapper.

She promised to tell me the secrets of her winning system when she was on her deathbed but not before, because I couldn't be trusted. If her secrets got out, everyone would be betting on *her* horses and driving the odds down.

Grandma was my dad's mother, a half Tlingit Indian from Alaska. She had a big family and I always met new relatives every time I went. Every relative on my dad's side of the family seemed to be in the fishing business, except my dad.

On racing days, Grandma and I got dressed up in our Sunday best. She never left the house without looking perfect. Her shiny black hair flipped up at the ends, like Marlo Thomas in *That Girl*. We could've walked through a hurricane and her hairdo would not have moved. We'd pay our twenty-cent fare and hop on the bus, because she'd never learned to drive. Our bus ride down Capital Hill always included two stops. First was a local bar on Broadway that sold the racing form. Then back on the bus, rolling past Dick's Drive-In. I saw the long line at the walk-up window and I wished that we could stop for a cheeseburger.

Next stop was Grandma's favorite department store, Frederick & Nelson. Grandma loved that store. I loved the Frango Mints, fancy mint-flavored chocolate truffles wrapped individually and sold in a hexagonal box. I could taste them in my mouth as we entered the glass doors. Unfortunately, we weren't there for the mints. Grandma had other things in mind as she invariably dragged me passed the Frango Mint displays to the perfume counter. I hated it, because I knew exactly what was coming next.

"Hold out your arm!" she ordered. Resigned to my fate, I complied and waited for Grandma to douse me with Chanel No. 5 or White Shoulders or some other perfume to see which one she liked. The process left me smelling like the youngest French hooker in Seattle, but my grandmother had a way of getting what she wanted.

When Grandma finally exhausted the patience of her grandson and the perfume counter clerk, we left the glories of the department store and boarded another bus for Longacres racetrack in Renton, sixteen miles south of Seattle. I usually sat in silence with my thoughts for the remainder of the ride.

I was an only child and my parents both had careers and hobbies that didn't involve me. I would see them at dinner, but then they were off to bowling nights, crafting classes and poker games. When I was really young, they'd take me along to the bowling alley and rent me a lane to bowl or a pool table. I was too short to work a pool cue on a full-sized table but I amused myself by rolling the balls into each other. Although I was quiet and introspective, I craved friendship and I remember wanting a brother or a sister like all my classmates seemed to have. It wasn't a bad childhood. I wasn't abused or neglected and I have no complaints. It was just my childhood; I soon learned to function on my own.

I was a picky eater and would only eat cheeseburgers or grilled cheese sandwiches. Since my parents were gone most nights, I fended for myself and could eat whatever I wanted. But when I was with my grandmother, I had to clean my plate no matter what nasty thing was on it. She'd make me sit at a table in the kitchen until I did, which was pretty much never. Many a night I'd sit in the kitchen staring at my cold peas until it was time for bed, while my grandmother sat watching a television program in the living room.

Grandma allowed me to take the bus alone to downtown Seattle when I was just ten years old. Unheard of, these days. I'd usually end up at First Avenue near Pioneer Square, in one of the seediest parts of town. It was filled with lowlifes and porn theaters, but it was also the location of my favorite store, a magic shop filled with gum that made your teeth turn black and pancakes of rubber vomit for practical jokes.

Although I didn't make friends easily, I loved my pets. My favorite dog was a Brittany Spaniel named Butch and we had a close bond. He slept on my bed and we spent a lot of time together. It was much easier for me to hang out with my dog or cat than another kid.

When I got a little older, I asked to stay home when my parents went out so I could watch TV or read my favorite magazine, *Famous Monsters of Filmland.* If the weather was good I played tennis against the garage door or played catch with baseballs as they rolled off the roof of our house. When you are an only child, sometimes a sturdy wall or the slope of a roof are your only playmates.

I had a few friends but didn't make new ones easily and, when we moved, I never kept in touch. I felt no need to. I learned that I didn't need other people to make me happy and I liked being alone. I could do whatever I wanted, whenever I wanted. I was already on my way to being a hermit.

I also learned I could teach myself anything I wanted just by reading a book. I didn't want to depend on anyone else, including my teachers, for anything. If I wanted to learn something, I'd go to the library, check out a book, read it and get my questions answered.

When Grandma and I finally arrived at Longacres, before we climbed out of the bus I would stare at the beautiful, one-mile oval track with brilliant green turf in the center. The track was surrounded by green fields and in the distance were the mountains, with a full view of mighty, white-capped Mount Rainier. Graceful poplar trees lined the track.

My grandmother shared a box with her friend, Irene. But since Irene didn't like kids in her box seats, especially a little kid who smelled like a prostitute, Grandma and I were usually banished to grandstand seats.

I loved collecting handfuls of the losing race tickets that were strewn all over the ground. I sat in the stands while Grandma talked to her friends and I read the horses' names in the programs, matched them to the tickets and tried to determine how much they paid out. I also liked trying to figure out how the horses got their names. Most of the time they were derived from their parents' names, which were also listed.

One time a stranger asked me which horse I would pick for a particular race, then wanted to bet me two dollars my horse wouldn't win. What kind of guy would want to take two dollars from a kid in a bet? I was a child wandering around in an adult world.

I'll never forget my first real bet. The horse's name was Coco's Pal. Grandma took my bet to the window and then Coco's Pal won. He was the favorite and didn't pay much, about enough to buy an extra hot dog. Unlike Grandma, however, I never developed a taste for betting. Somehow the racing form came alive for her. She could see magical patterns that came together and showed her how the race was going to play out. I just saw a tangle of numbers.

But what I *could* see were the horses dancing in front of the starting gate, muscled and gleaming in the Pacific Northwest sunlight, men perched on their backs in bright silk shirts. Then the anxious time, loading into the gates, jostling and rearing and harnessed energy ready to explode. I watched, my stomach clenching as I waited.

Finally, the bell! Gates opening, massive locomotives snorting and blasting out of the gates, then stretching out into long, graceful undulating lines as the pack strung out and drove through the cool air around the oval and toward the finish line. The crowd surged all around me, waving their tickets and yelling out the names of their horses while I reveled in the motion and the spectacle.

All in all, it was definitely worth being doused in perfume.

Chapter 2

Speed Plus Attitude

Metro, Year One

"If everything seems under control,
you're not going fast enough."
—*Mario Andretti*

On March 13, 2003, a new foal entered the world on a chilly spring day in Coxsackie, New York. His mother, Here Comes Nikki, was purchased for $2,500 in a foreclosure sale by Gus Schoenborn, who bought the bargain Thoroughbred for two reasons. He liked that she had placed fourth in a graded stakes race at the age of two, meaning she had matured early. He also liked her pedigree.

Here Comes Nikki had run in eighteen races and won only two. But while she was not a big success as a racehorse, she was a genetic treasure chest with double bloodlines stretching back to a very famous Canadian racehorse named Northern Dancer.

Northern Dancer won the 1964 Kentucky Derby in a record two minutes flat. Later, he went on to win the Queen's Plate, Canada's version of the Derby, by seven and a half lengths. When Northern Dancer died in 1990, his offspring had already banked over twenty million dollars in earnings. The Canadian superstar was also known for his aggressive personality.

When Here Comes Nikki stepped down from the van at Gus Schoenborn's farm in Coxsackie, New York, the first thing he noticed was her eyes. "She had what we would call the white eye, which took me by surprise. She was nervous, too, a little spooky and scared." Then, as the ranch help led her around to stretch her legs after the long drive, Gus noticed her personality. She laid her ears back, a bit aggressive for a mare.

Gus intended to breed Nikki to City Zip, a stallion he'd paid a lot of money for. At the age of two, City Zip was running and winning, earning himself a slot as one of the top two-year-olds for the year 2000. His career winnings eventually totaled over $800,000. When City Zip was ready to retire, Gus decided to go down to Belmont Racetrack to take a look. His confirmation was a bit suspect and Gus wanted to see him in person.

When City Zip was led out of his stall on September 8, 2001, Gus took one look, saw that one of his front feet turned out, and couldn't believe it. He turned to Linda Rice, City Zip's trainer, and said, "Come on, this is a joke. This isn't City Zip."

"Yes, this is him," said Linda.

Gus was flabbergasted. "This can't be the guy who reeled off five graded stakes races in a row in New York." When Linda assured him this was indeed *the* City Zip, Gus wanted to walk away but didn't want to seem impolite. Plus, he'd driven three hours to get there.

Gus turned to talk to his business partner, a New York financier, and the two men looked and looked and talked and talked. Not only was Gus enamored with City Zip's record, but he liked the horse's calm. He walked up to City Zip's shoulder and the horse didn't bat an eye. Next, Gus decided to examine his male parts, very important when purchasing a stallion for breeding. City Zip stood without reacting, allowing Gus to see what he needed to see. Nothing seemed to bother the horse. *Who is this guy?* Gus thought.

Gus was torn. The horse had a strong pedigree and blinding speed (even with his conformation issues) and could run on turf or dirt. Plus, he'd developed early and seemed easy to work with. That was important for a stallion, who can get all riled up when mares are around.

Gus decided to trust his instincts and buy the stallion, but the deal nearly came undone. Three days after his visit to Belmont to see City Zip, the World Trade Center attacks in New York City on September 11 turned the world upside down. In the aftermath, Gus's partner tracked the ups and downs of the stock market and wasn't sure if he still wanted to invest such a large chunk of money in a racehorse. Then, when someone started mailing envelopes of deadly anthrax spores to news media and senators, Gus's partner decided to pull out of the City Zip deal. He worried that if anthrax somehow got into the animal population, officials would close down the interstate transport of horses and mares wouldn't be able to be transported to Gus's farm for breeding to City Zip. Meaning: no stud fees.

It was a blow, but Gus had some time to round up alternative investors and in the end still purchased City Zip for $1.4 million. Even though he was disappointed in his partner's decision to pull out, he was grateful his partner had gone with him to Belmont to meet City Zip in person. He knew he wouldn't have driven to New York to see the horse without money in his pocket.

City Zip settled in and the first thing Gus noticed was how alert the stallion was. "He was probably the smartest horse I've ever been around," Gus said. "It was almost eerie. He was very observant and more aware of what was going on around him than most people."

One day, Gus got a call from a man named Rick Benas, an avid handicapper who lived about forty-five minutes away. With his glasses, trimmed beard and gray hair combed up and back, Rick Benas could have easily passed for a slightly heavier George Lucas. Minus the billions of dollars. Upon his retirement, Rick had made a deal with his wife—she would get to drive a Jaguar and he would buy a racehorse. Rick's colleague, Dave Engel, had suggested he get in touch with Gus.

Rick was a self-taught expert on racehorse bloodlines. He grew up in New York City going to Aqueduct Racetrack in Queens. He loved the challenge of analyzing the multiple variables affecting a horse's performance in a race, including bloodline, race history, behavior, jockey, weather and more. The complexities appealed to him far more than other types of gambling. And after seeing City Zip race at Belmont, Rick loved him. He was fast on grass and fast on dirt. Pure speed.

Rick called Gus, wanting to know if he had any City Zip babies for sale. It was too early, however. "He is just going to stud this year," responded Gus. With an eleven-month gestation period, City Zip's foals would not be born until 2003. "Contact me next year if you're still interested."

When the new crop of foals finally arrived, Rick Benas and Dave Engel showed up at the farm one July morning, the first day of the racing season at Saratoga. Dave would be a minority owner in the purchase. He looked like the kind of guy who arrived at his law office in a dark suit but left work in a sports jacket with the racing form under his arm. Gus showed the two men a group of twenty scampering foals, all of them less than six months old and all of them sired by City Zip.

Rick knew about Nikki's Northern Dancer bloodline and, not knowing how to evaluate a horse's conformation or athletic ability, Rick chose a lean reddish brown baby with a black mane and tail and three white socks, because of his mother's bloodline. Nikki's foal had white patches on his forehead and nose connected by a thin white strip. The foal was not yet weaned and Rick and Dave enjoyed watching him run around, shaking his head and having a good time.

Gus approved. "This is a good one, guys. He'll be a runner for you," he said. The purchase price was $15,000. Then later that day at Saratoga, Rick and Dave watched Ghostzapper, a three-year-old half-brother to City Zip, run in a seven-furlong allowance race. He won against a competitive field with a very good time. The men were happy; Ghostzapper's talent confirmed their confidence in the just-purchased foal. Before the end of the year, Ghostzapper was a graded stakes winner. The following year, he was named Horse of the Year in North America, acclaimed one of the fastest performers since the advent of speed figures.

One week later, trainer Linda Rice showed up at Gus's farm to visit City Zip and his progeny. She spotted Nikki and her foal, then asked Gus if she could buy him for herself. Gus told her that particular foal had already been sold to two gentlemen.

Linda promptly called up Rick and asked, "Can I at least train him?" Rick was not a horseman and knew he needed help, so he agreed to let Linda train his horse, sight unseen. It was better than picking a trainer's name out of some directory.

Rick didn't yet know it, but Linda was from a family with horse racing in their DNA. Her father was a leading trainer, her two brothers were jockeys and Linda was an excellent rider who had thought about becoming a jockey, too. But she had decided to become a trainer instead, not an easy job for a woman in a male-dominated sport. With a fierce work ethic and good instincts, Linda Rice had become one of the top horse trainers in New York State. Among the many successful racehorses she had trained was City Zip.

When City Zip's new colt was weaned, Linda sent him down to Indian Prairie Ranch to stay with her father, Clyde Rice. Clyde had a training facility in Ocala, Florida, with a small training racetrack and his own starting gate. The promising colt was ready to be schooled.

First, however, he needed a name. Playing off City Zip's name, Rick decided to name him Metro (for City) plus Meteor (for Zip) and ended up with Metro Meteor, his registered name.

Coincidentally, a few years before, the city of Paris had built a new subway line called the Meteor. Meteor was an acronym for **MÉT**ro **E**st-**O**uest **R**apide, meaning *Metro East-West Fast,* and it seemed to fit the young Thoroughbred.

With an evocative name, promising bloodlines and the prospect of expert training with the Rice family, Rick Benas and Dave Engel had high hopes for their very first (and only) racehorse. Their hopes grew as, early on, Metro Meteor started displaying plenty of attitude, just like his mother. He had also inherited her white-rimmed, spooky eyes. Clyde was willing to put up with the attitude for now, because he was seeing something else: it appeared that Metro Meteor had inherited his father's raw talent. The trick now was to control the colt's attitude without quenching his spirit.

Chapter 3

Alaska and Rock 'n' Roll

"Art flourishes where there is a sense of adventure."
—*Alfred North Whitehead*

While Grandma and I spent summers going to the races, Grandpa was up in Alaska fishing for salmon. During the off-season in Seattle, he was your typical, happy-go-lucky grandfather who enjoyed playing with his cats and spending time with me.

Grandpa's name was Del and he was a commercial fisherman as far back as I can remember. He worked his boat, the Pioneer III, for four months during the summers and made enough to take the rest of the year off. Grandpa and Grandma always got along and I never saw them argue. However, Grandpa was a totally different man when he was on the boat.

He was the last of the old-school salmon fishermen who pulled in their nets by hand, before hydraulics. All of my grandpa's boat captain friends were built just like him—solid as rock with hands of steel. "Ronny, shake my hand," he'd say, holding out his hand. If I dared to put out my hand, he'd squeeze it until I begged for mercy.

I hated being called *Ronny.* It was so childish, but my Grandma tagged me with that nickname from day one and it stuck. Since my grandpa and uncles called me Ronny, the fishing crew did, too. Even Opie Taylor was allowed to grow up and become *Ron* Howard, the famous director, but to my grandparents I was forever Ronny.

My first year fishing with Grandpa was the year I turned fourteen. I was replacing my Uncle Dan, a very good fisherman who had left to run his own boat. My dad's brothers were much younger than my dad, so I was almost like another brother rather than their nephew. I idolized my uncles and my grandfather.

On the boat, Grandpa was the old salt whose every other word was a cuss word. I served as his bartender. "Ronny, go mix me a drink," he'd order, which meant a whiskey and Seven-Up. He bought cases of whiskey and cigarettes tax-free, enough to last the whole year, because we traveled through Canada on our way up to Alaska.

My grandpa's boat was a purse seiner with a six-man crew. A purse seine is a large net set vertically down into the water, then drawn in or "pursed" in a circular fashion to trap the fish. I was trained to drive the skiff, the most important job next to the captain. It was also the easiest job to screw up; mistakes could cost thousands of dollars.

We fished for salmon, mainly Pink (although we called them Humpies), and they were headed for the cannery. The salmon you see fresh in the store is usually caught by troll line, because people don't like to buy fresh fish with net marks or mushy fish from the bottom of a hold.

Grandpa knew where to find the fish by studying which creeks the salmon were running to at certain times of the year. We would also go scout the fishing grounds, looking for fish jumping out of the water. We usually stayed around Ketchikan, catching a few hundred per set. Sometimes it was a bust and we'd catch zero (what we called a "water haul") and sometimes the stars aligned and we'd catch two to three thousand.

The heavy net, lined with floats, was carefully folded up on the back of the fishing boat. The skiff was a small, simple boat but had the power of a semi-truck. I drove it by myself to tow the net out into the water. I helped get the net into place against the beach while my grandfather was in the main boat, three hundred yards away, pulling on the other end. The tide brought the fish into the net and I had to watch carefully, know the tides and be ready to maneuver the net to unsnag it if it hung up on the rocky bottom.

With Grandpa in the boat and me in the skiff, we'd hold the net open for twenty to thirty minutes, then close the net by pulling in the purse line that ran through rings on the bottom of the net, drawing it up and closed. The salmon were now trapped inside and the crew on the main boat could begin to pull the net back in using an overhead hydraulic power block, dumping the fish on deck and then stacking the net back up.

In the 1970s, there was no two-way radio communication between me on the skiff and Grandpa on the boat.

Instead, I'd watch for his hand signals for direction. When Grandpa became animated, jumping up and down and waving his arms outside on the upper wheelhouse hundreds of yards away, I knew I was in for an earful when I got back on the boat.

"Ronny, how can you be so goddamn stupid?" Grandpa would shout. Then he'd tell me everything I did wrong, talking out of the side of his mouth with one eye closed, exactly like every caricature you've ever seen of an old time fisherman. Getting yelled at was just part of life on a fishing boat. I never took it personally; it just went with the job. And I made every mistake you could make.

My first couple of years were rough and I spent most of the time seasick and screwing up. But by the time I was sixteen, I had it down. My grandfather had groomed me into a real salmon fisherman. I was always the youngest one on the boat, but I was the boss by then and my grandpa depended on me to run the crew. Being bossed around by a kid called Ronny didn't always go over well with guys in their twenties and thirties.

One summer, my dad took a few months off from Boeing to spend a fishing season on the boat. It caused a lot of tension, because his own son was yelling at him and telling him what to do. But by then I was a seasoned veteran and he was the greenhorn.

We fished three to four days a week with very little downtime. On fishing days we worked from sunup to sundown and in Alaska the summer days are long, with only about four hours of dark. After a day of fishing, you'd unload your fish. That meant jumping down in the fish hold up to your chest in salmon, then pitching them two at a time into a basket to be lifted up out of the hold. Pitching fish was really slimy, the worst part of the job. Sometimes, if you had a lot of fish, when you were done pitching it would be light out and time to start fishing all over again.

When I could, I did some reading, played cribbage or went for a hike around Ketchikan. One of my favorite places was the garbage dump, the place to be if you wanted to see bears or bald eagles. But most of my spare time was spent doing laundry or waiting for showers. There was no shower on the boat so we'd go to the cannery, which provided showers and laundry facilities for the workers. There was always a line and sometimes it would be a week between showers. I never felt clean and spent all summer smelling like fish and diesel fuel.

I love everything about Alaska. It's my favorite place in the world, because you can travel around by boat and not see a house for days. Whales breached, bald eagles hunted and porpoises raced alongside the boat. My favorite part of salmon fishing was the night before we went out, anchored up and enjoying the dark and the quiet. You could hear a conversation on a boat a hundred yards away and see stars you could never see back home.

On the water, the crew traded off on wheel watches, a two-hour shift steering the boat. I got pretty good at reading a chart and guiding the boat in the dark by using the lighthouses. There were buoys and blinking lights on shore to use for navigation, along with radar to tell you how far away the shore was. Each light blinked at a different rate and the rate was marked on the chart so you could tell where you were.

One time I was outside and steering from up top, because there were lots of logs in the water. I could look down and see them in the moonlight. You don't want to hit a log, because it can get pushed down under the boat and damage the propeller. I was a little on edge, looking out for logs, when I looked to my left and saw something heading for the boat. Two glowing trails were moving through the water straight toward us. The glowing lines got closer and closer. *Are they torpedoes? Are we under attack?*

Just when I thought we were going to blow up, I finally recognized a familiar silhouette. The torpedoes were actually two porpoises looking for a late-night race with the boat. As they glided through the water, their bodies stirred up microscopic algae that emitted light when disturbed, causing phosphorescence. That explained the glow-in-the-dark trails.

Starting at seventeen, I began drinking beer in bars with other fishermen. Sometimes, to get a laugh out of the crew, I'd do a perfect impression of my grandfather in one of his yelling fits. But I was fiercely loyal. One time at a bar in Ketchikan, I overheard one of our crew down the bar telling someone my grandpa was a drunk. I immediately grabbed a glass ashtray and flung it at the back of his head. Then I ran down and got in his face. "The next time we're at sea, you better not go out in the dark, because you might accidentally fall overboard and no one will ever find your body."

The guy was ten years older and six inches taller than me but I must have looked all kinds of crazy, because he immediately ran to the boat, packed up his things, and quit. He told my grandpa I'd threatened to kill him. This got me in a lot of hot water with Grandpa, because we were set to leave port the next day and now we were short-handed. I set off back to downtown Ketchikan to find another crewman. By the time I returned with some college kid from Buffalo looking for adventure on the high seas, my Uncle Dan had already smoothed things over with Grandpa. He was trying not to look pleased that I had defended his honor. I had no plans to murder anyone, especially someone who could crush me with his bare hands. But I was a seventeen-year-old kid who just pegged Goliath in the head with an ashtray and he didn't go down. I figured "crazy" was the best defense I had for saving my own life.

Whenever I was back in Seattle, I resumed the role of a high schooler. It was confusing, because in Alaska I was a man who did man things in a man's world. My friends were working summer jobs at ice cream parlors for around $3.25 an hour while I was making thousands of dollars fishing. I paid for my first car, a '69 Ford Mustang fastback, with cash and I immediately equipped it with the best sound system I could find, Radial T/A tires and chrome mag wheels—the perks of being born into a family with high-paying work. I spent the rest of my summer earnings on records and concert tickets. Since I wasn't comfortable with girls, I fell in love with rock music. My first concert was Pink Floyd's *Dark Side of the Moon* tour when I was fourteen. I decided I wanted to be in a rock band so I bought a Fender Precision Bass, because I figured bass guitar was the easiest to learn and the quickest way to get into a band.

My first band was called Joe and the Jumper Cables, a throwback band playing old time rock 'n' roll. I tried to grease my hair back, but I was the youngest guy in the band and my hairline was still low and straight across and never looked quite right. The guys in their twenties and thirties had hairlines starting to recede and could groom their hair into an authentic ducktail. When we played in bars, I wasn't allowed to come down off the stage, because I was still underage. Whenever the band took a break and the other guys were inside having a beer, I had to go outside and sit on the curb until the break was over.

I was a child living in an adult world, usually the youngest in everything I did. As I got older, my trips to Alaska became more sporadic. I think my grandfather thought that I would take over his boat when he retired, but with the advent of farm-raised salmon, fishing was turning into a tough business to try to earn a living. But even during the summers when I stayed at home in Seattle, my day jobs were always fish-related. I was hired by a cold storage company to grade salmon and I was a hot commodity, because I could grade the fish by species and weight without even using a scale. It wasn't much of a skill, but I was good at it.

I did have one unwelcome souvenir left over from my salmon fishing days. I felt like I was going deaf from sleeping next to diesel engines and, later, being around loud music. I have spent most of my life smiling and nodding during conversations, because I can't hear most of what people are saying to me. It made me uncomfortable trying to talk to people, so I went out of my way to avoid conversation. My hearing issues, along with being an only child and being shy, have always made me want to withdraw from people.

By the time I was twenty-five, my grandfather was ready to retire. I had to make the decision about whether I wanted to take over his boat and be a fisherman for the rest of my life. I decided against it.

With no other marketable skills besides rock 'n' roll, I then chose to join the Air Force. Having decided against salmon fishing, I thought maybe I could use the time to figure out what I wanted to do with my life.

Chapter 4

The Winner's Circle

Metro, Year Two

"Some people say I have attitude—maybe I do.
But I think you have to."

—Venus Williams

Soon after Metro Meteor was weaned, Dave Engel went to Florida to visit his ailing parents. On a hot day in June, he took his dad out to Indian Prairie Ranch to see the colt. When Clyde Rice brought out Metro, the young horse refused to cooperate with the grooms, balking and pulling on the line. "He was a little scary," Dave remembers. Then, Clyde broke the bad news. Metro was such a hyperagressive, rambunctious horse, no one was safe around him. "If you're going to have him as a racehorse, I suggest we castrate him."

Oh, crap, Dave thought. *I don't want to geld him.* The idea was to buy a colt to race, then stand him at stud later for added value, almost like an annuity. Dave dreaded breaking the news to Rick. But Clyde was adamant. "If you don't do it, Metro's never going to be a racehorse or anything else. He's uncontrollable." Seeing Metro's attitude in real life, though, convinced Dave. He and Rick agreed with Clyde's plan and allowed Metro to be gelded.

Afterwards, Metro was a little easier to handle although he kept his wild-eyed look. He responded well to training, including getting comfortable with handling, walking on a lead line, grooming and accepting the saddle and bridle. Once Metro was used to having a saddle on his back for a week or two, next he had to get used to the feel of a rider on his back.

From then on, the exercise rider taught Metro how to go, stop, respond to the rider's aids and walk in a straight line. Next, he learned how to jog and then gallop. Other important skills included learning how to enter and leave the starting gate, how to gallop around a track and how to work with the pony horse, an amiable companion horse used to help guide racehorses back and forth to the track and keep them calm.

Metro was showing promise, although everyone agreed he was "back in the knee," like his father, City Zip. Instead of his front legs standing upright, perpendicular to the ground, Metro had been born with a slight backwards bow. If you looked at him from the side, his legs bent ever so slightly backwards at the knee, putting excess strain on various parts of his front legs.

A horse's knees are the equivalent to human wrists, with multiple small bones that flex in different places, supported by a complicated network of tendons and ligaments. Metro's back-in-the-knee problem meant his knees were under a great deal of pressure, especially when galloping at high speed. By virtue of his genetics,

Metro was a gifted runner with a great deal of heart, but his front legs would be especially prone to fractures, bone chips and soft-tissue injuries. Later in life, he would most likely face carpal osteoarthritis, a degenerative, debilitating and very painful condition. In terms of racing ability, Metro had won the genetic lottery. But with his knees, he had lost. Prognosis? Owners of horses like Metro are urged to restrict the degree of stress and strain on their horse's knees, not quite the ideal scenario for a colt with so much talent.

As Metro's training progressed, Linda and the owners decided his very first race would be at Belmont Park on July 3, 2005, for a Maiden Special Weight race. The jockey silks were white with large orange circles, in honor of Rick and his wife's alma mater, Syracuse University. The newly formed organization was named Obviously NY Stables.

When Metro was led around the paddock for the handicappers to get a look, Dave thought he still seemed pretty wild-eyed and distracted. Once in his starting stall, though, Metro came out of the gate like he'd been trained. He was still slightly distracted but on the run.

Overall, the first race was a disaster. In the five-furlong sprint with other two-year-olds, Metro broke sharply from the rail and battled for the lead. As the pack of horses approached the turn, a colt named Trading Pro came over and bumped Metro into the rail. Metro's jockey pulled him up, dropping back to last place in the eight-horse field.

"Metro Meteor has lost his action," intoned the track announcer.

Dave and Rick fought panic. "He broke down!" yelled Rick.

Dave could see Metro was okay, though he lagged way back. "No, he's fine," Dave replied. Sure enough, Metro gathered himself and finished strong. But even though he finished sixth out of eight horses and was seventeen lengths behind, he moved well. *He's going to be fine,* Dave reassured himself.

Four weeks later, Metro came back to Saratoga for another Maiden Special Weight Race. This time, Linda put blinkers (a hood with blinders) on Metro to keep him focused on the race and less distracted by the other horses. Blinkers had also worked for his father, City Zip. Once again, Metro came out of the starting gate with a flash of speed and ran in front, battling neck-and-neck for the lead with a horse named What's Your Edge. This time, Metro finished second, losing by just one length. The two-year-old colt was getting the hang of it. And he was showing what no trainer could teach—courage and desire.

Two weeks later, Metro figured it all out in another five-and-a-half-furlong race at Saratoga. It was a hot and humid Sunday. The track was giving away stadium blankets, not much help in the heat. But the giveaway meant the track was packed with a crowd of 63,000 people. Metro easily won his third race, pulling away in the stretch with jockey Cornelio Velasquez on his back.

Rick and Dave were thrilled, but the unexpectedly large crowd had clogged up the interstate and no one else was there to help celebrate Obviously NY's first victory.

Dave's son parked on the side of the highway and was running to try to catch the race. He phoned his dad. "When are they approaching the starting gate? Tell them to wait." Dave's wife and daughter were stuck in a traffic jam so bad they couldn't get within a mile of the track. When they heard Metro had won, they got out of the car and started dancing in the road. "I'm on my way to the winner's circle," Dave called to tell them.

Metro entered the winner's circle for the first time, along with his jockey, Rick and his wife, Linda, Dave and a friend who owned a small piece of Metro. Dave called his mother in Florida to tell her Metro had won. "Unbelievable," she said.

After that first win, Linda recommended trying Metro on grass, scheduling him for an upcoming stakes race at Saratoga called the With Anticipation Stakes. The purse was $65,000, but Metro's odds were 30–1. He would be racing against some other very talented two-year-olds and no one gave Metro any chance at all.

The turf condition was listed as "good" that day, but the track was definitely boggy. The tail end of Hurricane Katrina had just moved through the Northeast, bringing several days of steady rain. Rick and Dave were surprised that Linda wanted to run him in a mile-and-a-sixteenth race, but quickly endorsed the idea.

When the starting gate clanged open for his fourth race, Metro blasted out of the ten-hole in a ten-horse pack, running way on the outside. Metro took the lead around the first turn and every horse in the pack made a run at him down the backstretch, but Metro held them all off. His race records noted, "dug in gamely." Metro kept the lead in the stretch, but in the last hundred yards a horse named Stream Cat, with Hall of Fame jockey Gary Stevens aboard, caught him inside the sixteenth pole and Metro finished in second place.

The Obviously NY team was incredibly excited at Metro's performance, especially considering how hard it was to win on the front end, from an outside post, on an "off-turf" day. Their investment was starting to look like it would pay off. Metro Meteor was well on his way to establishing himself as one of the top turf sprinters on the East Coast.

Metro was also on his way to his first knee operation, however. In October, Metro was shipped back to Florida at the end of his two-year-old season to undergo surgery. He had bone chips in his knees.

Chapter 5

Pointy Head

"It's a helluva start, being able to recognize what makes you happy."

—*Lucille Ball*

I was a smart kid and learned things easily, whether it was how to run a fishing crew or play guitar. I didn't have much use for grade school and I skipped when I could, staying home to watch television programs. It was easy to do since my parents both worked. Once I found I could keep my grades up even though I missed a lot of school, it became a pattern. I never needed a note and for some reason was able to come and go to school as I liked.

After sixth grade, we moved to a different town a few miles away and I enrolled in junior high, where I didn't know anyone. I did go to school the first day but was absent the next two. Junior high was different and, on my return, I was asked for a note from my parents. My days of skipping school were over. I'd have to attend school like the rest of the kids.

Junior high was easy and I was good at many things but great at nothing. Math was my strongest subject and

I quickly moved forward into advanced math and algebra. Once I got to algebra, however, I was in for a rude awakening and hit a wall. I just couldn't understand it and I went from straight A's in math to flunking. Because everything had come so easy, I lacked the commitment to dig in and fight to learn, because I'd always followed the path of least resistance. So I gave up on algebra. *When am I ever going to use this?* I told myself. If only I'd known that in a few short years, I was going to find out exactly why I needed to know algebra.

In high school I fell in love with photography. My photography teacher, even though he was a hippie and a little odd, was my hero all through high school. He was an odd guy with long gray hair and a gray beard who drove a Volkswagen bus. His art seemed to revolve around naked men and I have no idea how he was permitted to be a teacher, but he was a strong artistic influence and he helped me learn how to look at the world through the eyes of a photographer and an artist. I took several classes from him, served as his assistant and spent hours in the darkroom. He allowed us a lot of freedom and I always had a camera with me. I didn't have to go to class as long as I did the work and turned in my photos.

I remember one particular series of his charcoal drawings. Naked men, of course, but just torsos, behind bars. The images stuck with me, because I realized an artist doesn't have to give the viewer all of the information. If he had sketched a complete body of a man, you would have looked at it, thought, *yup, it's a naked man,* and moved on. But by leaving out a portion of the important visual information, you are drawn in to engage with the art and figure out the rest of the story. Good art lets the viewer ask questions and fill in the blanks on his or her own.

What does his face look like?

Why is he behind bars?

Why is he naked and behind bars?

Why am I, a heterosexual male, staring at a picture of a naked man?

Did any of my friends see me?

When I graduated from high school, my life was mostly salmon fishing in the summers and rock 'n' roll the rest of the year. Then I got married and had a baby girl in my mid-twenties, while I was in the Air Force. The Air Force was the first job I ever had where I wasn't the youngest person on the team. By the time I got to basic training in San Antonio, Texas, I was the second oldest in my flight, which is what they called the fifty guys in your training group. The oldest guy was twenty-six and we called him Pops.

From basic training, I went to technical school at Lowry Air Force base in Denver. I scored very high on the entrance exam. Not that I was a genius, just very good at taking tests. I was offered just about any job I wanted and I chose electronics. Little did I know my disdain for high school algebra was about to catch up with me, because electronics was all algebra. I was forced to learn it or flunk out of Air Force technical training. I had always skated through life and taken the easiest route, so it was kind of a shock. I knew if I didn't work and learn, I wasn't going to be able to pay my bills and support my family, so I was motivated.

After nine months of training and finally mastering algebra, I was assigned to be an Avionics Technician on the EF-111 at Mountain Home Air Force Base in Idaho. The F-111 was a long-nosed bomber nicknamed the *Aardvark*. But the nearly identical EF-111 I worked on carried no weaponry. These jets, nicknamed *Spark Varks,* had been converted to carry electronic jamming equipment. Their sole purpose was to fly overhead and jam communications and surface-to-air missiles sites so that our fighter jets and bombers could get into enemy territory unmolested.

I was no warrior and there was nothing glamorous about the job. I didn't even touch a real airplane until I was deployed to Saudi Arabia in 1991 for the first Gulf War. I worked in a shop repairing electronic boxes pulled off the planes for maintenance. The guys on the flight line, who actually got to touch the planes, called us "Pointy Heads," because we went to war armed with nothing but books and O-Scope probes. We lovingly referred to them as "Booger Hookers," since in our view all they did was sit around, picking their noses and waiting for a plane to come back broken.

Occasionally, when I was tasked for guard duty, I was issued an M-16 but no bullets. I guess the Air Force was afraid I might hurt someone. Not even a courtesy Barney Fife bullet for my front pocket, in case of emergency.

The Air Force was the first time I had a full-time job that required discipline and a regular schedule. When I was young, I had quickly learned how to game the school system. Fishing in Alaska had mostly been in the summer and I never knew which days I'd be out fishing until Fish and Game told us. Playing bass in rock bands meant I never knew when I was going to play until someone hired the band. The Air Force was the first time I had structure and a job to go to every day.

It was the first time I had the close brothers and the family I had always craved, through the guys I worked with. But I also noticed it was starting to get hard to enjoy having a conversation, because I couldn't always hear everything the other person said. I was going to be forced to come to terms with significant hearing loss.

During training, when we were stationed in Idaho, we'd take off on the weekends and go camping and trout fishing. I chose the artistic approach to fishing. While my buddies were casting metal spinners and lures they had purchased, I went the fly fishing route, even tying my own flies. There is an art and a beauty to fly fishing. I felt as if I was creating little pieces of art out of feathers and fur. Stalking and catching a trout on a number twelve Royal Wulff that you created yourself is not just fishing, it's art.

I was homesick the first year I was in the Air Force and I tried to get home every chance I got. But after a while, I realized the world is a big place and there were other places I could be happy. My grandfather died from cancer when I was in the service. Back in my first year on the boat, he got hurt really badly when the tail of his jacket caught in the winch and he suffered several crushed ribs. I was fourteen and rode with him in the ambulance to the hospital. His lungs had collapsed and they were a mess from years of smoking. If he would have quit smoking then, he might have lived longer, but as soon as he recovered he went back to it. When he got cancer, no one told me he was dying. It pissed me off, because I would have gone home to see him one last time. My Dad later sent me a photo of the Pioneer III, clipped from the pages of *The Seattle Times*. The old fishing boat had sunk at the dock in Seattle after being accidentally rammed by a much larger crab boat. The photo showed it half-submerged, hanging from the lines holding it to the dock. It felt like the end of an era.

During my Air Force years, I stopped playing bass but still loved classic rock. There was a show on TV called *Rock and Roll Jeopardy,* hosted by Jeff Probst (now famous as the host of the *Survivor* series). I always wanted to be on that show. I'm the village idiot when it comes to regular *Jeopardy*, but I know I could have cleared the board on *Rock and Roll Jeopardy*.

When I was in the Middle East during the war, I had some extra time. Since camping and fly fishing were no longer an option, I needed something else to fill the time so I started drawing. I'd take a photograph from *Sports Illustrated,* like a football player on the field or Mike Tyson getting punched, and try to create a realistic drawing. Next, I decided to attempt watercolors. It wasn't easy, but I found it relaxing and I soon discovered my best paintings came quickly, when I lost myself in the work.

Sometimes I'd look over at the clock and see three hours had passed, when it felt like twenty minutes. My favorite paintings were the unfinished ones, leaving a little something to the viewer's imagination, and I found the hardest part was learning to quit before the painting was finished. It was like writing a song—so many great songs were written quickly but are still played forty years later. Keith Richards wrote "Satisfaction" in just a few minutes, then fell asleep. Luckily his tape recorder was running and captured the moment so he could listen to what he had created the next day when he woke up.

Usually when I faced a challenge I just called it quits and moved on to something else. I had no drive to solve problems and overcome obstacles. But as I learned how to draw and then to paint, it fed something inside of me that loved color and motion and speed and power. I was interested in creating paintings of racecars. At the time, eBay, the online marketplace, was a new phenomenon. On a whim, I decided to post one of my paintings and it sold for $45! It was just a hobby, but selling those car paintings on eBay planted a seed. Maybe when I got out of the Air Force I could possibly make a living painting and be my own boss.

Sometimes, when I look back at those early paintings, I think they're better than what I'm doing now. I believe art is better when you don't know much, when you're just being yourself and not trying to paint like someone else. Knowledge in art is not always a good thing. It's better if you learn to paint your own way.

I was still in the Air Force when my marriage ended. We'd had our second child, a boy, but I still hadn't overcome my selfish, only-child ways and I didn't know how to communicate or share my life with someone else. My fishing and softball hobbies didn't include my family, so eventually my wife found someone she liked better and moved on. Once again, I felt adrift and alone in the world.

Two years later, when I returned from the Gulf War, someone threw a barbecue for some of the guys from the electronics shop. We'd just returned from the deserts of Saudi Arabia and we showed up in our newly purchased clothes for our debut back into civilization. At the barbecue, I met a girl named Wendy who worked as a flight attendant. One of my friends was dating Wendy's roommate and they dragged Wendy to the barbecue to try to fix her up with one of the other guys I was in Saudi with. She wasn't interested in him, but we hit it off. I guess she couldn't resist the sight of me in my freshly pressed white pants and salmon-colored shirt, looking like I'd just walked off the set of *Miami Vice*.

Our first date was dinner and a movie, *The Doors*. During the meal, I asked Wendy, "So how long do you plan on being a flight attendant?" For some reason, I thought flight attendants had a shelf life and were only allowed to work to a certain age. She let me have it and she still reminds me of that stupid question.

Wendy and I really had nothing in common. I was five years older, which isn't a lot, but the cultural difference was huge in terms of music. Wendy grew up in the eighties, so while I'd been listening to Led Zeppelin, she had listened to Duran Duran. Her older brother is my age, so the only thing she knew about classic rock, which was so important to me, was whatever she heard coming through her brother's wall. Wendy had never been to a concert and I had been to hundreds.

But Wendy was beautiful and feisty and loved to talk as much as I hated to. We can have a conversation for an hour and I'm only required to contribute a couple of words. She does the heavy lifting. Plus, she is nosy and asks lots of questions, which I answer, so there is never an uncomfortable lull in the conversations. I was smitten and seven months later we were married.

I hadn't learned my lesson, though, and I quickly fell into my old, selfish habits of doing only what I wanted to do and not making the effort to communicate and build our marriage into a partnership. Wendy worked for a commuter airline out of Boise called Horizon Air, so when she was gone I did whatever I wanted to do. But Wendy wasn't one to give up. She is 110 pounds of pure intimidation and would have none of the old me and my solitary ways. I quickly learned I would be working hard to keep this marriage and to make it work. I had met my match.

Wendy never critiques my artwork and I have learned not to ask. I tell her she lacks a brain-to-mouth filter. Every thought that hits her brain immediately rolls off her tongue, so she has an uncanny ability to cut your ego off at the knees without even trying or knowing that she is doing it. One time she was flying and one of the pilots said, "Everyone says I look like Dennis Quaid."

"No, you look more like his brother, Randy," Wendy immediately responded. "You know, the loser guy from the *Vacation* movies?"

Awkward silence.

So, thankfully, she holds her comments on my paintings.

After Wendy and I got married, the Air Force transferred me to New Mexico. But all of its natural beauty happened to be a very long drive from Clovis, where I was stationed. Two years later, Wendy was hired as a flight attendant for Southwest Airlines and we decided to say goodbye to Air Force life and move to Phoenix, where she would be based.

Chapter 6

Chips

Metro, Years Three to Four

"Healing is a matter of time, but it is sometimes also a matter of opportunity."
—*Hippocrates*

After being sent back to Indian Prairie Ranch in Florida, Metro Meteor underwent surgery on his knees in October 2005.

DIAGNOSIS:

RIGHT KNEE

Moderate to large chip fracture on the distomedial radius

Moderate sized chip fracture on the opposing proximal radial carpal bone

Moderate chip fracture on the proximal intermediate carpal bone

Some minor remodeling on the distolateral radius

In the intercarpal joint, a small chip fracture on the distal radial carpal bone

LEFT KNEE

Moderate sized chip fracture on the proximal intermediate and proximal radial carpal bones

The surgery was successful and, after the recommended recovery period, Metro was rehabilitated and went back to racing for Obviously NY Stables. In the summer of 2006, when he was three years old, Metro raced at Belmont, Saratoga and Woodbine.

He was moved to turf sprints, races of five to seven furlongs, where he excelled. Linda thought the soft turf courses would be easier on Metro's knees and make for a longer career. Metro's style of racing also changed. No longer was he the horse who went for the early lead and set the pace. Metro would run at the back of the pack, waiting for the right moment to unleash a lightning-like burst of speed, passing all competitors in the homestretch and sometimes coming from twelve to fifteen lengths behind. His knees held up and he won four out of seven races.

In the fall of 2006, Metro went back to Florida for the winter. In November, he underwent a second surgery to remove more bone chips in his knees. This time, the damage was more extensive.

DIAGNOSIS:

RIGHT KNEE

Large, chronic chip fracture on the proximal intermediate carpal bone and a smooth osteophyte on the distolateral radius

The areas debrided at last year's surgery were filled with adequate replacement tissues

In the intercarpal joint there was a superficial chip fracture along most of the distal radial carpal bone and partial thickness cartilage damage on the opposing third carpal bone

LEFT KNEE

In the radiocarpal joint there was a moderate sized chronic chip fracture/osteophyte on the proximal intermediate carpal bone that was minimally debrided

The defect on the proximal radial carpal bone was filled with thick fibrous replacement tissue (debrided last time) and there was a smooth osteophyte on the distomedial radius

In the intercarpal joint there was a similar distal radial carpal chip fracture, but without any peripheral cartilage damage

NOTE: Even though there were multiple focal areas of damage in these joints, there was minimal peripheral cartilage damage in any of them.

Once again, Metro was rehabilitated and trained to prepare for his third season of racing, this time as a four-year-old. By now, his reputation was established. He was a very fast turf horse. But the ongoing knee problems were concerning and, in May, Linda suggested entering him in a $50,000 claiming race, where all of the horses are for sale for the same price.

The other owners on the track showed immediate interest in Metro and so many parties submitted a claim that the sale was settled by a five-way shake. In other words, five people wanted to buy him so they settled the matter by rolling the dice. The victor was Gary Contessa for Winning Move Stables.

Linda had seen this coming. Since City Zip had knee problems as a two-year-old, just like Metro, it was no surprise when Metro began to have knee problems, too. "We did the best we could while he was sound," she said. "Losing a horse like him is a very hard thing. I was involved since finding him as a foal, watching him grow up, training him and then watching him turn into a great competitor."

Rick and Dave were devastated when Metro was claimed and sold to a different stable. They didn't think anyone would pay $50,000 for a horse with knees like Metro's and they liked him so much they had been investing in other successful City Zip foals, including Metro's full sister, Cizi, his full brother, City Sneakers, and another mare out of City Zip named Canadian Ballet.

To this day, Rick and Dave have followed Metro's journey, making sure he is taken care of. Rick remembers Metro as the kind of horse who brings people together and he is still close friends with Metro's breeder, Gus.

Dave remembers Metro's social personality. "He would grab onto my sleeve. He liked attention and seemed to literally grab for it." He also remembers the horse as a bright spot during some major family crisis moments. Dave says knowing Metro changed his outlook on all animals. "I've not eaten any red meat for several years, because Metro taught me that all animals have a sense of self-awareness, emotional sensitivity and intelligence."

Metro only ran two races for Gary Contessa's Winning Move Stables, victorious in one of them, before being claimed again. Ownership turnover is common for racehorses in the latter stages of their careers, but Metro was a horse in more demand than most.

In June 2007, Metro was sold to California Dreamin' Stables in another $50,000 claiming race. Metro raced eight times for them, winning twice.

In July 2008, Metro was sold to Kenneth Ramsey, again in a $50,000 claiming race. By 2008, Metro and his still ailing knees were on the decline. Ramsey never came close to recouping his $50,000 investment.

In December 2008, Metro was sold in a private sale to Bob Oliva of Renpher Stables. He was shipped out from his glory days in New York to a lower-level track in Pennsylvania, in the hopes that he might excel against lighter competition. Metro raced twice without winning. He would never win again.

Although Metro bounced from stable to stable after those first couple of years with Obviously NY, he never lost his spirit. Rick and Dave both thought of him as a buddy. Rick and his friends loved to feed Metro carrots. "We loved him," he said. "Metro was the architect of the stable. His speed and his wins built Obviously NY and made it possible for us to buy other horses."

"Metro, no kidding, is one of the finest people I've ever known," said Dave. "He's a *mensch.*" Dave loved to visit him at Saratoga. When he walked into the stable area, he called out, "Hey Metro! Who's the fastest horse?" Metro always responded by popping his head out of the stall door and shaking his head. "We all loved him."

Linda called him "a great little horse." She went on to become one of the East Coast's leading trainers and a groundbreaker for women in racing.

And Metro? Well, he was really, really sore.

Chapter 7

Red Paw Prints

"It took me four years to paint like Raphael,
but a lifetime to paint like a child."
—*Pablo Picasso*

We lived in Phoenix for a while, where I proved to be the world's worst car salesman. I was working ten-hour days, six days a week, and pulling in a poverty wage. Not a good job for an introvert.

Another bad job for an introvert is working as a flight attendant, so I got the bright idea to try that, too. It wasn't a good fit but I liked going on trips with Wendy. On overnights, I brought my watercolors and painted in my hotel room. I was still mostly painting racecars and selling them on eBay, but one day, on a whim, I did a painting of Stewart, our gray tuxedo cat. Even though I'd made a modest name for myself selling the NASCAR paintings, the bidding for Stewart's portrait went through the roof. I thought maybe I'd found a way to make a living with art. It worked and soon I was making more money selling my animal paintings on eBay than working for Southwest, so I quit in 2005 to pursue art full time.

Wendy and I liked Phoenix and we did a lot of day trips, jumping in the car and driving around the state. We hiked in the Superstition Mountains and caught the occasional Phoenix Suns game. After a while, though, we got tired of living there. It was getting too big for us. We rode the housing boom, buying and selling a house every couple of years. Each time we'd move to the edge of town, upgrading to a better house, the city would overtake and pass us by, pushing beyond its boundaries. But Wendy and I started craving small-town life again.

"Let's try the East Coast for a little bit," I suggested to Wendy. It would be an easier move for me than for Wendy. My dad had retired from Boeing and my parents had sold their house and had been traveling the country in an RV for several years. Half the time I never knew what state they were in. We exchanged quick emails every couple of months, but we weren't the tight-knit family Wendy grew up in. She was close to her family and she was moving away from them and from Arizona, where she'd spent her teen years in Lake Havasu.

We decided to move to Gettysburg, "the most famous small town in America." Although everyone knows the history and the big battlefield on the edge of town, the population is only 7,500 and it has a compact, quaint downtown surrounded by rolling hills dotted with historic farms and stone barns.

Wendy was not socially challenged like me, so she quickly settled into life in Gettysburg. But I became even more of an introvert. I was working for myself and didn't have a job to go to or people to socialize with. No friends or family, just Wendy. I knew no one nor did I have any desire to know anyone.

One day, after we'd been in Gettysburg for a few months, I was painting alone at the table in my office with only Spencer, the cat, for company. Suddenly we heard a noise that made us both jump.

Is that the...?

Oh, no.

The sound of it made me cringe. I hated it. But there it was again.

I felt a slight sense of panic. It wasn't so bad when Wendy was home and could deal with it. But on the three days a week she was off working for Southwest Airlines, I was left alone to face it myself. Most of the time I just ignored it, but sometimes I couldn't hide and I had no choice but to face answering the door.

Spencer hated the doorbell, too. He usually ran and all you'd see was a glimpse of his fur as he streaked down the hall, a black feline blur looking for the nearest bed. He would jump up, wriggle underneath the comforter and stay there for the next couple of hours, a lump in the bed, until he felt safe to come out again.

Today, for some reason, Spencer didn't run. He seemed fascinated by watching me paint and he sat contentedly on my studio table.

"Probably just the UPS man," I told Spencer. We decided to ignore the dreaded doorbell. I remembered that a shipment of art supplies was due to arrive. *He'll just leave the package on the porch. He's just ringing the bell as a courtesy, to let me know he is dropping something off.*

Not because he wants to talk to me. That was the excuse I was going with to talk myself out of the agony of making myself walk to the door, find out who was on the other side and be forced to talk to them.

I dipped my brush into the red paint and made another large stroke across the canvas, much to Spencer's delight. He followed the movement of the brushstroke with his head.

It was my day to let loose and paint whatever I wanted to. I love to paint abstracts. I love to paint without feeling like it has to look like something. I don't have much passion for what is referred to as realism, making a painting that looks like a photograph. What's the point? That's what they make cameras for. To me, art is vibrant color and texture, emotion and feeling. Finding colors that harmonize, blending on the canvas or paper and making another beautiful color. I didn't want people to look at my artwork and say, "That painting looks just like a photograph." I wanted people to look at one of my abstracts and say, "Wow! That looks like it was a hell of a lot of fun to paint!"

But people didn't see my abstracts the same way I did. I had listed them on eBay but I had yet to sell one. Abstracts weren't going to make my truck payments. That's why I painted pet portraits. And my abstracts? They were for my eyes only.

Pet portraits weren't my passion, but I didn't hate them and they did pay the bills. Over the years I have built a pretty successful pet portrait business. Customers email me photos of their dog or cat, choose a background color and then I send them back a watercolor rendition of their pet. I've never met any of my customers in person. I am just a faceless individual in an email and that's the way I like it. I consider myself fortunate to earn a living as an artist. I'd be a starving artist if I was painting what excites me, the abstracts no one wants to buy.

The world is filled with artists much more talented than I am who refuse to bend to what the public wants to buy. I am all about paying the bills, so I paint what people want. The abstract paintings that give me so much joy eventually get painted over, morphing into a marketable, soulful beagle or a charming Bichon Frisé, helping us make the mortgage payment and survive for another month.

Ding-dong. It was the doorbell again. *Dammit!* Whoever was out there was still there. And they must've known I was home. I had my music on loud, my old friend Sammy Hagar blasting from the speakers. Sammy must have given me away and told the world I was hiding in my house.

It's not that I hate people. I don't. I just don't feel comfortable around them unless Wendy is by my side. I don't know how to have a one-on-one conversation. I can do okay in a group, injecting the occasional witty or sarcastic comment, but alone with another person I instantly feel the pressure of having to carry on a conversation, something I am not comfortable with and avoid at all costs.

Ding-dong! There was the doorbell again and whoever was pushing the button was clearly not going to go away.

I looked up at Spencer, hoping he would save me and volunteer to go and see what was so important to the person on the other side that they had to torment me. But he was content to sit there and gaze earnestly at the freshly painted canvas lying down flat on my table.

I finally caved. "I'll get it. You stay here and hold down the fort." I dropped my brush and headed down the hallway toward the front door. Then I had an idea. I turned left, into the laundry room, hoping that maybe whoever had been ringing the bell had now given up and was retreating up the sidewalk away from the house. I peered out the laundry room window but saw no one. I wheeled around and headed back into the hallway. A few more steps and I took a left again, this time into the dining room. If I was quiet, I still might be able to retain the option of not giving away my presence and not having to open the door.

I slipped silently toward the dining room window and carefully pulled back the curtains, just enough to position one eye in the crack and hopefully see who was at my door. I pulled the curtains back just an inch or two. I still couldn't see who was there but I did see a woman in her thirties standing out on the sidewalk, looking at my front door. Then the woman turned her head and looked in my direction.

She's looking right at me!

My cover blown, I could no longer pretend I wasn't home. Now I *had* to answer the door. I took a deep breath and forced myself to walk over, turn the knob and pull it open.

"Do you want to buy some Girl Scout cookies?" said the sum of all fears. I looked down at a ten-year-old girl holding out a green box of Thin Mints.

I let out my breath and caved again. "Sure. I'll take it. And a box of Samoas." I pulled out my wallet. Transaction completed, I said goodbye and headed back to my office. I felt a little ashamed, my shoulders slumping. A neighbor had once called me a recluse. At first I recoiled but then I realized she was just telling the truth. Without Wendy, I probably would be a hermit and never leave the house. As I trudged along, I looked down, feeling defeated.

Wait. What is that on the carpet? I paused my walk of shame for a moment, right in front of my office, and stared at the little red blotches. *Is that blood?*

I stooped down, looked closer and realized it was red paint. The more I looked, the more red I saw. I was very careful never to splatter paint. I stood at the doorway to my office and peered in. Then it finally dawned on me as the red paint splotches came into focus. Tracks. Spencer's paw tracks. And the abstract painting I'd been working on was now covered in little smeary red paw prints. Spencer had walked across the wet painting and then jumped to the floor.

Where is he? I have to find him before he tracks paint all over the house. Paint on the floor of my office was one thing. Wendy had given up on it long ago and allowed me to make a mess in there. But the rest of the house was pristine, kept up to Wendy's standards. If Spencer tracked paint throughout the rest of the house, I would be the one to answer for it. I started to panic again when I heard a rustling underneath my table. I bent down to find Spencer staring back at me.

"What have you been up to, little guy?"

All I got was a muted meow. I reached down, picked him up and plunked him back in the middle of my wet canvas. *Ironic. I'm an animal artist and now my cat wants to be an artist, too.*

"I can't sell these. You paint it. Maybe you'll have better luck."

Chapter 8

Last Race

Metro, Years Five to Six

"The blood and guts of horseracing isn't the Kentucky Derby and the Arlington Million...It's the six-, seven-, and eight-year-old horses that have been passed around more times than blame itself."

—*Dave Feldman, Woulda Coulda Shoulda*

Metro's newest owner, Bob Oliva of Renpher Stables, quickly grew attached to his new horse. Bob always talked to his horses and felt like they listened back. "He was one of the very few who would stand there and listen to me," he said. "But he definitely had an attitude. He thought he was the boss."

Bob had purchased Metro with another horse in a package deal and shipped them both to Penn National, the racetrack where Bob kept his horses. While Bob had a background in telecommunications, he'd always loved horse racing and had been going to the track with his father since he was twelve years old.

In high school, he often cut afternoon classes and headed to the track. One day at the window, the man who was taking Bob's two-dollar bet asked, "Why are you here every day? You could do anything you want in the city. Why do you come here?"

"One day I'm going to be the leading rider in New York City," said Bob.

"The leading rider, huh?" the man said, thoughtful. "How'd you like to work at the racetrack?"

While Bob never did become a jockey, he was able to work with a Hall of Fame horse trainer for a while. Then, when he needed a more substantial paycheck, he got a job in the telecom world. But he always wanted a racehorse for himself. When he got older and made some money, Bob bought his first horse. He got lucky and, in just two weeks, made $6,000 on that horse. Once again, he was hooked.

From that first successful investment, Renpher Stables grew into an organization running ten to twenty horses and began developing extensive racehorse partnerships. Partnerships offer percentage ownership in a racehorse, as little as 3 percent, for an affordable cost, and Renpher had over one hundred partners. Metro was purchased for one of Bob's partnerships and among those partners were Ron and Wendy Krajewski.

The trainers for Renpher Stables were David Lupo and Therese Schirmer.

David was not completely bald, but still clung on to the hair that formed an arc over his ears. He looked like he was no stranger to hard work or to combing through a racing form over donuts and coffee. He could have easily blended in with trainers on the backside as well as the bettors on the other side of the rail. Therese was tall and blonde. She gave you the impression that she was meek and powerful all at the same time. She was quiet and polite but you knew she could hold her own with a feisty Thoroughbred.

David had worked in finance and insurance and made a lot of money as a young man, but after his brother passed away, he decided to make a change and do something he really enjoyed. He'd grown up with horses, but his remaining brother, a trial attorney, advised him to try out training and make sure he liked it. He started with the meanest horse in Detroit, a mare so aggressive he took his life in his hands every time he entered her stall. After a week of training, she was his best friend. Within a few months, David and his brother purchased a string of New York-bred racehorses and set up shop at Hazel Park Raceway in Detroit.

David later worked as a trainer in Cleveland, then ended up at Penn National with Renpher Stables, where he crossed paths with Metro Meteor. David knew about Metro's pedigree and, more importantly, his successes. Metro was in the twilight years of his career, with his knees a mess. But even so, David gave him the royal treatment. "Horses like Metro have earned that majesty. I treat them differently from the other horses, because they give everything to racing." David kept Metro down in the middle of the barn, right across from the feed room, so he could feed him first. "Metro earned it."

With Metro's sore knees, both Bob and David knew he needed to be racing on turf. They got him a dirt race in February and he didn't even come close to winning. But with the unpredictable spring weather in Pennsylvania, they couldn't find a turf race for Metro until June 11,

2009. It was an $8,000 claiming race. However, rains had forced the race to be moved off the slippery grass track and onto the dirt. When this happens, owners who don't want their horses racing on dirt have the option of scratching their horses from the race without penalty.

Metro's training was going as well as could be expected, but David could tell his knees were very sore. When David heard Metro would not be running on turf, he confronted Bob. "We've gotta scratch this horse. He can't even *walk* on dirt." David wanted to wait another month or two to allow Metro's knees to heal. But Bob, feeling pressure from the partnership to run the new horse and earn some money back, didn't feel he could spare the time.

Racing is tough on horses, says David. "You're taking a field animal and putting him into a nine-by-nine or twelve-by-twelve box. Add the strain of being around the track all the time, plus the food, supplements and medications, and most racehorses get ulcers. On top of that is the pain. Horses can't run through pain, so they're subjected to all sorts of treatments so they will run."

But even though it's tough on the horses, David loves the sport. Winning a race with a horse you've purchased or trained is intoxicating. "Nothing can touch that feeling when your horse crosses the wire. It's a weird thing, but that's the mystique of horse racing."

In his sixth year, Metro ran that race on the dirt and it's the race that broke him down. His battered knees could no longer take the punishment and, although he did finish, he came off the track a different horse.

David watched as Metro limped back to the barn. Then he started cursing. "Why did we do that to this horse? He didn't deserve it. The racing Gods make you pay if you do that." Later, David told his assistant, Heather, "We're not going to run him again."

"I wish I would have stood up and said 'No. Let's wait one more month.' But I didn't," said David. "If there's a God, he'll punish me for letting Metro Meteor run that race. After that, he was just a big-kneed cripple."

It just so happened, however, that an artist named Ron and a flight attendant named Wendy were looking for a horse. When David and Therese heard this, they began to formulate a plan. Maybe, just maybe, Metro had a way off the track.

Chapter 9

Meeting Metro

"God forbid that I should go to any Heaven in which there are no horses."

—R.B. Cunninghame Graham, letter to Theodore Roosevelt, 1917

Wendy used to say she'd always wanted a horse. But she says she wants a lot of things. If we watch *Game of Thrones,* she'll say she wants a dragon. Nevertheless, I love to spoil her. If she says she wants a dragon, I'll try to find a small, friendly, affordable one for her.

When Wendy was in grade school in Needles, her best friends Sheila and Chris Jennings owned a mustang from the wild herds of horses managed by the Bureau of Land Management. Smokey the mustang was laid back, very tolerant and gentle with little kids. Wendy and her friends used to take turns riding Smokey bareback through the desert. Every year, Smokey tolerated them dressing him up and marching him in the parade through downtown Needles.

My early riding experience, however, was limited to the pony ride at the Woodland Park Zoo in Seattle, where they made you wear a seatbelt as the pony trudged around a circle at a glacial pace. When I was twelve, I did have a trail ride experience at a dude ranch in British Columbia called Lucky Strike Ranch. Since I didn't know anything about horses, I was assigned to an old gray draft horse (also, in a strange coincidence, named Smokey). But because Smokey had a chronic flatulence problem, ol' Farty and I were banished to the back of the line. It wasn't quite the thrilling equine experience I was expecting, when I compared it to watching the jockeys and horses at Longacres with Grandma.

During my later teen years, my mom owned a horse named Like a Dime. Her horse kept her busy in the evenings while my dad enjoyed his hobby of Texas Hold 'Em at his favorite poker room. I never rode my mom's horse, groomed it or even touched it. I was all about photography and rock music during those years, although I did go out one weekend and take photos of her riding in a weekend horse show.

So Wendy and I couldn't really qualify as horse people. Neither of us knew much, apart from Wendy's bareback rides as a kid. But we had exhausted most of the typical sights as we drove around Pennsylvania, looking for something to do in our free time. One of our Friday evening drives took us to Harper's Ferry, West Virginia, about an hour away, to visit a small casino. The casino had a horse racing track called Charles Town. We planned on getting dinner at the buffet and maybe catching a couple of races, just for fun. I hadn't been back to the races in thirty-five years, even though we always made an effort to watch the Triple Crown on TV.

We found we really enjoyed the energy of the racetrack and the intense, athletic beauty of the horses. Watching horse racing as an adult was much different. When I was a child, it all seemed so much grander—the people, the track, the pageantry. Racetracks and casinos had been magical places. I had visions of James Bond playing baccarat in his tuxedo in Monte Carlo, a guy in a red jacket with tails playing a long trumpet as the horses marched on to the track, coolly observed by women in big flowery hats holding mint juleps.

When you go to a racetrack in person and it's anytime except Derby Day, James Bond in a tuxedo begins to morph into an obese man in Birkenstocks driving a motorized scooter or an elderly woman dragging a cart with an oxygen bottle. Many of the people were there for a good time and to drop a few bucks, like the smiling, happy faces you see in the ads. But some reeked of desperation, people unhappy with their lives and placing bets with money they couldn't afford to lose in the hopes of hitting it big and scoring a chance at a better existence. I've been known to play blackjack but, if I had a million dollars in my pocket, I'd probably still only make a two dollar bet. Gambling isn't about trying to make my life better; it's just about having a little skin in the game to make things more interesting.

But the horses were the same, just as beautiful as they had been when I was a kid. I especially loved the way the horses danced in the paddock before the races, all legs and quicksilver movements, energy and passion sparking off their hooves as necks bowed and tails twitched in excitement. You couldn't get the same experience watching a race on TV, so Wendy and I began to make Charles Town and other tracks within driving distance our regular Friday night dates.

I worked hard to learn the art of handicapping. Surely it was in my blood, as my grandma had done so well. But since she never shared her secrets, I still struggled to read a racing form, trying to make sense of the numbers on a horse's past performance so I could pick a winner. I could never seem to get the hang of it. It felt like high school algebra all over again.

Wendy, on the other hand, developed her own trademark betting system. She bet on any horse that was gray in color, had the word "bear" or "cat" in its name or gave her a special, knowing glance in the paddock. There was no research involved, no sweating over the forms. She usually ended up winning money.

My hours wasted trying to decipher the endless numbers on a racing form could never compete with Wendy's system and I quickly gave up on betting. So while Wendy was busy making money, I simply enjoyed the spectacle of the sport. I loved the sight of Thoroughbreds running all out at full speed. I looked forward to every Friday visit to the track and I couldn't get the horses out of my mind.

"Let's buy a racehorse," I said to Wendy on a whim one Saturday morning. If I couldn't be successful betting on horses, maybe I could be successful owning a horse. I'm not really sure where the idea came from, but I knew

I enjoyed watching the horses in the paddocks more than the races and I didn't want to wait anymore to only see them on Fridays.

"We can't afford a racehorse," Wendy said.

"Not a whole racehorse. We can buy shares." I had done my research and found a stable that operated out of Penn National called Renpher Stables. We could own part of a racehorse for as little as $300.

I'd also done twenty years of research on Wendy and I knew what to say next. "If the horse wins a race, you get to be in the winner's circle photo."

Her eyes got big. Wendy loves being in the center of the action. She was in.

We bought small percentages in a few of Renpher's horses and it made going to the races even more fun. One night, on our way to an evening of racing at Penn National, Wendy knew we were going to see one of our horses and asked me about it in the car.

"Who's running tonight?"

"Metro Meteor," I answered. Metro was the fourth horse we'd bought into and so far, we had yet to buy a winner. We owned about 3 percent of Metro. I figured that was about thirty pounds of a thousand-pound horse, the equivalent of the bottom part of one leg.

"Is he any good?" Wendy asked.

Fair question. "I don't know. His morning odds were six-to-one, so he has as good a chance as any."

"Hopefully this one will win," Wendy said. She was probably thinking about how to pose in the winner's circle and which friends she was going to show the picture first.

We got to the track early so we could see Metro in the paddock before the race. Even though we were officially owners of Metro and had the badges to prove it, we were asked by Bob not to come into the paddock before the race. It's different when you're the sole owner, but this was a partnership. Metro had twenty owners and it could get a little crowded. So we watched Metro from outside the paddock and tried to pick out which 3 percent of him we actually owned.

Metro put on a show. He looked different from the other low-priced claiming horses. He had the look of experience, of a horse that had done this before. At the time, I was not aware of his history in New York, that he was once worth more than our first house, or of the problems that funneled him into a low-level claiming race at Penn National.

After a few laps around the paddock track, the horses were led into their assigned saddling areas. This was always an interesting part to watch, as excited, nervous horses were now asked to stand in an enclosed space, surrounded by three walls as they got tacked up. Some kicked the walls in nervousness and others spun in circles while their handlers tried to slow them down long enough to throw a saddle on them. But Metro stood perfectly still. Not that he wasn't difficult. He was, but Metro gave you the sense that he wasn't being difficult because he was nervous but because he enjoyed it. It was a game he played with his trainer. He threw his head wildly up and down as the groom and trainer tried to pull the hood and blinkers over his head. When the girth to his jockey saddle tightened around his chest, Metro turned and bared his teeth at his trainer to let him know the saddle was plenty tight enough.

With some last-minute instructions, the jockey cocked his leg at a ninety-degree angle as the trainer effortlessly lifted the slight man onto Metro's back.

Wendy and I left reluctantly and hurried to the rail, not wanting to miss the starting bell. The race was a short one, just five furlongs or five-eighths of a mile, and it was over in less than a minute. Metro Meteor lagged and finished in sixth place, never even close to winning. Some of the other syndicate partners left the rail after the finish to watch the replay on one of the monitors mounted around the track. I stayed to watch the horses come back as they cantered easily along the rail on their way back to the barn.

Metro was one of the last in and I noticed his jockey was trotting him, not having him canter like the other horses. Metro bobbed his head up and down as he passed slowly by and I had a flash of insight. *Is Metro in pain?*

When I'd looked at him in the paddock, I'd noticed his front knees were bumpy and swollen, not smooth and flat like those of the other horses. But I'd dismissed it. *That's probably normal for him.*

I felt badly for Metro as he limped awkwardly back to the barn. This was not the same proud, dancing horse that had left the paddock, ready to thunder his way around the track just a few moments before. His striking white-rimmed eyes were tired and looked a little distant, like his mind was off somewhere else.

I wasn't the only one on the rail. Other people were standing in the tangle of discarded race tickets as they watched the horses come back in. Someone nearby spoke up as Metro limped by. His tone was observational, jaded, like he'd seen it all.

"Looks like that one is done being a horse."

I was stunned, not quite understanding the words. I had just seen Metro run a race. Sure, he wasn't flashing around the track at lightning speed, but he made it all the way around in one piece. As I turned to watch him disappear into the shadows, he reminded me of an aging Mickey Mantle at the end of his career, hobbled by old injuries and unable to chase down the fly balls that used to be so easy. But he still carried the swagger of greatness.

I knew in my gut that Metro wasn't done being a horse. I had seen a different side of him in the paddock. But I didn't yet know that I had just seen his last race and soon I would own more of Metro than part of a leg. I'd learn about his racing career, find out what had happened to his knees and begin to forge a relationship with one of the jackass-iest racehorses that ever ran a race. I'd experience Metro as lightning bolt, going from zero to forty miles an hour in a split second. Or Metro as rocket ride, able to levitate and shift position while in the air. Or Metro as cranky old man, looking for someone to bite, because he was having a bad day and didn't want to play nice. Soon, I would live, breathe and die for this horse who was supposedly done being a horse. He was about to climb under my skin and stay there.

Chapter 10

You Could Put a Five-Year-Old on His Back

"A horse doesn't care how much you know
until he knows how much you care."
—*Pat Parelli*

Even though I'd just met Metro, I was anxious to hear how he was doing. The sight of him limping back to the stable after the race played over and over in my head like a bad home movie.

I tend to do a lot of thinking and I spend hours in introspection, problem solving and worry. Metro was my new worry. *How bad are his knees? Will they have to put him down?*

Within a couple of days, we received an email from Renpher. Bob's group messages went out regularly to all of the partners to keep us informed on how the horses were doing, along with their racing status. The email reported that the track vet had observed Metro in pain and put his name on the vet's list. He wouldn't be allowed to race again until he was healthy.

I thought back to Friday night, right before the race. "Wendy!" Bob had yelled as we approached the paddock. Everyone always seems to be more excited to see Wendy than me. But that's okay, because Wendy is a lot more fun to be around.

Bob loves horse racing and he loves his horses. Besides managing his horses and the people who train and care for them, he has to deal with over one hundred partners who think they know more than he does and who second-guess everything he does. Everyone thinks they can make money from horse racing, but only a select few do.

I sensed that Bob liked Wendy and me. We were the perfect partners, because we had no preconceived notions about making money. We just wanted to have an adventure. Plus, we didn't really know anything about horses and didn't pretend to. We were Bob's students and he liked teaching us about the sport he loves.

Bob had led us to the paddock to point out Metro. "Which one is he?" I asked.

"The one with the white socks." That was the first time we'd laid eyes on him. Bob explained that Metro was about to run in a low-level, $8,000 claiming race.

Claiming races usually draw horses that are older, not in great shape or not as competitive for one reason or another. In a claiming race, any of the horses entered can be purchased before the race by another licensed owner. When a horse is purchased or claimed, one of the race-track officials will attach a large *CLAIM* tag to the horse's halter before the race, meaning the horse will be going to a new barn.

If someone had wanted to buy Metro on Friday night, all they would have had to do was go to the racing secretary's office, fill out a claim form before the race and deposit the money with the bookkeeper. Anyone willing to part with $8,000 could have claimed him before post time. But no one did.

I was surprised, because Metro just seemed to move with more class and confidence than any of the other horses. "Do you think he will be claimed?" I asked Bob.

He shook his head. "Look at his knees. No one is going to claim a horse with those knees."

I knew it had been four months since Metro's last race. I didn't know why he'd been out of competition so long, but I had a feeling those knees had something to do with it. Maybe that is why some of the other partners were selling their shares in Metro to unsuspecting buyers like Wendy and me.

I read Bob's email again. Even though Metro had only raced a couple of times for Renpher Stables and had not even earned back his purchase price yet, Bob was announcing Metro's retirement and looking for a new home for him. Wendy and I, along with the other owners, would still be responsible for Metro's expenses until Bob could find a suitable home. As I read the message, I felt relieved. I didn't know the extent of his injuries, but I was happy they weren't going to put Metro down. And I didn't mind paying our share of the expenses until they could find him a good home.

The newsletter also announced the retirement of another horse named Bamboo Shade or "Boo." He'd be running a couple more races and then retiring at the end of the summer. We'd met Boo before. Being a partner meant we were allowed to come visit the horses at the stable, as long as we made arrangements in advance and brought baby carrots for the horses and donuts for Bob and the crew.

Wendy was already in love with Boo. His official color was Dark Bay but he was really a glossy black. Wendy was putty in his hooves. On our stable visits, she could never tear herself away from Boo to visit the other horses. She spent her time in front of his stall, rubbing his head until he fell asleep. It was the first time I'd ever seen Wendy around a horse and it transformed her. Happiness shone in her eyes like I had never seen before.

Wendy is low maintenance and always has been. She makes a good living and doesn't spend a lot of money on herself. She had never asked to purchase anything for herself as long as we had been married, even though she had every right to do so. But I knew she'd always wanted a horse of her own. I could hear it in her voice when she talked about riding Smokey in the deserts of California. And I could hear it again when she talked about Boo.

I told her about Bob's email. "Boo is retiring at the end of the summer, after a couple more races. Do you want to ask Bob if we can have him?"

"Seriously?" Wendy looked shocked.

"It's a couple of months away, which would give us plenty of time to find a place for him. There are lots of barns that give lessons. You don't even need a horse to get started. While you're waiting for Boo, you could ride the lesson horses and get some riding under your belt before we bring him home."

I didn't have to hear her *yes*, because I already knew the answer from her eyes.

Due to our schedules, we had to wait two whole weeks before we went back to the track. We knew Bob was inside, up in the box he rents out for the partners to use when it's raining or too hot and humid. But first we decided to go watch the horses parade in the paddock before the next race. We spotted Dave and Therese, Bob's trainers, near the paddock. We'd gotten to know them over the past few months and they were always friendly and approachable. They looked up and smiled.

"You guys see Boo every day," said Wendy. "What's he like? Would he be a good horse for a beginning rider?"

"Why?" said Dave. "Are you thinking about taking him when he retires?"

"Yes," said Wendy, a note of excitement in her voice. "If Bob will let us have him."

We were pretty sure it was a lock, unless one of Bob's other partners got there first. When Bob retires one of his horses, he gives the partners first crack. He never asks for money, just a good home.

Theresa piped in. "Boo is kind of standoffish, a loner," she said. That surprised me. I pictured Wendy rubbing Boo's head as his eyes drooped in relaxation. "If you want a horse that is going to be your best friend, you want Metro."

Metro?! That surprised me. Metro seemed like a very powerful, intense horse. *And what about his knees?*

"What kind of riding are you going to be doing?" Dave asked Wendy.

"Just trail riding."

"Metro will be good for that." Dave nodded his head. "He's sound. Just needs some time off."

"Yes, and Metro will be your buddy," Therese added. "He's friendly and gentle."

We left the paddock and climbed up to Bob's box to watch the race. My mind was on overdrive. If I didn't know better, I'd think the two trainers were giving Wendy the hard sell on Metro. She was all ears and seemed to forget about Boo.

From reading Bob's emails, I surmised it was proving difficult to find a new home for Metro. There must be a reason. But I decided to stay out of it. This was Wendy's horse and Wendy's decision. Deep down, though, I knew they were pushing her buttons. She wanted a horse that would be her best friend and the trainers were telling her what she yearned to hear. But I also got the feeling that they were thinking more of what was best for Metro, not us. We knew nothing about horses. To us, one horse was as good as the next. Plus, he was free. *Where's the down-side to that?*

So I wasn't surprised when, up in the box, Wendy didn't waste any time. "Bob, can I have Metro?"

Five simple words that changed my life. But I didn't know that yet.

Bob turned around in his seat and stared at Wendy, seated on the steps. His eyes widened and he paused for a minute. He must have known how little we knew about horses. But maybe he sensed we were good, responsible people. We could be trusted. Plus, we brought him donuts.

"You want Metro?" he said, finally. "You got him. But here's the deal: No jumping. No dressage. His knees can't take it. He's a good horse. I wouldn't hesitate to put a five-year-old on his back."

Wendy's face started to glow as she began to smile.

"Do you have a place to keep him?" asked Bob.

"Um, not yet."

"Well, you better go home and find one, because he is ready to go now."

In shock, we turned around and left after thanking Bob. We didn't even stay for the races, but hopped right in the car and headed back to Gettysburg. Our two-month plan of finding a barn and learning how to ride had just jumped out the window. We now owned a real racehorse, but we weren't close to being ready.

The shock started to settle in on the way home. I couldn't help but wonder if we were doing the right thing. We'd come with one plan and left with a completely different one. *This isn't the first time we've done something on the spur of a moment,* I fretted. T*he worst that's happened before is we bought something we didn't need and lost a little money. But a horse? That's a twenty-year commitment!*

We scoured the phone book, the Internet and the local papers for a stable and Wendy saw an ad for Stone Hall Stables. It sounded nice, like something out of a

PBS special on English country living at the turn of the century.

Stone Hall Stables was a couple of miles from our house and we stopped in for a tour with Karen, the owner. She showed us a stall up front and center, right in the middle of the action. This would be Metro's new home.

Karen was an abrupt, to-the-point person. She seemed to rule her stable and her household with an iron fist. She had competed in hunter jumper. We just nodded our heads as if we knew what she was talking about, although we didn't. We had no idea there were different kinds of riding. My frame of reference was old Westerns and I thought everyone used a Western saddle and rode like Clint Eastwood.

Karen said she didn't compete or ride anymore and I noticed she used a golf cart to get around the property. She told us that, besides running the barn, she kept busy giving English lessons. I considered that for a minute, confused. Then I had an a-ha moment. *Oh. She must be talking about English riding, not about teaching the English language.*

Karen gave us a list of shots Metro would need, along with a Coggins report for a viral disease called Equine Infectious Anemia, before he'd be allowed on the property. He also needed two bales of hay from Renpher so he could be slowly weaned off his racehorse diet and acclimated to the new menu.

Nothing to worry about—it all seemed pretty simple and straightforward. Bob arranged transportation for the following day. We could hardly sleep with anticipation, but Wendy and I showed up at Stone Hall Stables the next morning to wait for our horse to arrive. We tried to act cool but we couldn't stop smiling.

Stone Hall was at the top of a small rise, with a gravel drive leading about 300 yards down to the highway. The farm was about thirty-five acres, mostly pasture with trees on the borders. The barn had eighteen stalls and there were indoor and outdoor arenas.

Wendy and I stood next to the barn, looking down the gravel drive, waiting for the truck and trailer to arrive with our precious cargo. It was ten in the morning and sunny. The humidity was already getting to me. I wasn't quite used to it and would rather be in Phoenix at 110 degrees than Gettsyburg at 90. I started to feel my shirt getting damp as Karen rolled up in her golf cart. We were excited and hoping she was, too. After all, she was getting a champion Thoroughbred racehorse at her barn. What a privilege, right?

Karen didn't waste any time on niceties. "Do you have a halter and lead rope for your horse?" she barked out.

Wendy and I looked at each other. *Whoops.*

"No," said Wendy.

"Do you have brushes? A grooming bag? Tack locker? Anything?" Karen asked again.

No, no, no and no.

"We don't have anything," Wendy admitted. "We don't know *what* we need."

I started to feel like it was going to be a long day.

Chapter 11

Horses for Dummies

"Horses are uncomfortable in the middle
and dangerous at both ends."
—*Ian Fleming*

Upon discovering we had not even a single, solitary hoof pick to our name, Karen let out a huff. I was starting to get the feeling she didn't have much tolerance for novice horse owners.

"Well, you are going to have to get all of those things immediately if you are going to have a horse," she said with a dramatic sigh. I knew from experience that when a woman sighs, she has just called you an idiot without actually saying it. I don't know if this is an inherited skill or a required class in high school.

Karen collected herself for a moment before taking on an artificially calm and even tone, as if speaking to developmentally challenged children. "I will make you a list of what you need. Then run up to the tack shop off Highway 15 and pick it up." She blinked her eyes to punctuate. "Today."

I guess I couldn't blame her for being annoyed with us. We truly were not prepared. Becoming horse owners had happened so fast and we hadn't had the time. We were doing the best we knew how to do, but now Karen was kind of raining on my parade. The excitement and anticipation of Metro's arrival quickly melted away and turned into embarrassment. I felt like a guy showing up for a big, elaborate wedding and realizing I'd forgotten the marriage license, the tuxedo and the ring. *What an idiot,* I thought, figuratively smacking myself in the head. *Of course we need some horse stuff.*

It was too late to go now, as the horse trailer would arrive any moment with our precious cargo. We spent the next ten minutes in awkward silence, unable to take our eyes off the little stretch of road we could see at the end of the gravel drive. I felt Wendy's hand slip into mine and I looked down at our clasped hands. *At least we're in this together.*

Then her hand tightened and I looked back up and to the left. It was a horse trailer, coming south. I had been looking to the right, expecting the trailer to come from the nearest freeway exit. Wendy gripped harder as the trailer rolled closer to the entrance but didn't slow down. Her hand relaxed as the trailer passed by. *It's not Metro.* A lot of horse trailers traveled this road. *Relax.*

Five minutes passed, then a horse trailer approached from the south. I recognized the truck and trailer as the same one that had just driven by. *This must be it!* The driver had probably missed the turnoff and continued on to find a place wide enough to turn around. This time, the truck and trailer slowed, then turned onto the gravel drive and continued toward us. My heart started to beat harder and I wondered if Wendy could hear it. But hers was probably pounding, too.

Dust billowed up as the truck came closer and followed a slight curve to the left. As the side of the trailer came into view, I could just see the silhouette of a horse's head through the open window. The horse raised his head and sniffed the air. Then his mouth opened up and he let out a loud whinny to announce his arrival. My heart jumped in response. *Metro!*

I looked over at Wendy. Her eyes were starting to well up. "I think I'm going to cry," she said.

The driver stopped the truck and went around to open the back door, securing it on the side so it couldn't swing back. There was a safety chain draped across the opening, covered by a black rubber protector so the horse couldn't get hurt. The chain kept Metro inside until we were ready to unload him. Metro moved around a little, shifting his weight from side to side. His feet made hollow thumping noises against the padded metal floor and the trailer rocked a bit. Overall, he seemed calm. He was probably used to being transported from place to place and he knew the drill.

The driver opened a small, upper window at the front of the trailer, untied Metro's lead rope from a metal ring and let it hang down. Then he came back around, climbed up into the other compartment next to Metro and grabbed the rope.

"Okay, buddy. Time to go," he said in a quiet but firm voice. "Back, back, back." Metro slowly backed out, lowering his head and stepping slowly but gracefully down from the trailer with each foot. As soon as he was out, he arched his neck and raised his tail, flicking his ears from side to side and then pointing them forward again. His nostrils flared and he snorted, looking proud and excited.

Are we ready for this? I looked at Wendy and her eyes were glued to Metro. She looked like a kid about to unwrap the biggest Christmas present under the tree.

I looked back at Metro, then down at his feet, and noticed he had lost a shoe. Two shoes were still attached and a third was loose, barely clinging to his hoof. I admired his face, the two white patches that made up his blaze held together by a pencil-thin strip. He wore a faded olive-green halter probably worn by a hundred other horses. I wondered what had happened to them. Then the driver handed me an eight-foot nylon rope attached to a ring at the bottom of Metro's halter. I stared down at the rope in my hand. I had never held a thousand-pound animal by the end of a rope before and the look on my face must have told everyone the truth.

"I'll take him to the paddock for you," said Karen's husband, Mike, taking the rope from my limp hands. I was more than happy to let him.

As Metro walked away, following Mike to his new home, Karen said, "He looks thin. And his knees look swollen."

But to Wendy and me, his brand new owners, Metro looked stunning. Wendy's smile was huge and I wanted to shout, "It's a boy!" Instead, we decided we'd better hustle to get to the tack store before it closed.

At the store, we followed Karen's list to the letter and started piling up a big stack of equipment at the register. First, though, we had to negotiate color, and to Wendy's delight there were several ultra-bright colors available. I shook my head as she kept picking up bright pink and purple halters and brushes. Every horse item was apparently available in a be-dazzled version, covered with glitter. I had my work cut out for me if we were to leave the tack store with Metro's manhood still intact.

"Geez. Give the boy some dignity," I said. I didn't want our mighty racehorse to look like he'd popped out of a pink cardboard box labeled *Barbie's Dream Horse.*

Wendy reluctantly agreed and we compromised on a royal blue lead rope, hoof pick and blue brushes, among other things. We also splurged on a soft leather halter. After we paid, we headed to the bookstore for some books on basic horse care. Wendy was about to head out of town for her regular three-day flight assignment and I figured I could learn how to take care of our new horse on my own while she was gone.

I had no doubt that I could learn how to take care of Metro. Although I had zero horse experience, other than from watching horses at the track, I was confident that I could become a horse trainer just by reading books and teaching myself. I had learned everything in the privacy of my own home. How hard could it be to become a master horseman?

Wendy, as usual, brought me down to earth. "This book says horses need to be groomed every day," she said, flipping through the pages of a copy of *Horses For Dummies*. "You need to go up to Stone Hall and groom Metro while I'm gone."

"Don't worry," I said. "I'll take care of it." *No problem. I can brush my hair, so I'm sure I can brush Metro's, too. Simple.*

We took everything back to the barn and stood and watched Metro as he got acquainted with his stall. He walked around, sniffing everything, pausing often to listen to the new sounds. Every once in a while he'd come over and take a look at us, bobbing his head a bit. As it grew dusky, Mike came along with his tractor, towing a small trailer filled with hay. He stopped and threw a chunk of hay, packed into a rough rectangle, over the door and into Metro's manger. Happy munching and crunching sounds filled the evening air as Metro dug into his dinner. His tail flipped up and down in excitement and his front hoof arced out and pawed the ground as he ate. *Typical guy. Food comes first.*

We knew we wouldn't get any more interaction out of him so we reluctantly said our goodbyes and left, starry-eyed and still in shock. Not long ago we had owned 3 percent of a racehorse. Now we owned 100 percent. He was all ours. Yes, we were inexperienced owners, but we could learn. And it was a heady feeling. We owned a Thoroughbred, a racing machine created and trained to conquer the track. I couldn't believe it.

Wendy took off early the next morning and I headed to the barn after a night of not much sleep. To my relief, mine was the only car in the parking lot. Karen had explained how most of the other owners came after work to spend time with their horses in the evenings, so I planned to come during the day when no one else was around. That way, I could just do what I needed to do and slip out without anyone noticing. As a bonus, I could avoid having to make small talk.

I parked my car and headed into the barn. As I approached his stall, Metro must have seen or heard me and he let out a sound that reminded me of Scooby Doo. "Ah-ah-ah, uh-uh-uh," his voice starting at a medium register and then going lower down into his chest, ending in a throaty murmur. I could almost feel the vibration in the air. Later, I'd find out this was called a *nicker* and it's how horses greet each other. Whatever it was, I loved it and was surprised to be welcomed with such a friendly sound. Maybe this was all going to turn out pretty great, no matter what Karen thought.

"Hey, Metro." Metro's stall, like all the others, had a box fan on the bars to give the horses a little additional air circulation. I listened to the quiet hum and breathed in the scent of warm fur, sweet hay and horse manure (which smells almost as good as sweet hay to horse folk). I'd gotten used to the scent at the training barn and it was starting to feel like home. Metro stuck his head out over the door and began to bob his head up and down, a big floor-to-ceiling type of nod.

"Aren't you a happy guy?" The artist in me immediately thought, *I bet if I could teach you to hold a paintbrush in your teeth, you could paint a fence like Tom Sawyer.*

I turned and looked down the row of stalls. All the other horses had their heads out, doing nothing. They looked a little bored, standing quietly and watching. Metro was the only one putting on a show. Without a doubt, I knew we had the greatest horse in the barn. We certainly had the horse with the best history and racing credentials. I smiled to myself. This was going to be an adventure.

I turned back and reached out to stroke Metro's head, my hand running down his white blaze. I stroked him again, feeling his warm, silky hair over the angular bridge of his nose. Then, on the third stroke, my reverie was rudely interrupted when he suddenly jerked back his head and lunged forward, snapping at my arm, white teeth flashing.

What?! Without thinking, I jumped back and pulled my hand away, adrenaline rushing through my body.

Did Metro just try to bite me?

Chapter 12

The Sweet Spot

"You need to learn to go with the horse
so you can get the horse to come with you."
—*Tom Dorrance, True Unity*

Right after Metro snapped at me, still not quite believing what I'd just seen, I tried again. He was standing quietly, with a "Who, me?" look in his white-rimmed eyes as I slowly lifted my hand again and gently stroked his face.

Snap! I jerked my hand back just in time as his teeth snapped together.

Are you kidding me? Don't you know I'm your new owner? I'm here to help you.

I decided to give Metro the benefit of the doubt. He was new around here. So was I. Maybe it was nerves or even simply that horses didn't like their heads stroked more than twice at a time. *I'll have to remember that. Two strokes max.*

I grabbed Metro's brand new blue halter with the shiny silver buckles and snapped the lead rope onto the tie ring at the bottom. I coiled the lead rope and held it in my left hand along with the halter as I unbolted the stall door and slid it open. To my surprise, Metro's happy-go-lucky demeanor quickly vanished. His ears, pointing forward when there had been a half-door between us, now did a one-eighty and folded flat back and down against his head. I knew from my horse books that this was not the sign of a happy horse. The white rings around his eyes stood out and he seemed to glare at me with an intensity that made me very uncomfortable.

Cover me; I'm going in. I wasn't about to give up on day one.

After unbuckling the halter, I slipped the noseband up and over the bridge of Metro's nose and the crown piece over the top of his head. While I buckled the halter, I kept a close eye on his mouth, in case he tried to bite me again. I clipped the lead line to the ring on his halter and led him out of the stall. As soon as we emerged, his ears came back up and pointed forward again.

We took a few steps down the aisle and stopped in front of the cross ties, short pieces of rope attached to rings along the wall. I lifted the cross ties and clipped one to his halter. Next, I grabbed the cross tie on the other side of the aisle and clipped it on. Metro was now secure and I felt a little more secure as well.

Now that we were in the aisle and away from the gloom of the stall, I caught my first real glimpse of the canvas Metro had prepared for my introductory grooming experience. The left side of his body was entirely caked in thick mud. It had dried onto his coat and was now stiff, smelly and separated into clumps. I had no idea where to start.

"Looks like you had fun last night, big guy!"

Why does Wendy always do this to me? She has a habit of adopting a pet the day before she is scheduled to fly away on a three-day trip. She had done this with Spencer, leaving me to pull him off the curtains and walk through my own house in fear as he swan-dived off every cabinet onto my unsuspecting head.

I knew Karen wanted to slowly introduce Metro to the other horses, so for the first few days he would have a small, paddock-sized pasture to himself. It was about the size of an average suburban backyard. The nice grass in the paddocks had been overgrazed, leaving mostly dirt. With the sporadic rains we'd been getting, there was plenty of mud and it looked as if rolling in the stinky muck was going to be one of Metro's new hobbies.

I couldn't get mad at him, though. I figured being stuck inside a racetrack stall didn't give a horse much opportunity to have a good roll in the mud. *Enjoy, Metro. This is the first day of your new life.*

For the moment he was quiet, soaking in his new environment. I stepped over to the shiny tack box we'd purchased yesterday. I felt like a greenhorn—I knew our unblemished equipment was an advertisement to all of the other boarders that we were brand new to all of this. *Note to Self: Next time, drag shiny new tack box behind truck for twenty miles.*

I was glad no one could see me as I opened the box and pulled out my copy of *Horses For Dummies,* spreading it out on top of the box. I turned to a chapter called "Keeping Your Horse Clean and Pretty" and read. "Few things make a horse lover happier than being up on a horse that looks really good. Mane and tail flowing, coat glowing—you'll feel proud passing other riders on the trail as you sit astride such a glamorous beast."

Horse lover? *Check.*

Feeling proud? *Check.*

Glamorous beast? *Oh, yeah.*

I kept reading. "Of course, your trusty steed isn't going to come out of the pasture looking so great—you have to make it happen. Although cleaning up a half-ton animal after he's been milling around in the dirt for days may not sound like a picnic, we consider grooming as one of the most enjoyable parts of horse ownership. And besides, most horses absolutely love the attention."[1]

Okay, this was clearly going to be a positive experience for both of us. The book said so. I scanned the next few pages and got down the basic concept. It didn't seem too difficult. I picked up the currycomb, a small hard rubber tool with serrated ridges to remove dirt. Starting with his shoulder, I began applying circular strokes to Metro's body. But every time I touched the currycomb to his coat, Metro's head swung around to bite me. The first time I jumped back, but the cross tie thudded against the wall as the slack pulled taut, stopping his head from getting close enough to make contact. *Okay. You don't want me touching your shoulder. Fair enough.*

I moved farther down his body and started to curry near his hip, keeping a close eye on the dragon's jaws.

He seemed a little calmer, looking around with his face pointed forward. Then Metro lifted his rear leg and began twirling it around like Reggie Jackson twirling his bat in the batters box of the '77 World Series. I remembered Reggie had hit three homers that night and I jumped back just before Metro kicked out, trying to slap me over the right field fence. *Whoa! That was close.*

I had been under the impression that horses only kicked behind them, like the bucking broncs in the rodeo. I had no idea they could kick to the side. I would have to watch those feet. I could just picture his steel-clad hoof striking out and hitting my kneecap. It would be like breaking open a coconut shell with a sledgehammer. My dream of becoming a master horseman might be over before it ever began.

I tried the currycomb once again, more gently, while monitoring his leg. *Whoosh!* He kicked out again, almost like I was pushing a button that activated the lightning-quick movement. I was starting to get the impression this horse did not like to be touched anywhere. I consulted my book again (I was now thinking of it as *HFD*, because I didn't really identify as a dummy), hoping to find a chapter on "What to Do If Your Horse Is Trying to Maim or Kill You." I couldn't find one.

I did see a chapter called "Making the Big Buy" and it cautioned against taking a free horse. There were three possible reasons a horse might be free, the book explained. One, the owner just doesn't want to deal with selling a horse. Two, the owner wants the horse to go to a good home. Three, and I quote, "A horse is such a big pain in the neck that no one will buy him."

Gulp. We might be looking at a number three here.

I glanced back at Metro, standing peacefully between the cross ties and still covered in smelly mud. I decided to try again, touching the currycomb ever so gently to the middle of his side, halfway between his mouth and his back leg. It was a sweet spot, a safe little sanctuary that would become my base of operations for grooming. Before long, I had cleared out a small cleanish area on the middle of his body. I wasn't sure how I was going to groom his front or his back. I was going slow and giving myself time to figure it out.

The aisle darkened. "What are you doing?" asked Karen. I looked up and saw that she had parked her cart in the doorway, blocking the sunlight.

"What are you doing?" she asked again, stepping from the cart.

I thought it was obvious, but maybe not. Maybe her eyes hadn't adjusted and she couldn't see what I was doing. "Grooming Metro," I answered.

"I don't want you working with this horse when no one is around. He's dangerous."

No kidding.

"I walked into his stall last night," Karen continued in an exasperated voice. "When I went to clean it out, he tried to bite me."

"I can't help it if no one is here when I'm available to come out," I explained. The truth was, I could come in the evenings when more people were around, but I didn't want to. I preferred coming during the day, when I could avoid people.

Karen conceded. "I'll try to keep an eye on you when I am home, but if I'm not here, you be careful. This horse could kill you."

I didn't know what else to do, so I kept brushing the small, safe spot on Metro's side, even as he simultaneously turned his head and lifted his leg again.

Okay, might as well ask the expert. "Do all horses act like this when you groom them?"

"No," said Karen. "I don't think this one is right in the head." She looked over and saw *HFD* sitting on my tack box. "You ever groom a horse before?"

"No, but I'm figuring it out." I hated to admit my inexperience but I didn't think I could fake it with her.

Then Karen decided to take pity on me. "Start with the metal shedding brush when the mud is caked on like this." She went to the tack box, picked out the shedding brush and began to groom Metro in front of me. Then she explained how to use each brush and in what order. Next, she demonstrated how to lift his feet and use the metal pick to remove the embedded dirt and pebbles. Metro twitched and bent and tried to kick out with his back legs, showing Karen about as much tolerance as he'd shown with me. I was glad to see that Wendy's horse didn't just hate me. He seemed to hate everyone.

As Karen worked on Metro, I couldn't help myself and began to tell her what I'd found on the Internet the night before when I'd stayed up late and researched Metro's history. For once, I had plenty of words and I rattled on and on about Metro's history, how many races he had won, how much money he had earned and what price he had sold for.

Karen said nothing. Stone-faced, she kept right on working, clearly unimpressed by Metro's illustrious past. She could only see what Metro was now. "I think you should have a veterinarian do an evaluation on him," said Karen. "He might have more problems than you think."

My heart sank. It had taken Karen about ten minutes to transform Metro from a glamorous beast to a worn-out, used-up hack.

"I can make a call and have a vet out tonight, if you want," Karen said.

I gave in. She was the expert. "Let's do it," I said, as Karen handed me the soft brush. I gave Metro a few more strokes on his now-clean coat as Karen left in her golf cart. I unsnapped the cross ties and led him back to his stall, wondering what the vet was going to say. I knew his knees were not so good, but I hadn't considered the possibility that Metro might have other issues. Maybe there were serious problems. I didn't want to think too much about it, especially since I didn't even have enough knowledge to speculate about what could be wrong.

As I pulled the stall door closed, Metro came forward and hung his head out of the opening again. No head bobbing this time. A glutton for punishment, I tried touching his head again, mindful not to exceed Metro's two-stroke policy. He pulled his head back a little and I leaned against the door and rested my arm on top. Metro leaned forward and lightly rested his whiskery lips on my forearm.

The logical part of my brain screamed at me to pull my arm away in case he tried to bite me again, but I overrode the danger signal and relaxed my arm. Metro began to move his lips, lightly nibbling my arm. He never used his teeth, just his lips. I liked the sensation.

I lifted up my left hand and carefully touched his upper lip with my index finger. He raised his head slightly and tried to catch my finger in his mouth. As he raised his lip, I caught a glimpse of his big, clenched teeth and rubbed my finger across them. These were the same teeth that had tried to take my arm off just a few moments before.

Metro seemed sweet and playful. I could sense no danger or evil in him, just a gentle soul who needed someone to figure him out. I wanted to get inside his head and see who was in there. He was a puzzle, one I needed to assemble.

I leaned in close to his ear, talking quietly. "You're not dangerous. You're just misunderstood."

Chapter 13

Bad-i-tude

"Maybe it's like Mac says.
Every man winds up with the horse that suits him."
—*Cormac McCarthy, Cities of the Plain*

While I waited for the vet to arrive, I thought back to the night before, when I had spent hours on the computer. When I searched *Metro Meteor* on the Internet, I got either a horse from New York that could run up to forty miles per hour or a train in Paris that could travel up to fifty miles per hour. Both were fast, but only one was flesh and fur and bones and blood.

Looks like Metro comes from good racing stock. Maybe he is *part meteor.*

I had discovered Metro's racing record, with eight wins. He had earned just shy of $300,000 in his racing career. He started out with Obviously NY Stables and on their website, Metro was described as "a bay that seemed to have a bit of an attitude."

No kidding.

Metro later went on to be claimed three times during the course of his career, each time with a price tag of

$50,000. He was a proven money earner and everybody wanted him.

However, when Metro got off the horse trailer on his first day of retirement in July, 2009, he no longer carried a $50,000 price tag. Instead, he was free to a good home and that good home was ours. At six years old, just a young adult in horse years, Metro's glory days were behind him and he didn't look like much anymore. But to two brand-new horse owners taking delivery of their very own horse, he was the most beautiful animal they had ever known.

I was jolted from my reverie when Dr. Mason finally showed up about an hour late. I haltered Metro and proudly led out Wendy's shiny new horse for inspection. Surely the vet would immediately ascertain what a fine specimen of horseflesh he had before him. Surely, there would be shock and awe. I readied myself to receive the accolades.

The vet took a long look at Metro, then walked around him in inspection mode. He narrowed his eyes, nodded his head and said "Hmmmm." Then he began to talk. No accolades, just pointing out each of Metro's many flaws. He acted more like he was negotiating the price of a used car I was trying to sell him, not looking at the greatest horse the world has ever seen.

He showed me two scars on the back of each front leg, where Metro had been subjected to knee surgery. Twice. At this discovery, Dr. Mason and Karen exchanged a few knowing words in horse-speak. I had no idea what they were talking about.

Then the vet squeezed each of Metro's knees and said, "Bone chips." Apparently Metro had knees like Joe Namath. Metro was underweight, probably the result of having an ulcer. "I don't have a scope with me to tell for sure, but I do have some ulcer treatment called GastroGard. It's fifty dollars a tube and he'll need one tube a day for thirty days."

Are you joking? What's in that stuff? I did the math. Ulcer treatment was going to cost $1,500 a month!

While I was counting the draining of my savings account on my fingers, the vet removed Metro's three remaining horseshoes and took him into the arena. Then he hooked a twenty-foot line onto Metro's halter and began moving him around in a large circle, a maneuver known as *lunging*. I wanted to enjoy the sight of Metro moving, but at the trot it became clear, even to a newbie like me, that something wasn't right. Metro limped.

By this time, my happiness and pride at uncovering Metro's legendary racehorse résumé were long gone. I was speeding down the track from disappointed to a place called despair. *Is Metro lame? Is it possible to get him healthy again?*

I was about ready to go home and binge on the Girl Scout cookies, feeling all was lost, when Dr. Mason did something really strange. He got a running start, slammed into Metro's side and tried to knock him over. At first Metro looked shocked. But by the third time, Metro just glared at the vet out of the corner of his eye and gave him a, *Dude, what is your problem?* look. Apparently it was some sort of cow tipping/balance test. Then it was time for the vet's findings.

Bad knees? *Check.*

Underweight? *Check.*

Probable ulcer? *Check.*

Possible neurological problems? *Check.*

The exam was over within a half hour and the vet concluded by presenting me with five tubes of gastric ulcer preventive, a can of powdered analgesic for horses and my first equine vet bill of $600 (the vet's next truck payment).

"These cheap claiming horses don't get the best of care," Dr. Mason said in a matter-of-fact voice as he began to pack up.

Wait. EXCUSE ME? Cheap claiming horse?

His dismissive words stoked my temper and I wanted to shout at him: *Don't you know who this is? This is Metro Meteor, stakes horse, winner of $300,000 and one of the best turf sprinters on the East Coast. This is son of City Zip, nephew of Ghostzapper, a Horse of the Year. I can watch the Kentucky Derby on TV and point out no less than five jockeys that have had this beautiful horse underneath them in the past. And YOU just called him a cheap claiming horse?*

I said none of this. I couldn't even lie and shout, "At least he has a nice personality!" But I knew with every last cell of my being that Dr. Mason would never get another dime from me. I watched as the vet got into his truck and headed off down the long gravel drive.

Good riddance to you, Doc. You will never touch our horse again. Metro and I don't like you.

I led Metro out to the large pasture, where he would spend the evening with the other horses. He stepped gingerly, like he was walking on hot coals. It was probably the first time in years he had no shoes on his feet.

The sun faded, leaving a rosy glow on the trees as I unbuckled Metro's halter and turned him loose. His days in the mud paddock were over and this was the first night he was to be turned out in the larger grass pasture. He pranced around with his tail high in the air, letting out long snorts as he explored. Then he stopped, surveying the large space. When he realized how much room he had, the fuse burned to the end and the rocket took off, burning white hot. This skinny, damaged horse with ulcers and bone chips shook it all off and he came alive, running. I wasn't looking at Metro anymore; this was Metro Meteor.

He sprinted the 300 yards or so to the other end of the pasture, tucked his shoulder down and made a wide sweeping turn, then sprinted straight back. *Strange. When Metro runs, there is no limp.* I could only pick it out when he was going slower. And he sure seemed to be enjoying himself. I wondered how long it had been since he had grass under his feet.

Metro picked up speed, then at the very last second he came to a sliding stop right in front of me. My heart jumped. It wasn't a long run. Just enough to show off what he still had under the hood and it was the most beautiful thing I'd ever seen.

Cheap claiming horse, my ass.

As soon as Wendy came home from her trip, we went to the barn so I could show her a few things. "Watch this," I said, opening the door to the barn.

"Metro!" I called out.

"Eh-eh-eh, uh-uh-uh," he answered back, poking his head out.

"He does that every time I come in the barn!" I was so excited to tell Wendy everything I'd learned about horses in the three days she'd been out of town. I'd made the most of my time and enjoyed every mostly idyllic minute. I'd created my own new routine, bringing a folding chair to sit right in front of Metro's stall, reading my horse books. Metro would hang his head out and read along with me, periodically planting his lips on top of my head and running them through my hair.

To return the favor, I groomed Metro every day. I no longer minded his habit of caking himself in mud. It just meant I could spend more time with him outside of his stall.

Showing off my newfound horse-handling skills, I haltered Metro and led him out of his stall. I hooked him up to the cross ties and started showing Wendy how to groom him.

"Let me do it!" she said immediately. Maybe Wendy was a little jealous that she had to be out of town those first few days. However, Wendy would get off easy, as Metro had been turned out on grass last night and didn't have a speck of mud on him. When I groomed him, he looked like he had just returned from three days at Woodstock. I'd already almost forgotten how Metro was really Wendy's horse and maybe I was coming across as just a tad possessive. I realized it was best to step aside and turn him over to Wendy.

"He's all yours," I said, handing Wendy the currycomb. Wendy began to run the brush in circular strokes across Metro's body as he started to bob his head up and down. The movement was violent, straining the anchor bolts attaching the cross ties to the wall.

"Does he always do this?" Wendy stood back and watched Metro's show.

"I'm not sure what his problem is. He seems like he really doesn't like to be touched." I'd been doing some research and thinking about Metro's behavior. Maybe spending your life at the track meant not much personal attention. Everything was fast, because there were hundreds of horses to attend to. The grooms probably just wanted to get their work done as quickly as possible, then move on to the next horse.

On her first day grooming him, Karen had noticed how Metro always raised his right front hoof immediately after you cleaned out his left front hoof. "The grooms at the track don't walk all the way around the horse," said Karen. "They pick out all four feet from the same side. It's quicker."

Wendy stared at the eyebolts beginning to wiggle as Metro continued jerking his head up and down. "I'm afraid he's going to pull those bolts out of the wall and piss Karen off," said Wendy. "You know how she is."

I did. Karen had seemed to be constantly looking over my shoulder the last few days, disapproving of everything I did.

"I'll try holding him by his lead rope." I unsnapped the cross ties from his halter and gave Metro plenty of slack so he wouldn't rip my arm out of the socket with his movements. I thought I might be able to calm him, so I reached my hand out to lightly stroke his head.

Just then, his big head and neck stopped bobbing up and down and snapped to the right, toward his hip. Instantly, I heard Wendy scream.

What just happened?

Metro's head swung forward again and I quickly grabbed a cross tie and hooked it to his halter. Then I ran around his back end and saw Wendy lying on the ground, both hands gripping her upper right thigh. Tears streamed down her face.

"He...bit...me!" she said in between gasps and sobs.

I'd already known, before she said anything. I knew what he'd done, because I knew what he was capable of.

In the past few days, I'd learned how to deal with Metro. I knew where to stand to stay out of danger and what parts of his body would spark a violent reaction when touched. I'd taken it all in stride and even found humor in his crankiness. But this was different. He had hurt my Wendy and I suddenly saw Metro in a whole different light.

As Wendy cried on my shoulder, I looked over at Metro. He stood there quietly. No more head bobbing; he just stared off into space. He didn't so much as glance at my wife, crying uncontrollably from the pain and the shock. Metro had attacked her and hurt her and he was showing zero remorse.

When the shock wore off and Wendy was ready, she stood balanced on one leg as I unhooked Metro and returned him to his stall.

Maybe he is *a dangerous horse. Karen warned me.* And now, Metro had clearly demonstrated he was more than capable of hurting someone.

I helped Wendy hobble to the car, looking back at Karen's house to see if she was watching us out the window. This time I didn't see her and I felt relieved. I didn't want this incident to stack up another piece of evidence in her case against Metro.

As we drove home, I could tell Wendy was still in pain. I was quiet.

"I don't want to send him back to Bob," Wendy said.

I knew that Wendy feared that my first instinct was to protect her and that might make me want to return Metro to Renpher Stables and then find her a more friendly, less dangerous horse. But that wasn't my plan. My first instinct *was* to protect Wendy, but the thought of returning Metro never crossed my mind, either.

"When we took Metro off the track, we made a commitment," I said. "We're going to take care of him the rest of his life." Returning him was not an option.

I started thinking about what to do with Metro and how to make him a safe horse for Wendy. In our relationship, I was always the researcher and the planner, the behind-the-scenes guy. I planned everything out for our trips: how to get there, where to stay, what to eat and what to see. So even though Metro was Wendy's horse, she trusted me to come up with a plan for how to make him into a safe and teachable horse. Wendy trusted me to figure Metro out and transform him.

But there wasn't much time. I knew that I had to get Metro figured out before he got us kicked out of the barn or hurt someone again. The next time, it might be more serious.

Chapter 14

A Horse Named Pork Chop

"There's not a word yet, for old friends who've just met."
—*Jim Henson*

Over the next few months, the Internet became my best friend as I spent hours and days researching horse behavior. I learned how horses can tell you what they're feeling through body language. For example, if a horse's ears point forward, he is alert. If his ears fold back tight against his head, the horse is angry or giving a strong warning. Signs of relaxation include cocking a hind leg, sighing or lowering the head. I also studied the dynamics of the horse herd and how horses organize themselves into a pecking order from top to bottom.

I took everything I was learning with me to the barn and watched Metro alone and with the other horses. If I observed the horses out in the field long enough, I could determine where each horse fit in the hierarchy of the herd, from the leader all the way down to the whipping boy. Unfortunately, Metro was the horse on the bottom. I didn't understand why, but I wasn't too worried.

I was curious, though, because he acted so dominant with humans but so subservient with the other horses. Was it Metro's upbringing? Since he had started his racing career when he was still quite young, maybe he was short on horse etiquette. Or was it because of his injuries? In the wild, the weak and injured were always the ones that ended up becoming dinner for the predators at the top of the food chain. If so, with his arthritic knees, Metro would have been dinner.

Two months galloped by as I studied Metro and got to know him better. Wendy had learned how to avoid Metro's bites and kicks and had started taking riding lessons from Karen, for when his knees got better. But there wasn't much progress in Metro's mobility. We had been hoping that what our equine athlete needed was rest. We made sure he got plenty of it.

But after three different vets came out to the barn to evaluate him, it was becoming clear that rest alone wasn't going to cure Metro's knees. I kept hoping for a different answer, for some small shred of hope, but each time the prognosis was the same: "This horse may never be rideable again."

One vet prescribed a drug which I was to inject into Metro's neck muscle every four days for twenty-eight days, then once a month for the rest of his life. Two months ago I'd never touched a horse. Now I was giving injections into a horse's neck. Metro took it all in stride and I had a feeling he was familiar with a needle. I once read that Hall of Fame trainer Jack Van Berg told a

Congressional subcommittee that training racehorses had become "chemical warfare."[2]

We also started adding various joint supplements to his feed. We scoured the feed stores and tack shops and if a label said it was good for joint health, we gave it to Metro.

We sent his x-rays to New Bolton and Virginia Tech, hoping an equine surgeon would sign on to remove the bone chips in Metro's knees and give him some relief from the pain and swelling. But each time, the results were the same. Since Metro had already had two previous surgeries to remove bone chips, he wasn't a candidate for a third. There just wasn't enough healthy bone left in his knees.

Not only was our health regimen not working, but neither were Wendy's riding lessons. Wendy wanted to learn the Western style of riding, but Karen only taught English. And the lesson horses were a problem. Since most of Karen's riding students were kids, the lesson horses were small and very stubborn from being kicked in the sides by too many little kids in riding boots. Each week Wendy tried a new horse, hoping to find one she liked. But what she really wanted was to ride her own horse. She wanted to ride Metro.

Even though Wendy had first asked for Metro and we had planned for him to be her horse, I was starting to fall in love with him instead. I loved his cranky attitude and his stubbornness. In my mind, I had taken possession of him. I just hadn't told Wendy yet.

I enjoyed the days when Wendy was out of town and I could have Metro all to myself. I led him out of his stall and together we searched outside the pasture fences for untouched patches of juicy grass and clover. I stood for hours holding his lead rope while he dined, talking to him out loud while he grazed.

"How was your night in the pasture, Metro?"

Crunch.

"How are those knees doing today?"

Munch.

"What did it feel like to be the fastest horse on the track?"

Chomp.

I also took to reciting the race calls from his greatest moments on the track. I had watched his races so many times on YouTube, I could recite the announcers' play-by-play verbatim.

"And here comes Metro Meteor!"

"He's just inhaled the field!"

"Metro Meteor rockets by them all!"

"Oh...He just blew them away!"

"Metro Meteor wins by three and a half at the wire!"

I usually ended our conversations with, "Someday, Metro, you'll be a great horse again."

Finally, I could take it no longer and one day I broke the news to Wendy. "I think we should get a second horse."

"You want your own horse?" Wendy looked surprised.

"No," I said. "I want Metro."

She stared at me, speechless. It is not too often I see Wendy at a loss for words.

"Metro isn't going to be ready to ride anytime soon," I explained. "It makes sense, because I'm in no hurry to ride and I have no problem giving him all the time he needs to get better." I was channeling my car salesman days and starting to get into the rhythm of a sales pitch. "You're ready to ride now, so you should have a horse *you* can ride. I think you should start looking for one."

Once she got over the shock, Wendy agreed. And we decided to do it right this time. Wendy and I knew a little more about horses than we had two months ago and we vowed not to buy the first horse we looked at. We also thought it might be a good idea to get a vet check before we brought the new horse home, not wait until afterward.

Well, all of those good intentions were tossed aside when we met Pork Chop. He was the first horse Wendy looked at and we didn't get a vet check. Pork Chop's racing name was "Snared," the worst name ever for a racehorse. He was everything Metro wasn't. Pork Chop was huge, measuring 17.2 hands, and looked more like he should be pulling fancy carriages in downtown Gettysburg than running against other Thoroughbreds. While Metro had skinny little chicken legs built for speed, Pork Chop had big, thick legs, more like a draft horse than a racehorse.

Pork Chop had only run six races total, finished last in just about every one and earned a grand total of $360 in his career. Not even enough to pay his food bill. After he retired, he was purchased by a pony rider and spent eight months at Penn National, parading horses to the post. It was at that track that we met Pork Chop and his current owner.

He introduced us to Pork Chop's breeder and original owner, who also happened to be at the track the night we met Pork Chop for the first time. He referred to Snared as a gentle giant and had entertained thoughts of training him to be a "timber horse" when his racing career didn't pan out. We didn't know what a timber horse was, but we assumed Pork Chop came that close to a career as a lumberjack. We had visions of him in his little metal hardhat and flannel shirt, pulling fallen trees through the forest. We would later learn that timber racing was a form of steeplechase where the horses raced through a course, jumping over immovable wooden objects.

Pork Chop was like a big Golden Retriever, lovable and slouching through life with a *Yup-yup-yo* kind of attitude. He was easygoing and you could stroke or brush him anywhere on his body without worrying he was going to snap your hand off at the wrist. Pork Chop took everything in stride. He was the anti-Metro.

When we were wrapping up the sale with the pony rider, Wendy asked him how he came by such an unusual name for his horse. "That's what I was having for dinner the night I got him." At least he wasn't eating turkey.

Wendy did consider changing Pork Chop's name. If she wanted to show him at some point in the future, he might need a more regal title. She settled on "Longstreet," after one of the generals who fought here in Gettysburg. It was certainly a regal name, but Longstreet didn't seem to fit the big chestnut-colored goober. After just two days of ownership, Wendy gave in. "You know, he really is a

Pork Chop," she said, and with that, his true name was restored.

Pork Chop moved into his new home in the stall right next to Metro and they soon became best friends. With his problems fitting into the herd, Metro really did need a friend. And it was the beginning of a great love affair between Wendy and Pork Chop, as it soon became clear he was the perfect horse for her and she was the perfect human for him. Wendy finally had the equine best friend she had hoped for.

Not only did Wendy love him, but so did everyone at the barn. The boarders loved him, the stall muckers loved him, even Karen loved him. But everyone hated Metro. His reputation as a dangerous horse had solidified and hung around his neck like an invisible *CLAIM* tag.

I just couldn't see it, though, because he was my horse now. Maybe I was looking at him through rose-colored glasses, but he was more than just a good horse. In my eyes, Metro was a great horse.

The evidence was there, however. The girls who mucked out the stalls were warned not to go into Metro's stall when he was inside. Many times when I showed up during the day, I found Metro tied up in the aisle while his stall was being cleaned. I could understand, because he was intimidating even to me when I entered his stall. His ears would pin back and he'd glare at me with hatred. *He's just a product of his upbringing,* I'd tell myself. As a racehorse, he'd once spent twenty-three hours of every single day in his stall. Every day, he'd be pulled out to work for an hour, then back he'd go. His stall was his sanctuary and his castle. I could understand why he was so protective, because his stall was the only thing truly his.

One day, I realized just how much Metro was disliked. Another boarder stopped by to talk and made the mistake of resting her arm on the opening of Metro's stall door. Immediately, Metro came forward and rested his lips on her arm, just as he did with me every day. She turned and slapped him across the face.

"Did you see him come after me?" she practically shouted.

"He wasn't doing anything, just being friendly." I was trying to control my own anger. I glanced at Metro, who retreated a few feet, afraid to come back to the door.

"That horse is not friendly! He tried to bite me!"

I looked over at Wendy and saw outrage in her eyes, too. But we said nothing. We were afraid to speak up. Our status at the stable was already shaky.

It got even shakier when Open House day came around. It was an annual tradition for the horse barns in Pennsylvania to polish up the facilities once a year and put their barns on display for anyone who wanted to come and take a look. Karen had been preparing for weeks, with plans for riding demonstrations, hot dogs cooked up by the riding club and the Girl Scouts selling cookies. She expected a big turnout.

Metro's stall would be right in the middle of the action, as he happened to inhabit the most high-profile stall in the barn, right at the front. It was the first stall you saw when you came through the barn door and it was the stall you stood in front of to watch the riding demonstrations in the indoor arena. On this day, Metro would be on display, too.

The morning of Open House day, we visited a couple of other nearby barns first, so we could see what the other facilities were like. Wendy was just curious; I was secretly looking for another home for Metro and Pork Chop. Next, we planned to swing by Stone Hall Stables to visit the boys and join the festivities. It had been raining on and off, so we figured our horses would be in their stalls.

The rain had paused when we pulled up to the barn, but the ground was still too soft so there were no horses in the pasture except one. Metro. My heart sank. Not a good sign. There had to be a reason for the exile.

"Metro was a bad boy today." Karen's voice startled me. There were quite a few people milling around for the open house, but she had quickly spotted us. "He went nuts in his stall. He was running around in circles, kicking and bucking."

Wendy and I listened in horror.

"I was afraid he was going to get out and hurt someone, so we had to hold people back to get Metro out to the pasture."

Apparently, Wendy and I had already missed the show. What she said next really got me, though.

"It's the carbs. Metro is eating too many carbs and it's making him crazy. We are going to cut his food in half from now on, to settle him down."

Metro, you've finally done it. You ruined the party and pooped in the owner's punchbowl.

I shook my head. I just couldn't see it. Karen must be blowing this out of proportion. Her description of the human chain of volunteers separating the crowd from the psychotic, bloodthirsty horse being led to pasture seemed a tad dramatic. I'd spent many hours observing Metro and I had never seen him act the way she was describing. I could almost imagine what she must have been thinking—that Metro was just seconds away from bursting through his stall door, trampling the guests, stopping briefly at the cookie table to scoop up a Girl Scout in his teeth and carry her into the woods to dine on her Thin Mints. But let's face it, who doesn't like Thin Mints?

Still, I couldn't see it. This didn't sound at all like Metro. He had his quirks and vices, but going ballistic in his stall wasn't one of them.

After Karen walked away, I felt like a problem child being released from the principal's office. Chastised, I headed out to the pasture to visit my boy. Metro walked over to me, lowered his head down into my chest and let me rub his ears. Sweet as can be.

"I know you didn't do anything bad," I said.

Within weeks of the new low-carb diet imposed by Karen's staff, Metro was losing weight. It had taken significant effort and time to get some poundage on him and now it was melting away. He was starting to look like skin and bones again, just like when he'd come off the track.

One night, as I was standing just outside Metro's stall watching him eat his hay, it started to rain. I was surprised by the noise. The aluminum roof wasn't insulated and it sloped just a few feet above Metro's stall.

It was one of those warm rains, where the water dumps hard for a couple of seconds, stops and then starts again. Every time it started to pour, Metro would stop eating and run circles inside his stall, kicking out. When the rain stopped, he'd calm down and go back to eating his hay.

I stood watching him for a few of these rain and run cycles. The rain acted like a light switch, turning Metro on and off. Then a switch suddenly flipped for me. My mind flashed back to Open House day, when Metro had been accused of going nuts. I let out a sigh of relief. Metro wasn't crazy; he was afraid of the noise the rain made when it pounded down on the roof.

Metro, we have to get you out of this place.

Chapter 15

Strawberry's Field

"Horses were never wrong.
They always did what they did for a reason,
and it was up to you to figure it out."
—*Jeannette Walls, Half Broke Horses*

I couldn't wait to get back and see Metro. I'd been away visiting family for a few days and as soon as I returned to Gettysburg, Wendy and I made the short trip to the barn to see the boys.

Metro was right there at the gate. My ego told me he was waiting for me. *What a good boy.* However, as we got out of the car and walked up to the fence, something seemed off. No friendly whinny, just a vacant stare as he paced back and forth. Was he hurt? Angry? Scared?

I got closer and took a look, knowing what I was probably going to see. Another ragged, bloody gash on his chest. It was becoming a regular event. My gut feeling was that Metro was anxious, because he wanted to get out of that pasture.

The horses at Stone Hall inhabited several different pastures, with mares and geldings separated into groups. Metro and Pork Chop, now fast friends, shared a pasture with five other geldings. But for the past couple of weeks, our horses had been coming in from the field with open wounds, apparently inflicted by one of the other horses. Every day we dressed their torn flesh with goopy antiseptic stuff from a blue jar, hoping the mayhem would soon end. *Surely someone will notice and put a stop to it,* we thought, but the beatings continued.

I emailed Karen to let her know I was concerned about the safety of our horses. "Can anything be done?" I asked.

"If you don't like the care your horses are getting, here is a list of other horse barns in the area. Good luck."

Okay, so Karen wasn't going to help us out here.

No one seemed to know who was tearing up Metro and Pork Chop, but one of their pasturemates was kicking ass and taking their lunch money and I was going to find out who it was. I knew about the herd's pecking order, with biting and kicking a normal occurrence—that's why they sell the goopy stuff in the blue jars. But our horses were covered in wounds and after this latest occurrence and Metro's trauma, I just couldn't take it anymore.

I assigned myself to surveillance duty and staked out the pasture to try to identify the culprit. It didn't take long until I discovered the evil one in action. He was a little horse named Strawberry, twenty-six years old, a randy older gentleman. He had once shared a pasture with the mares and although he'd been gelded late in life and had no use of his naughty bits, he still seemed to know exactly what they were for. After Strawberry was caught trying to mount all of the mares, he was summarily banished to the gelding field. Not yet ready to give up his girlfriends completely, he patrolled the fence line next to the mare field like a North Korean sentry, making damn sure no other horses got near his girls.

I almost wanted to laugh as I watched him strut back and forth, his short little legs punching the ground. But my smile left when he spotted Metro. Metro was at the other end, as far away from Strawberry as he could get and still be in the same pasture. Metro tried to hide his nervousness by grazing but always kept one white-rimmed eye trained on his little nemesis.

Strawberry didn't seem to care that Metro was just minding his own business. Maybe Metro's movie-star good looks challenged Strawberry's ego (is there such a thing as small horse syndrome?) and he felt he needed to protect his reputation with the ladies. I watched Strawberry take off at a gallop, bee-lining it toward Metro.

Before I could say or do anything, Metro looked up from the grass, spotted the furry blur making straight for him and panicked. He pivoted on his bad knees to the left, then to the right, not knowing which way to run. Then he bolted, with the smaller horse right on his heels. He was closing in on the fence, about to run out of room, when he went into turbo-Thoroughbred gear and hit the fence. I gasped as Metro impacted the fence at a dead run. *He's trying to run through it!*

To my surprise, the boards held and Metro bounced back. But there was no escape. Metro turned around just as Strawberry started kicking. Metro was pinned, helpless, against the fence. The little Palomino Mike Tyson had him against the ropes and was now pummeling Metro, trying to end the bout.

I ran over to the pasture, yanked open the gate and marched in. Strawberry backed off as I grabbed Metro's halter and led him out of the pasture. He was cut and bleeding from shoulder to shoulder, his chest ripped open where he'd run into the fence. I took Metro into the barn, opened the jar of blue goop and started the daily ritual of cleaning and dressing his wounds.

Karen golf-carted over, took a look at my bloodied boy and said, "He doesn't need stitches. He'll live."

My blood began to boil. She hadn't shown the least bit of concern that Metro's chest was torn apart. I tried to describe what I'd just seen, but she brushed me off.

"That's just what horses do," she said. The message was clear; I was a newbie horse owner and didn't know what I was talking about. My concerns meant nothing.

However, luck was on my side and another boarder had witnessed the attack. She had more credibility with Karen and she backed me up that Strawberry was a terror and needed to be moved to another pasture.

I was still outraged, though. Strawberry was put in another pasture, not because my horse was getting the crap kicked out of him or because Strawberry might end up killing Metro, but because another boarder asked for the transfer. It was frustrating. I was a new horse owner, but with the amount of research I'd been doing and the amount of time I spent at the barn, I probably knew more about horses than some of the other boarders. However, Karen still treated me like I knew nothing and treated

Metro like he was nothing but a bother. I knew there had to be a place out there that would appreciate Metro as much as I did and I couldn't wait to find it.

In the meantime, now that Metro had been off work for five months, it was time to ask him to do something else besides convert grass to fertilizer and drain our savings account. I had done nothing with him besides try to push the two-stroke limit, groom him without losing a limb and lead him from Point A to Point B (when he was in the mood).

Metro wasn't really that hard to handle. He respected personal space on the lead line and didn't try to run me over. But periodically, he would stop, plant his feet and play a game called *Let's-See-If-You-Can-Make-Me-Move*. To correct the behavior, someone suggested I walk along his side and tug on the lead rope, throwing him off balance in order to get his feet moving. It worked well, but two steps later he'd stop again.

It became a ritual. Instead of walking in a straight line, we created a snake-like path as I tried to get him to where I wanted him to go. Other times, I stopped and tried to wait him out. I'd walk away and just stand there, waiting for him to join me. We were like two gunfighters in a stand-off, separated by a twelve-foot lead line and waiting to see who was going to draw first. Eventually, Metro would give in and come toward me. But it was only after a five-minute stare-down and always with a grudging attitude.

Metro didn't do this dance with Wendy or Karen or anyone else but me. He'd figured out I was his owner and even though others might handle him from time to time, he knew I wanted to be in charge. But he had decided he wanted to be in charge.

Even though he was a marshmallow with Strawberry, with me he worked hard to let me know he was actually the boss in our relationship. He wouldn't have cared if I was leading him to the all-you-can-eat carrot buffet at the Bellagio. If he wanted to stop ten feet short, he would, just because he was Metro and he didn't like to make anything easy for me. Metro had clearly appointed himself the boss in our little herd of two. He was stubborn and ready to fight me every step of the way, with our days a battle of wills. And Metro was winning.

I couldn't even begin to know how to work out the respect issues. Metro had 800 pounds on me and I knew that I would lose any battle of strength. I realized that I'd have to learn how to outthink him, but the problem was I had no idea how his mind worked. He obviously knew more about me than I knew about him. It was time to bring in the big guns.

I was ready to try something new. I did want to be partners with Metro, but I didn't want to be his manservant. One of the other boarders suggested I look up Pat Parelli and try Natural Horsemanship.

I conducted some research and watched videos of Parelli on horseback, no saddle or bridle, galloping around the arena, jumping obstacles and spinning his horse in circles. He did everything with his horse but dance the Macarena. I was under no illusion that I'd soon be galloping Metro bareback down the beach with my arms outstretched and my gray hair blowing in the wind, but I did like the sound of the groundwork program.

Parelli suggested some exercises to do with your horse. He called them the Seven Games, but basically it was just teaching your horse to move forward, backward, left and right at the end of a lead rope. What appealed to me was that all the exercises looked low-impact, something a horse with bad knees could do. Up until this point, the only groundwork I had ever observed was Karen lunging her horses in a circle for endless hours. Metro's knees would never hold up to that.

I also discovered that Parelli wasn't the only Natural Horsemanship expert. There were others, such as Buck Brannaman and Clinton Anderson. They were horse whisperers and they all taught the same basic concepts, but each with his own unique twist.

I eventually gravitated to Clinton Anderson. He seemed to have the most no-nonsense approach and something he said really hit home with me: "You've got to earn your horse's respect." Instantly, I knew that's what I was missing in my relationship with Metro. He respected Strawberry, but he didn't respect me.

I invested a few hundred dollars in Natural Horsemanship instructional DVDs, along with a rope halter (better for training), a lead line and a stick with a line on the end of it. I watched the DVDs over and over until I had a grasp of the basics and then started working with Metro in the outdoor arena. The first exercise was nothing more than getting your horse used to the tools you were going to use to train him. I couldn't wait to try.

On the first day, I began with gently throwing the lead rope over Metro's back. To a human, a rope over the back is nothing to worry about. But to a horse, with the instincts of a prey animal, a rope thrown at him can look an awful lot like a giant anaconda. In the DVD, a horse had dragged Anderson around an arena for ten minutes when he tried this exercise, until he accepted the rope was not going to kill him and he calmed down. I was ready for Metro to drag me around the arena, too. The first time I threw the rope at him, however, he didn't react. Metro just stood there quietly, not caring about the rope one bit once he got used to it and relaxed.

While I worked, focused on trying to learn how to understand and communicate with my horse, I didn't realize I was being watched. Karen had been observing us from her guardpost at the kitchen window. Within a few seconds she'd hopped in her golf cart and zoomed over to the arena. "No. No. No!" she said. "I don't want beginners self-teaching at my barn!"

What? I just spent several hundred dollars on the best instruction available, I'm willing to spend the time and the energy needed to work with my horse to curb his questionable manners and you're telling me I can't?

I just wanted to work with my horse. I wasn't some kid, taking risks and going at this blindly. I was a fifty-year-old man who'd pretty much learned how to do everything by reading books, watching instructional videos and teaching myself how to do things. I'm good at figuring things out. But I knew it was no use arguing with Karen on anything to do with horses. She was the self-appointed ruler of her own little insulated equine kingdom. It was a monarchy and Metro and I were the court jesters.

I had a flash of inspiration. Maybe there was a way. "How about if you watch the Anderson videos and then teach me how to work with Metro?" I asked, hopefully. "I'll pay you to do it. If you don't want to teach me, you could at least supervise me. Would that work?"

"No."

Off she zoomed. Karen was a hunter jumper instructor and didn't believe in all that natural horsemanship stuff. In Karen's world, there was her way and the right way and they were the same thing.

If I had wanted to learn how to ride and jump Metro, Karen was my girl. But neither Metro nor I had the desire or the knees to go that route. So I was at a barn where I was allowed to do nothing with my horse but lead him out to the pasture and back.

I had had enough of the Wicked Witch of Stone Hall and her flying monkey, Strawberry.

Chapter 16

Dream Barn

"The ache for home lives in all of us, the safe place where we can go as we are and not be questioned."

—*Maya Angelou*

Back at Stone Hall Stables, life had gone from bad to worse. Since Karen didn't seem to want to help me, I tried to bring in my own horse trainer. Wendy had been over at the local tack shop and spotted a flyer that read, "Natural Horsemanship Training, Emily Barker Horsemanship." Emily said she would be happy to come out to the barn and teach me how to do groundwork with Metro. I was ecstatic. I was finally going to get the help Metro and I needed. But after I explained the situation and answered a few questions, Emily asked me something strange:

"Is the barn owner okay with me coming out to the barn and working with Metro?"

What? Why wouldn't Karen be okay? This struck me as truly odd. Karen said I needed supervision. What problem could she possibly have with a trained professional like Emily? I shook it off. *For once, I'm not going to worry. It will be fine.*

After I finished talking to Emily, I was walking on air. I was going to start working with my boy and all would be right in the world. Excited, I called Karen to give her the good news. "I've found an instructor willing to come out to the barn. She's going to teach me natural horsemanship and then supervise me while I do the exercises with Metro." I waited, hopeful. Her response shouldn't have blindsided me, but it did.

"No outside instructors," she said forcefully. "How *dare* you bring another instructor to my barn! This is my barn and my rules and..."

Her angry voice drilled into my head and went on and on but I stopped listening. Then, I apologized. I reminded her I was new to the horse world and didn't know the etiquette for horse trainers. I had no idea bringing an instructor into the barn was frowned upon. All I knew was that Karen had refused to teach me what I needed to know, so Wendy and I had discovered someone who would. I apologized over and over, but the more I apologized, the more she went on.

Finally, I'd had enough. "Well, will *you* work with me? Will you teach me groundwork? I want to start working with Metro. All I want to do is work with my horse." My questions were turning into desperate pleas.

Karen literally started sputtering into the phone. The only phrase that penetrated my skull was "failure to communicate." Karen was refusing to take me on as a student, because of failure to communicate? She reminded me of the prison warden in *Cool Hand Luke*. And the more she talked about failure to communicate, the more she sounded like a warden.

That was it. There had to be something better out there. I'd hit my tipping point with Karen and we decided to find a new barn, as of yesterday.

After a thorough search, we found a guy named Tom Josford who had some stalls opening up at the end of the month, so we decided to go take a look. The facilities were similar and I liked Tom; he even kept a racehorse he owned at the stable. He ran it at Charles Town Racetrack for small purses, seemed to really like horse racing and asked me lots of questions about Metro. I wondered if he'd still like Metro after he ventured inside Metro's stall. But for once, it was nice to have someone take an interest in my horse. Right now, all Metro had was his history. His future was still uncertain.

Tom gave us a tour of the property on a Saturday, always a busy time for a stable with lots of horses and owners out and about. I watched the other boarders with their horses. Would they be more accepting of Metro? I knew there was no guarantee. *Maybe a change of barns won't help. Maybe the other owners will always hate Metro, wherever we go.*

I did see a number of people riding with Western saddles, something we never saw at Stone Hall, where everything was English. *Will Western people like Metro better?*

Feeling hopeful, we made an appointment for Tom to come and pick up our horses in three weeks. It felt good to have an exit strategy and things were easier at Stone

Hall now that we knew we were leaving. I felt like a prisoner with just a few short weeks left on his jail sentence, ready to emerge into the sunshine to try and start a whole new life.

Karen didn't say much those last few weeks, which was fine with me. I didn't like her, I didn't want to talk to her and I knew she didn't like me. The last days at Stone Hall Stables, I simply enjoyed taking Metro out of his stall and going for walks so he could enjoy grazing on what good November grass we could find.

I was looking forward to a new start for us and for Metro. This was not his home and none of the humans or horses liked him. It felt like having your child bullied by the other kids at school and then called into the principal's office every day of the week.

Because Pork Chop was higher in the pecking order, even he did his fair share of chasing Metro around in the pasture. But if any other horse started to pick on Metro, Pork Chop stepped in and chased the offender away. They were brothers and Pork Chop wasn't going to let anyone pick on his brother but himself. I could live with that. He never hurt Metro, just herded him around to whatever side of the pasture Pork Chop preferred.

I started counting down the days and, three days before the big move to Tom's place, I emailed him to confirm. I preferred email over phone calls, not only to avoid talking, but also because my hearing had worsened to the point that I couldn't always make out what other people were saying.

Tom emailed back: "I am really sorry, Ron, but the stalls I promised you are no longer available. The person who was supposed to move his horses out has decided to stay."

I yelled, "Wendy!" She came running. I don't think she had ever heard that much panic in my voice before.

"Are you okay?" She looked into my eyes.

"Read this." I pointed to the email.

She looked up with a frown. "What are we going to do?"

"I don't know," I said. "Will you call him and see if there are any other options? A small stall? A field? A closet? Anything at all?!"

I paced around my office as Wendy talked to Tom. I was aching with disappointment. Why didn't he just tell the other person he had promised the stalls to someone else? Tom had committed. It wasn't our fault the other boarder decided to stay. And the last thing I wanted to do was beg Karen for more time. I knew she'd make my life a living hell.

As soon as Wendy hung up, I peppered her with questions. "What did he say? Does he have any ideas? Is field board available? We can do field board until stalls open up."

"Calm down," Wendy said in a soothing voice. "He feels really bad and was all apologetic. He gave me the number of a friend who owns a barn close by. Tom has already contacted him and told him we were nice people, and the guy agreed to take the horses."

"A friend's barn? I don't want to go to a friend's barn!" I yelled. I pictured an old farmer with a broken down barn three times as old as he was. I could just see Metro standing in the rain, mud up to his knees, competing with a bunch of goats and chickens for his food. *This is not going to work.*

In a cool, breezy tone, Wendy settled it. "Let's just check it out, Ron. It's only a couple of miles away from Tom's place."

"Now I *know* that the place is a dump." If there was another barn in the area, I would have known about it, with all of the Internet research I'd been doing. I knew for a fact there were no other stables listed online. This one must be so bad the owner wouldn't even post photos for public inspection.

"Well, I'm going to call the guy." Wendy took the number and walked away.

"Fine," I said. "I'll be here on the computer looking for a real barn."

Wendy won and the next day we were driving, following the GPS instructions to Tom's friend's barn. We ended up at a mailbox with *17505* painted on the side. "Well, we're in the right place." I looked for buildings or at least a driveway. Nothing. "Did you see a sign?"

"No, but I did see a gravel drive about a hundred yards back. Maybe that's it."

I gave Wendy a look, spun the truck around and backtracked. As I turned left into the gravel drive, I saw an old faded piece of plywood nailed to a board fence. Scrawled in paint that looked like it had been lettered by a three-year-old were the same five numbers: *17505*. I was starting to feel vindicated. Clearly, this barn was going to be a dump and we were wasting our time.

We followed the road as it curved to the left through a stand of colorful maple trees. When we emerged from the trees, I stopped the truck and put it in Park. We sat in silence, staring.

In front of us sprawled a beautiful pasture, so lush and green it looked like the eighteenth hole at Augusta. Crowning the pasture were four buildings. The largest, cream colored with a magenta roof, was a huge enclosed horse arena. To the left was another large, matching building with a glossy green tractor in front. Another pair of buildings sat across the drive, facing the arena. The smaller one looked like a cottage with a chimney. A thin ribbon of smoke curled up into the cool November air. Across the field I could see board fences bordering several grassy, rectangular pastures, including an outdoor arena with a pristine, sandy surface.

Okay, this is pretty nice. But where are the horses?

I shifted back into Drive and we rolled slowly down the drive and through the pastures, finally parking in a small lot in front of the arena. A bear of a man with a mustache and goatee emerged from the darkness. He was over six feet tall and dressed in work clothes with an old ball cap. On his feet were worn-out rubber boots and he wore a heavy khaki jacket that had seen better days. *Must be the barn help.*

A palomino and a gray grazed on the grass in front of the cottage by the arena. They weren't tied to anything or fenced in and looked like they were free to roam and do whatever they liked. I was in awe and I felt like Dorothy in *The Wizard of Oz* when she woke up in a strange, new land with everything in Technicolor. My much anticipated *I told you so* melted away as I realized I was looking at Metro and Pork Chop's new home.

Ed came out to meet us and I let Wendy do all the talking, fearing I might say something stupid and ruin our chances. "Beautiful place you have here," Wendy said, glancing at the horses on the lawn.

"That's Poco and Sunny," he said. "They're my horses. I let them free range once in a while so they can mow the grass. They stay pretty close, unless I have corn growing on the upper field. Then they usually make a bee-line for it."

Ed had a laid-back demeanor that I immediately liked. The atmosphere at Stone Hall was so stressful and I couldn't ever imagine Karen allowing a horse to roam free there.

"Come on in to the main barn and I'll show you around," said Ed.

I took a deep breath and let the peacefulness and beauty of the place steal into my soul. Maybe Metro could have a chance to heal in this place and live the happy life that had eluded him so far. Maybe I'd learn more about natural horsemanship and be able to work with my horse. And maybe Metro's damaged knees would rejuvenate enough for me to be able to ride him. This magical place had surprised me. Maybe Metro was about to surprise me, too.

Chapter 17

Metro, Meet Emily

"Your horses are a mirror to your soul.
Sometimes you won't like what you see;
sometimes you will."

—Buck Brannaman

Ed led us into the indoor arena. The sand footing was pure and white, like a Caribbean beach. I could almost hear the steel drums and taste the Piña Coladas. On each end of the arena was a huge, pyramid-shaped stack of windows, letting in a massive amount of light. Across the sides were three more big windows that slid open, allowing in plenty of fresh air. Above it all was the biggest ceiling fan I've ever seen in my life.

Everything about Ed's barn was big and beautiful and he was proud of it. He told us about every piece of wood in every building. He explained how many kilowatts of electricity he was saving through using solar panels and windmills, the details of which went right over our heads. Every last detail of Ed's arena was thought out, planned for and executed with excellence. I couldn't find one thing I would have done differently.

Finally, he led us into the barn. "There are nine stalls in this barn and nine stalls in the other one," Ed said.

I looked down the row of stalls. *Funny. They all seem empty.* The stalls looked brand new, like no horse had ever stepped foot inside.

"Where are all the horses?" If they weren't in here and they weren't outside, where were they? Free ranging, out in the woods?

"There are none," said Ed. "Just Sunny and Poco, and you met them already."

I had a thought. *No horses means no boarders. No people I'll have to make small talk with. No people to hate Metro. This is paradise. I want to live here!*

"Tom sends me people when he doesn't have stalls available," Ed explained, "or if he meets someone he doesn't like. I cooperate by giving them a tour of my place and if they seem high maintenance or if they have screaming kids, I just tell them we're full."

Would we meet Ed's criteria? I suddenly felt a sense of fear that he was about to send us packing, too. How odd that he'd built the Taj Mahal of horse barns and didn't seem to care if he made any money by taking in boarders. But maybe he didn't need it. Looking around at the high-end construction and the top-notch farm equipment, I sensed that Ed had money and lots of it. He didn't build this place to generate income; he built it because he could. The boarders were just an added option, when suitable.

I was afraid of offending him but took the plunge anyway. "So, I take it this isn't your only source of income?"

Photo courtesy of Jeanne Benas

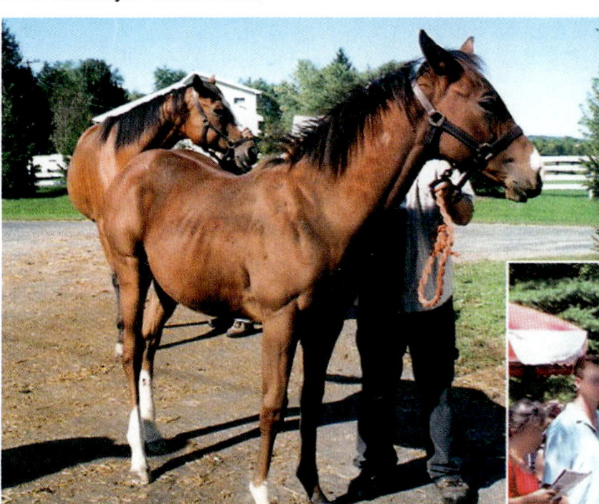

At left, the yet unnamed colt, Metro Meteor, with his mother, Here Comes Nikki.

Photo courtesy of Lois Dworkin

At right, two-year-old Metro Meteor parades to the paddock at Saratoga.

Below, one of Metro's many wins, at Belmont Park.

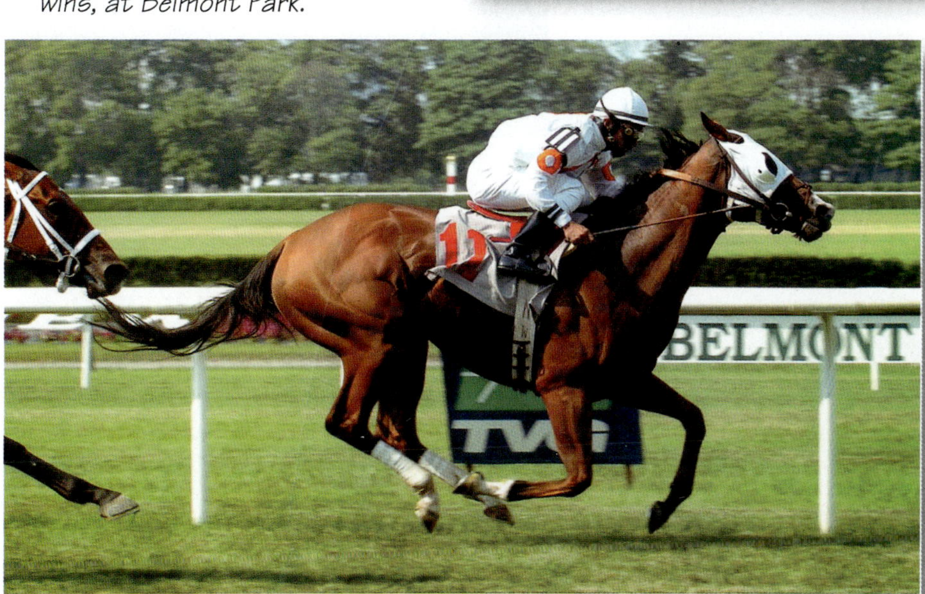

Purse $45,000

Belmont Park, New York
Obviously NY Stable owner
Linda Rice trainer
Drinkwater 2nd

METRO METEOR

July 1, 2006
Cornelio Velasquez up
7 furlongs time 1:21:4
Buff Naked 3rd

Photos courtesy of Ron Krajewski

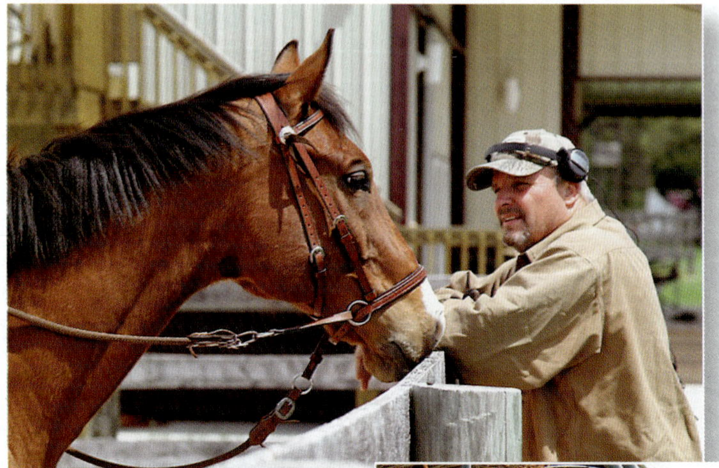

*At left,
Metro and
Ed O'Neill.*

*At right, Pork Chop
and Metro enjoy
a bale of hay on
their first day
at Ed's farm.*

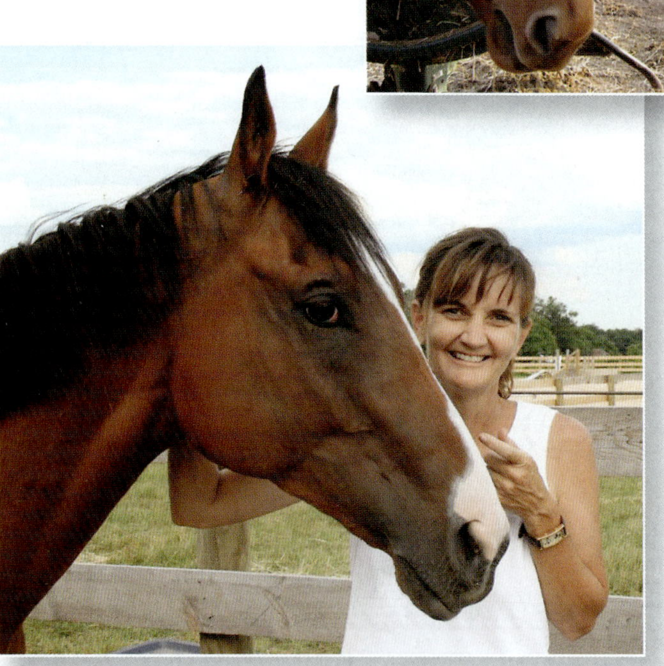

*At left, Wendy
Krajewski and
Metro on his
first day
off the track.*

Photos courtesy of Ron Krajewski

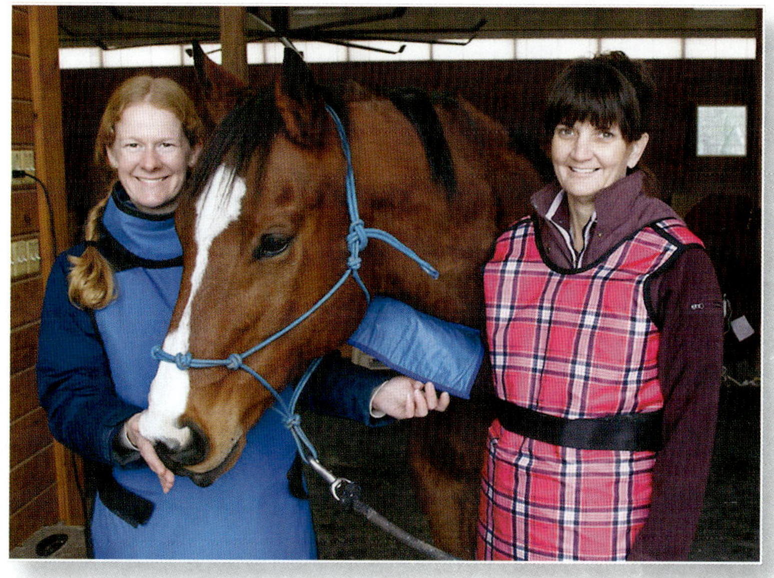

Above, veterinarian Kim Brokaw and Wendy wear their lead aprons to take x-rays of Metro's legs.

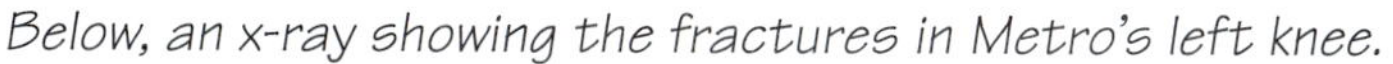

Below, an x-ray showing the fractures in Metro's left knee.

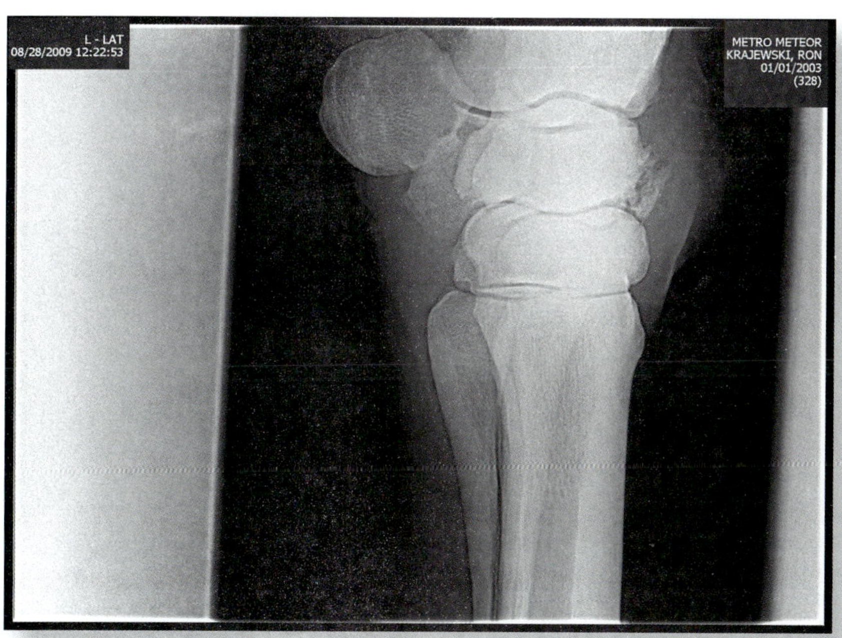

Photos courtesy of Ron Krajewski

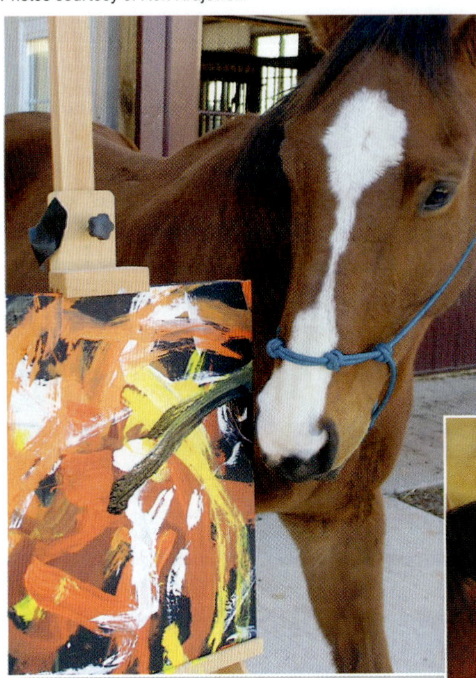

At left, Metro poses with his very first painting, "Jump Into the Fire."

Below, Metro shows his technique with a paintbrush.

Photo by The Picture Escape, photographer Heidi Geraci

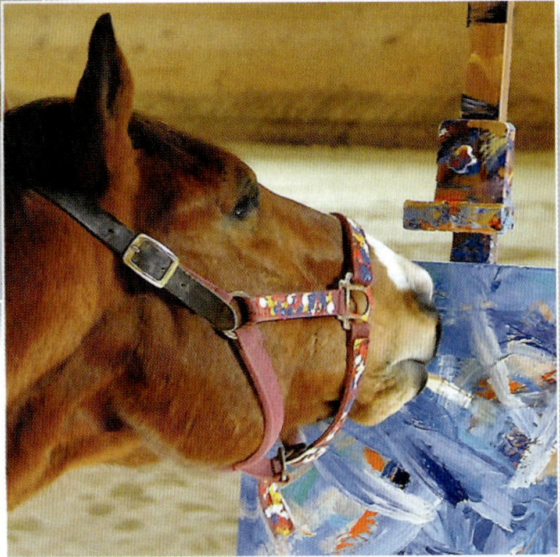

Below, Metro's first two paintings on their way to Gallery 30: "Jump Into the Fire" (left) and "Caramel Sundae" (right).

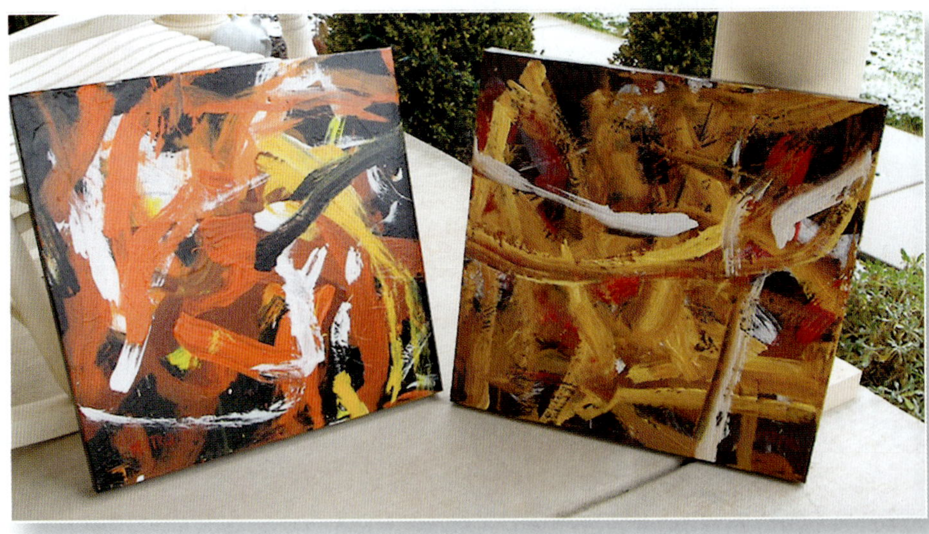

Photos courtesy of Ron Krajewski

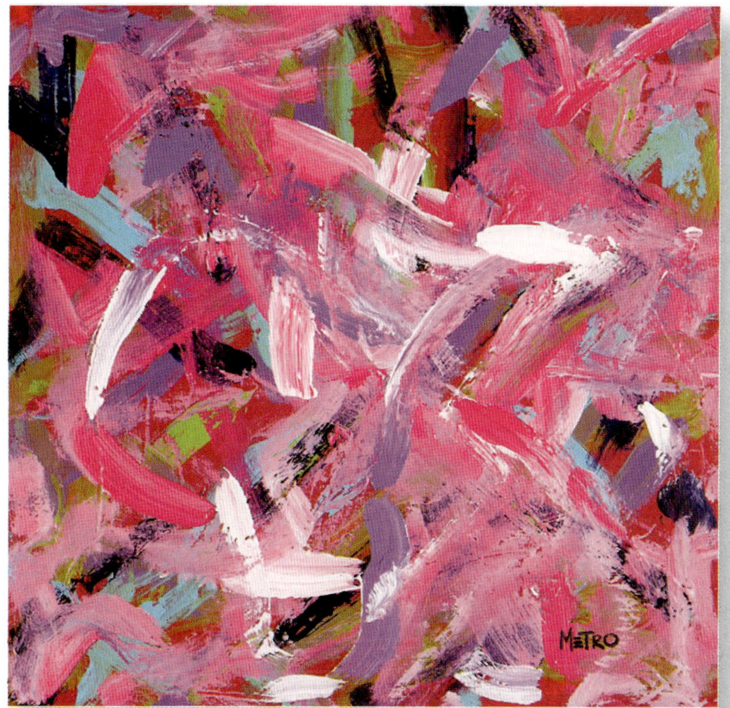

At left, "Flamingos in the Park."

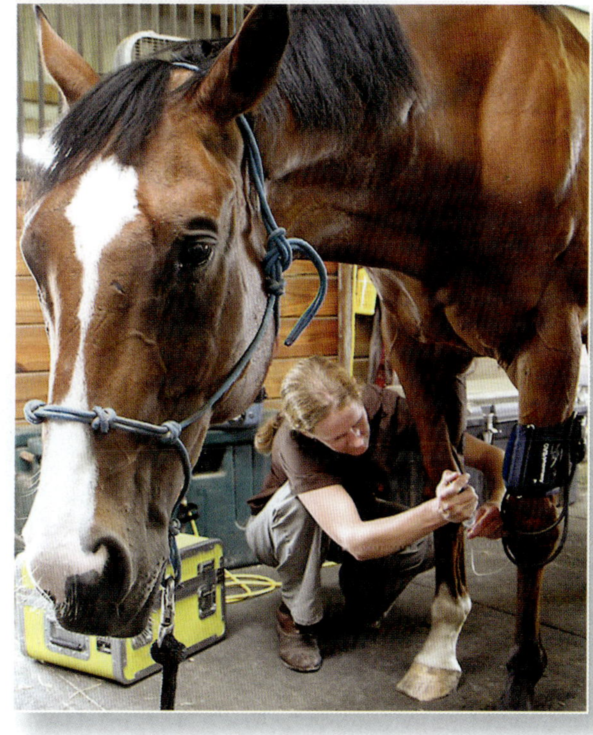

At right, Dr. Kim Brokaw administers a Tildren treatment to Metro's knee. These treatments would save his life.

Photos courtesy of Ron Krajewski

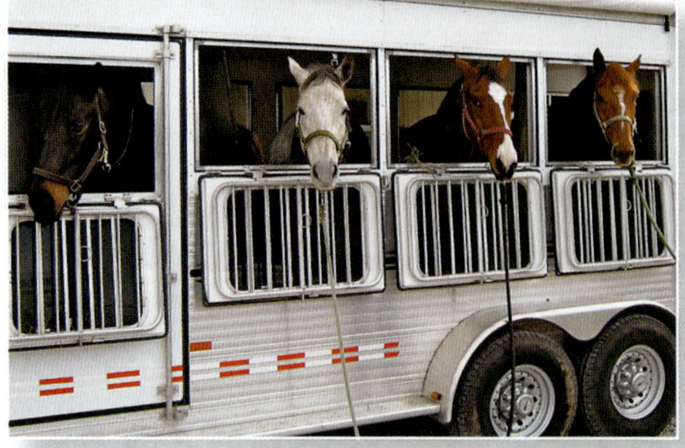

At left, Bart, Poco, Metro and Pork Chop in the trailer heading out for a trail ride.

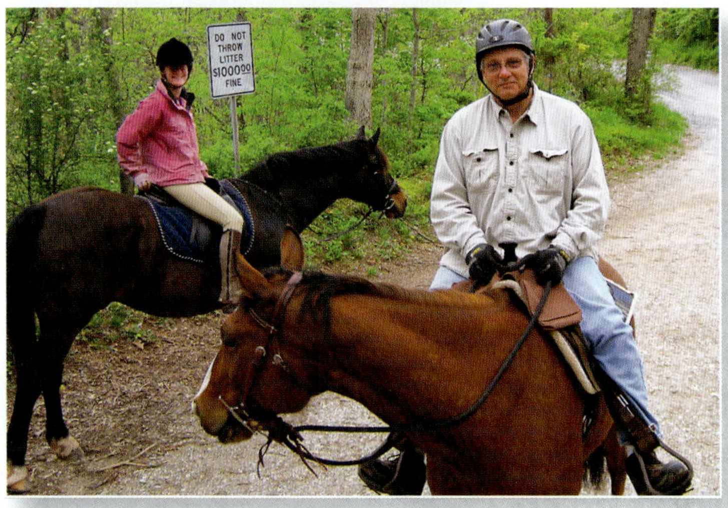

Above, Kim on her horse, Bart, and Ron on Metro at the trailhead to Union Mills.

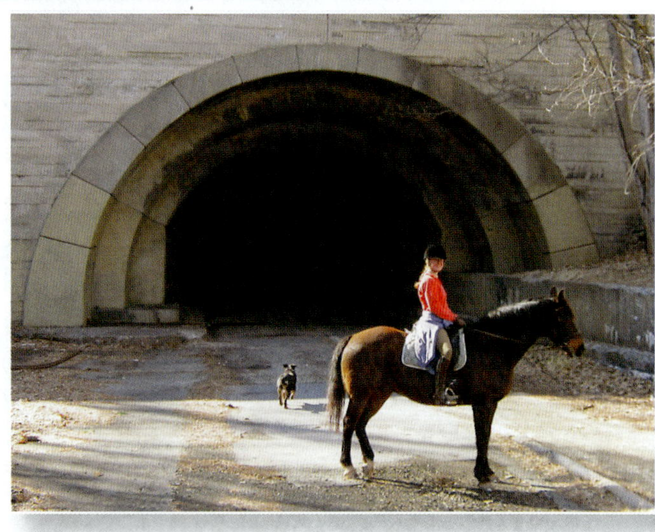

At right, Kim on Bart at the entrance to the old Pennsylvania Turnpike tunnel.

Photos courtesy of Ron Krajewski

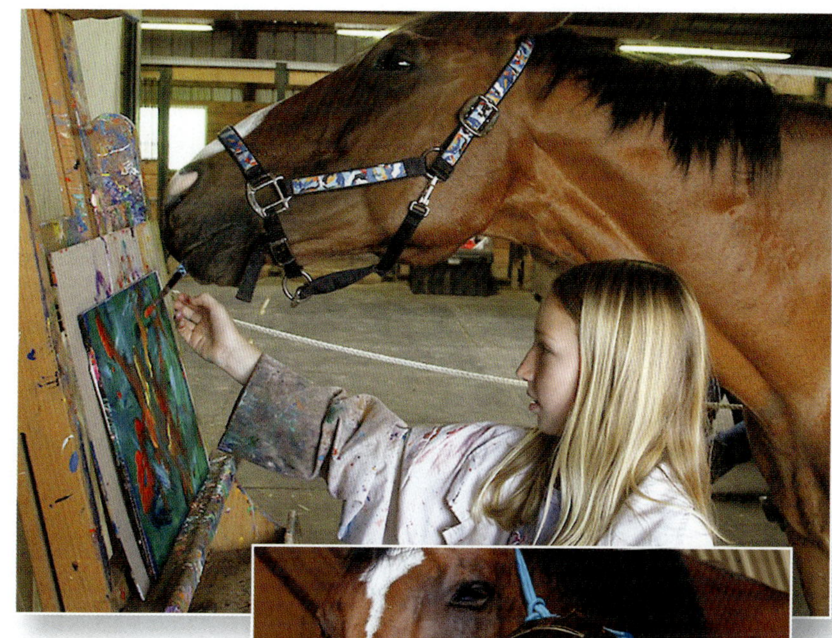

Above, ten-year-old Hailey Williams assists Metro with a new painting.

At right, Metro shares a laugh with his farrier, Sandy Zeigler, during a hoof trim.

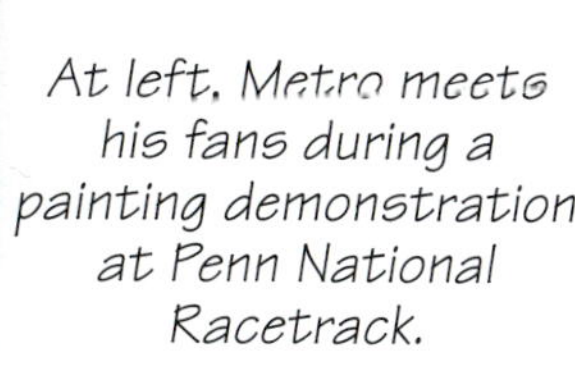

At left, Metro meets his fans during a painting demonstration at Penn National Racetrack.

Photo by Wendy Wooley/Peeps and Paws Photography

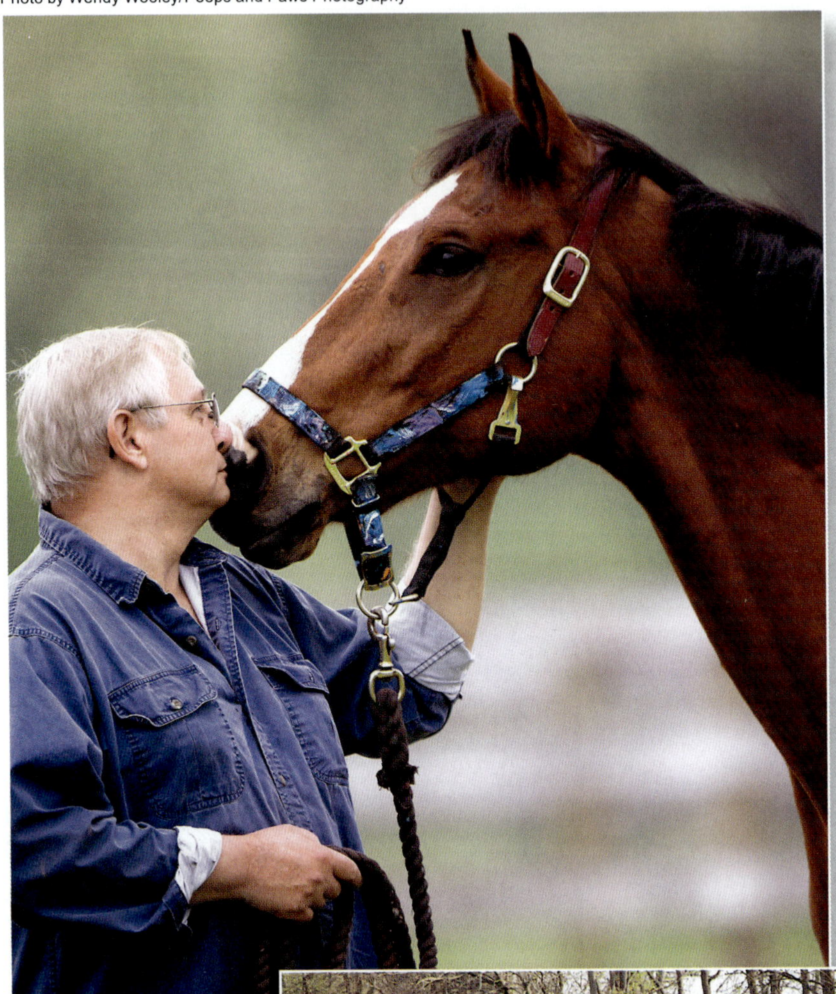

Above, Ron Krajewski and his buddy, Metro Meteor.

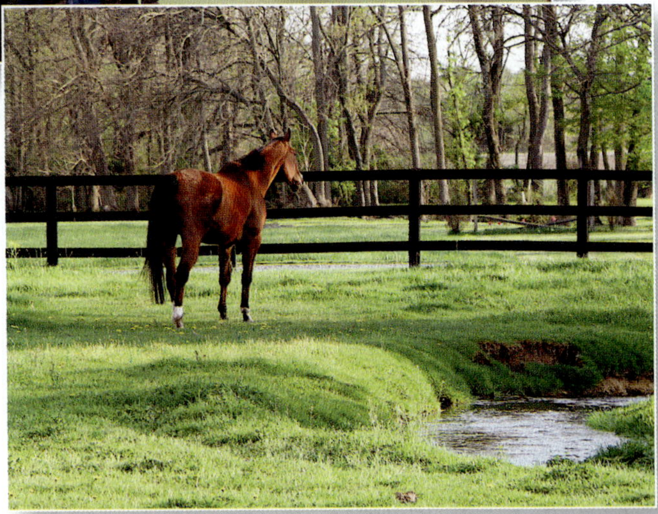

At right, Metro is enjoying his retirement at his new home in Gettysburg.

"No, I own a glass company," Ed said. "We get contracts for commercial and government builds and facilities in and around the Washington, DC, area."

Now that I knew Ed liked showing off his barn to potential boarders more than he liked actually taking in boarders, I was afraid we had no chance. Maybe this was all just a game to him and he had no real intention of allowing us in. I pictured us driving away, heads hanging low, locked out of heaven. No other barn would ever compare to what we had just seen.

We had to make this work. I was just about to plead our case when Wendy jumped in and beat me to it. "Ed, we're very low maintenance and we don't have any kids. Do you have any room for us?"

No one can refuse Wendy when she sticks out her bottom lip and looks up through those big puppy-dog eyes. Not even Ed.

"Sure," he said. "I do have room for you. Let me show you where the stalls are for your horses."

I let out the breath I'd been holding and looked over at Wendy. We exchanged a quick grin and followed Ed. Metro and Pork Chop's stalls were light and airy and each had a back door, opening into a shared paddock. The boys would have their own backyard. We walked through one of the stalls and out into the paddock. I noticed a large, cylidrical, green steel contraption sitting on a base in the paddock.

"What is this?"

"It's a bale feeder," said Ed, with a hint of pride. "You load a round bale of hay into it and the horses feed through the sides. I have them in every pasture, too."

This would be great for Metro. At Stone Hall, they rolled a round bale out into the field and all of the horses would gather around to eat, except Metro. He was always the odd horse out and had to wait for his turn. Now he and Pork Chop would have their own hay bale all to themselves.

I admired the quality of the feeder. You could tell much thought had gone into its design and construction. I glanced up at the top and saw a logo stenciled in white paint against the glossy green: *O'Neill Bale Feeders.* I glanced over at Ed and even though I didn't say it out loud, my eyes must have asked the question.

"I designed it and I own the patent on it," said Ed.

Clearly, we had just scraped the surface and I had much more to learn about Ed.

It was Metro's Parole Day back at Stone Hall Stables and déjà vu as we waited for Ed's truck and trailer to arrive, then watched him miss the turn-off. It was just a few minutes more before he turned around and came back. Stone Hall was about to become a distant memory.

Although she was usually watching at her window, today Karen was absent. I knew she wouldn't come out of her house to say goodbye.

"Let's get the horses," I said, turning my back on the house. "Ed will be here in a minute."

Pork Chop was the first to load. After he was secured inside the trailer, it was Metro's turn. He was standing quietly, head down. I handed the lead rope to Ed and he looked at Metro. "What a nice horse," he said, as he guided him up and into the trailer.

At last.

Wendy and I loaded the last of our gear in the Jeep and headed out. At the bottom of the driveway I braked, waiting for a car to pass by so I could make the right turn onto the main road. Not once did I glance in the rear view mirror. It was time to move on.

The horses settled into Ed's barn quickly, excited with their new home. Neither Metro nor Pork Chop had ever had a back door before. They ran in and out of the stalls, out into the paddock, over to the twin stalls and back out again. Eventually they figured out it was one stall per horse and Pork Chop chose first, selecting the left stall. Metro took the right.

Ed slid open the door to Metro's stall. As he walked in, I started to worry. I'd been through this scenario before and it usually didn't end well. "Be careful going into Metro's stall. He can be pretty territorial."

"Really?" he said.

Metro did the usual, treating Ed to his patented, evil-eye death stare and pinning his ears flat back on his head.

Ed walked over, threw one big arm around Metro's neck and began vigorously rubbing Metro's head with his other hand. He looked like a big brother giving his little brother a noogie until he cried "Uncle!"

Metro began bobbing his head up and down, trying to get away from Ed's loving torture. I figured the alligator bite would come next.

"He's a good horse," Ed said.

I couldn't believe it. Did he actually like my horse? Then the shock faded and a sense of relief and gratefulness began to flow through my veins like a trickle of cool spring water on a humid Gettysburg day.

Ed released his grip and lightly stroked Metro's head. "He just needs to learn who is boss."

Metro's ears came forward and he lowered his head.

I think Metro just cried Uncle.

We stayed at the barn all day. It was impossible to leave. We couldn't believe we had this beautiful place all to ourselves. Wendy took the horses out one at a time and gave them a tour of their new home. While she was busy, Ed took me around the property, explaining how everything worked so we would feel at home when he wasn't around.

"Let's go bring in Poco and Sunny," Ed said to Betty, the dog who had been following us everywhere. Part Rottweiler, part Labrador and a lot of pancakes and syrup, Betty stayed glued to Ed.

As the three of us approached the gate to the pasture, we saw Ed's horses grazing way at the other end. It would be a pretty good walk to retrieve them. "Get 'em, Betty!" he shouted. She scooted under the lowest fence board and took off running. Within a few seconds, Poco and Sunny came running toward us, bucking and kicking with Betty at their heels. All three of them looked like they were enjoying the game.

"Stand back." Ed opened the gate to the pasture as the horses approached. They ran through the gate and headed toward the barn, moving right into their stalls. We followed and closed the stall doors behind them. Clearly, things ran a little differently here than they did at Stone Hall Horse Penitentiary. Then we walked back across the drive to where Wendy was standing, holding Metro's lead rope while he grazed on the lawn. He was standing in just about the same place where we saw Ed's horses on our first visit.

"Everyone settling in?" asked Ed.

"Yes. We love it here!" Wendy looked down at Betty with a smile.

Betty was still excited from her round-up game and she began circling Metro. After herding Sunny and Poco into their stalls, she was pleased with herself and wanted to try her skills on Metro. But Metro continued to graze, not giving the dog a second glance.

When Betty couldn't get a rise out of Metro, she darted up to his front and tried to nip at his nose, buried in the grass. With a flash, Metro struck out with a front hoof, connecting with Betty and sending her flying across the grass. The dog landed with a yelp six feet away. She quickly rose to her feet, shook herself off and stared at Metro. He returned to leisurely grazing, as if nothing had happened.

I looked at Wendy and she looked back at me, wide-eyed. Had Metro just tried to kill Ed's dog? *Not good.*

"I'm so sorry! I didn't see that coming," said Wendy.

Is Ed going to kick us out on our first day here?

"It's okay," he said, with a gracious smile. "Betty needs to learn how to pick her battles. I think she just got her first lesson."

Not only did Betty learn a lesson, but it was time for Metro to learn some lessons, too. And after he got settled in, those lessons were going to be delivered by Emily. Ed was amenable to her training us in his barn, as long as she had her own insurance and signed a waiver. I couldn't wait. Finally, some training for Metro so he could start his new life.

Emily was much smaller than I was expecting. She could not have been more than five-foot-three and her blonde hair glimmered in the light as she got out of her truck. She strode into the arena and pulled out a four-foot stick with a six-foot string attached to the end. The rubber grip on hers looked worn, like she'd trained many a horse with it. She was quiet and didn't seem to like to talk much, which was fine by me. I gave her the rundown on Metro's knees and how he wasn't rideable yet. I wanted to learn how to do groundwork properly so I could keep him active.

I also confessed his biting problem, but nothing seemed to faze her. Her flyer at the tack shop had claimed she worked with problem horses, so I didn't feel I had to struggle to hide Metro's vices.

"The biting will go away once we start working with him," Emily said.

There's hope!

I had Metro attached to the cross ties and had already groomed him. I walked him around to demonstrate his problems. "He still has some spots that make him go nuts," I said as I walked around Metro, touching each spot on his body that sparked a reaction. Every time I touched a forbidden zone, Metro turned his head to try to bite or kicked out with a rear leg.

"We'll work on that, too," Emily said in a matter-of-fact voice.

What a relief. Emily didn't recoil in terror at the attempted bites or kicks. She didn't seem to see Metro as a dangerous horse, just one that needed some work.

But Emily didn't look like she weighed a whole lot more than Betty and look what Metro had done to that poor dog.

A small, blonde woman against a half-ton horse. Let's see who wins.

This was about to get interesting.

Chapter 18

Does He Always Do That?

"If riding was easy, it would be called football."
—*Unknown*

Emily led Metro out onto the Caribbean sand and got to work. She positioned herself to the side of his head and began tossing the lead rope over his back, then pulling it off. He didn't flinch. "Looks like he's done this before."

"Yes, but that's about as far as we got," I said. I left out the part about how the rope exercise hadn't fazed Metro in the first place. I didn't mind Emily thinking that I had actually tried to do some training with him, rather than just letting him run amok.

Emily tried the rope work on both sides, then moved on to the next exercise in Clinton Anderson's method. She stood beside Metro, looked at his hind end and used the stick she'd brought to lightly tap the air just to the left side of Metro's rear end. *One, two, three, four.* No response from Metro. She tapped the air four more times, this time a little more dramatically, but not touching Metro with the end of the stick. He still didn't move.

The third time she made contact, using the stick to lightly tap Metro on the butt. He immediately responded, taking one step to the side. Emily relaxed her body language and rubbed Metro on the butt with the stick to let him know that was the response she wanted.

I shook my head. *Metro was asked to do something and he did it?* It was the first time I'd ever seen Metro move without protest. For me, asking him to move meant I had to keep one eye on his teeth and the other on his hind feet. But with Emily, one step turned into two steps, then four, and soon she was able to get Metro's hind end to step around in a full circle while his front feet stayed put.

Soon Metro caught on and began to move when Emily just tapped the air, with no tapping on the butt required. Within minutes, she was able to wiggle a finger or walk toward Metro's butt and he would move out of her way. I learned the secret was in the body language. If Emily had a relaxed posture, Metro relaxed. If she changed her posture to read, "I mean business," Metro knew it was time to move.

I was amazed to learn how to communicate with a horse just by changing your body language. It's the same way they communicate with each other. When a horse pins his ears back, the other horses know it's time to move. The little blonde girl was metaphorically pinning her ears back at Metro and he responded every time.

She quickly had him backing up and trotting in circles, all through non-verbal communication and body language.

I watched in amazement as Metro did everything Emily asked of him. I couldn't wait to try it myself, but she wasn't taking the time to explain exactly what she was doing. Clearly, she spoke Metro's language and she communicated with horses much better than she did with people, but I had watched Clinton Anderson's DVDs so many times I knew most of what she was doing and why. I'd never had a chance to do it myself and now it was my turn to try.

Emily gave me a quick rundown on how to carry out the first three exercises and within moments, I got the same results as Emily had. Joy bubbled up inside of me as Metro responded to my cues. For the last seven months, since Metro had come off the track, he'd consistently fought me whenever I asked him to do something. Now, he was listening and doing everything I asked. I couldn't believe it.

Every time I wiggled the lead rope to ask him to back up, he did it. Every time I pointed to ask him to trot, he'd take off trotting in the right direction. Every time I tilted my head and looked at his hindquarters, he would stop trotting, swing his butt around and walk toward me with a lowered head. I wouldn't have believed it if I weren't actually there experiencing it. I was communicating with Metro!

I still got the feeling he was performing under protest, though. Metro has a way of doing everything you ask but making you feel like he's flipping you the bird while he's doing it (which I'm sure he'd be doing if he had fingers). But I was happy to take it. It might be Metro's way of letting me know I may have won the battle, but not the war, and I wouldn't want it any other way. While other horse owners might not put up with a horse with Metro's cantankerous spirit, I found it endearing. Every day with Metro was a new adventure. While I wished he had healthy, functioning knees, I would not ever change anything about his attitude. From the beginning, I loved his crankiness and I embraced the challenge. Yes, I wanted him to be better behaved and stop trying to bite me so much, but I still wanted him to be Metro.

Metro is like the crotchety old man in the neighborhood who keeps your baseball when it accidentally lands in his yard, but his family still loves him for who he is.

Emily's work was a huge breakthrough and I was reenergized with hope for Metro's future. For the next two months, I drove to Ed's barn and worked with Metro daily. I faithfully practiced the exercises Emily taught me and I continued to learn from her, even though we worked in silence most of the time. Between watching her carefully and continuing to review my Anderson DVDs, I began to understand the rudiments of horse-speak. I became pretty fluent with groundwork and, to my surprise and delight, Metro's knees were tolerating it well. I did detect a light hitch in his step during some of the trotting exercises, but it was short in duration and it didn't seem to bother him. It wasn't a heavy workout, just getting him to move when I asked.

I learned that horses are prey animals, born to be wary of anything that moves or makes a noise. A horse's first instinct when surprised is to turn and run away, so even something like a crinkly plastic shopping bag can become terrifying. I learned how to systematically expose Metro to situations that could potentially scare him. Besides shopping bags, I introduced him to a bouquet of helium balloons, cracked the stick and string like a whip to get him used to loud noises and walked him over a vinyl tarp.

Wendy and I spent hours in the arena, setting up obstacle courses with scary objects to help Metro and Pork Chop get over their fears. We had so many obstacles and balloons in the arena, we were just a bear riding a unicycle away from being our own three-ring circus.

Being trained to race meant the boys had been sheltered and their experiences limited, so now it was important work to get them used to whatever they might encounter while out on the trail. Not that we were in any danger of encountering tarps and Happy Birthday balloons on the trail; it was more about what those items represented. They were objects that moved and made a noise, a horse's worst nightmare.

Getting the horses to step on a tarp spread out on the floor of the arena turned out to be a major task. As far as Metro was concerned, it was a massive hole in the ground that was going to send him plunging down into Hades. The worst part was the crunching noise when he first stepped on it. But soon I had Metro walking on it, wearing it and dragging it behind him. It wasn't long before he was carrying Mylar balloons around in his teeth. Clinton Anderson says, "Heart attacks are free. Give your horse one every day." It seemed counterintuitive at first, but the more I gently scared Metro and helped him get over his fears, the calmer he would be.

Within two months, Metro had become the horse I'd dreamed he could be. He was well behaved, respectful and obedient. He began looking at me as his leader and stopped trying to dominate me. He still had some of that trademark Metro bad-i-tude, though. When I groomed him, he wasn't above letting loose a little kick or nip, but he got better. I didn't want him to lose the attitude completely, because it's what I fell in love with. I didn't want a different horse, just a better one.

I enjoyed our groundwork so much that I'd almost forgotten about riding him. I still wished I could, but I was happy just working with him, spending time together and helping him to become a better horse, a horse with some manners.

Ed's property was crisscrossed with wooded trails and we spent hours and hours just walking in the woods. Metro had his favorite patches of grass where breaks in the trees allowed in some light. I'd take Metro's lead rope off, pull up a log to sit on and watch him graze. Metro loved his walks in the woods and I often wondered what kind of trail horse he could have been. I wished he'd been dealt a better hand of cards. *Why wasn't he born with better knees that could stand up to the speed the rest of his body could generate? What kind of second career would he have had?* He was a beautiful horse and could have been a flashy competitor. I would love to have seen Wendy riding my Metro in the show ring. He'd been a great racehorse, but he was still just a young adult. He could have been great at so many things, if only he had his knees.

On the day of my last scheduled lesson with Emily, I lost track of time and ran late getting to the barn. I liked to have Metro groomed and ready to go by the time Emily arrived, but this time she beat me. When I arrived, I found Emily standing in front of Metro's stall, watching him.

"I am so sorry. I got involved with finishing a pet portrait and didn't realize I was late."

Emily was staring at Metro. She didn't look up or even acknowledge my apology. "Does he always do that?"

"Do what?"

"Does he always scrape his shavings into a pile and stand on them?"

I looked in and saw scrape marks on the floor of Metro's stall. It looked like he'd used his front hooves to painstakingly pull the shavings into a pile and now he was standing on the top.

"I never noticed," I said. "Why would he do that?"

"He's looking for comfort. Standing on the pile lets him stand with his hooves pointing down. Maybe toes down is a more comfortable position for him."

I learn something every day about this horse.

"Ask your farrier to put wedge shoes on him," Emily continued.

"Wedge shoes?"

"Horse shoes with an angle to them, higher in the back than the front."

"I'll ask Sandy," I said. "She'll be out here in a couple of days."

Sandy had always been great with Metro. We'd tried two different farriers at Stone Hall, but neither seemed to care that shoeing Metro was painful. The bending and twisting of his knees always caused him to fling his head around in pain. On shoeing days, I often found myself fighting to hold back tears.

I'd tried letting him go without shoes, especially since he wasn't being worked hard, but I found out he has especially soft feet. Just walking around on a gravel drive could make him footsore, so we continued to have his front feet shod.

Sandy, however, actually listened and understood. She had always treated Metro's knees with a great deal of care and she agreed to try the wedge shoes.

A few days later, I took Metro out for a round penning session, also known as an attitude adjustment. The round pen was a small arena, about sixty feet across, where I asked him to trot and canter circles around me. I'd found it was the best way to correct him if he started to slip back into his old, defiant, biting ways. He always started off his time in the round pen by pinning his ears back and kicking out when I asked him to pick up the pace. After a few rounds, he'd generally drop the attitude and become more cooperative. Often, he'd start out trotting with a slight limp, but I always watched his body language carefully to make sure he was in no pain. Round pen sessions were short—just enough to get the point across.

I looked at the new shoes as I led him into the pen. They had such a slight wedge, just two degrees, that I could barely detect it. I took him to the center of the pen, unsnapped his lead rope and pointed. Metro began to walk in a circle, hugging the fence. Then, without me asking, Metro sped up into a trot and then he went into a canter.

Hmmm. That's unusual. Metro never went into a canter on his own. And if I asked him, he usually kicked out a hind leg in protest. I stepped toward his front end and pointed in the opposite direction like Emily had taught me. Metro obliged by turning and trotting the other way. I didn't want him to pick up too much speed and hurt himself.

As he trotted, I watched carefully. *Where is the limp?* I couldn't take my eyes off his legs. I watched him for any sign of pain or stiffness, but there was nothing. Metro was trotting like a normal horse. *Can it be the shoes?*

I spotted Wendy strolling by with Pork Chop about fifty yards away. "Wendy! Come here for a second."

"What is it?"

"Just come and watch Metro."

Wendy led Pork Chop over, then stopped to watch Metro trot around the round pen. Pork Chop went back to nibbling grass.

"Where is his limp?" she asked.

"I don't know," I said happily. "He looks great. Maybe these new shoes have something to do with it."

Two days later, Emily agreed to come over and check on Metro. She watched him in action, then turned and said something I did not expect. "Do you want to start riding him?"

My heart jumped. "Do you think he's ready?" I stammered.

"He sure looks like he's ready."

My nerves kicked in. "I don't want to ride him yet." I wasn't sure *I* was ready, even if Metro was. "Wait. Why don't you train him under saddle for a month?" I had taken some lessons on Pork Chop and felt pretty comfortable on him, but Metro still seemed unpredictable. I had no idea what he'd be like with a saddle on his back. Or with me on his back.

One time we tried out Pork Chop's Western saddle on Metro, just to see how he would look. Racing saddles were tiny and lightweight, so it was the first time he had a heavy leather saddle on his back. As soon as the saddle settled into place, he started bucking and kicking like a mountain lion had jumped him. Would he do the same if I climbed up on him? I knew he was used to having jockeys on his back, but they had a lot more experience with controlling a temperamental racehorse. Plus, I was about the size of two jockeys.

Emily agreed to ride him first and I showed up at the scheduled time with video camera in hand, expecting a show. I imagined it would be like a Western movie, when a cowboy gets on an unbroken horse for the first time. I watched in awe as she did the necessary groundwork until Metro was calm and responsive, then put the saddle on him and worked him in the round pen again until he was used to it. Then she just climbed up on his back and rode him. To be honest, I was a little disappointed; Metro gave up too easily. No bucking. No kicking. His spirit was still unbroken, but I could tell Emily knew exactly what she was doing.

Emily went on to ride him daily for the next month and I showed up to watch them every single day. I enjoyed seeing Metro looking healthy and carrying a rider on his back. It was as it should be. He was putting on muscle and starting to look stronger and more toned, like he did in his old racing photos. He was starting to look like Metro Meteor again.

Finally, it was time. "Are you ready to get on Metro?" Emily asked.

"I've been waiting for nine months." I strapped on my helmet, took the reins and walked Metro to the plastic mounting block. I climbed the two steps and stood on top, then lifted my left foot to place it in the stirrup before I swung my other leg up and over his back. Just then, Metro took a step sideways away from me. I felt like it might have been his way of reminding me that he hadn't forgotten our never-ending struggle for supremacy. He wasn't about to let my first ride be an easy one.

I climbed back down the mounting block and wiggled the reins to back Metro up a few steps. I brought him forward again, next to the mounting block. This time, I made it up and onto his back without incident.

It was the moment of a lifetime. I settled down into the saddle, made sure my hands were positioned properly with the reins snug, then gave him a little squeeze with my legs. We began walking around the arena. It wasn't a ride into the sunset with my hair blowing in the wind, just a short, slow walk around the arena on a horse I never thought would allow me on his back.

I couldn't believe it. I was riding Metro.

Chapter 19

Rocket Horse

"There is something about riding down the street on a prancing horse that makes you feel like something, even when you ain't a thing."

—*Will Rogers*

While Metro was well on his way to becoming a calm, respectful saddle horse, Pork Chop was already there and Wendy was having a blast riding him. Together they were doing so well that she decided to enter her horse in a trotting class at Fun Day.

Fun Day was hosted by Rick Long, the owner of Double Rock Farm, just a couple of miles down the road from Ed's barn. A rail-thin figure with a cowboy hat and ears that seemed just a little too big for his head, Rick had leathery skin from years of being outdoors. A cigarette dangled from his mouth, ash drooping.

On Saturday nights, Rick and his wife, Bev, hosted cattle cutting and penning events drawing a mess of cowboys, cowgirls and wannabes. Double Rock was a great place, filled with happy people wearing flashy Western shirts and good-naturedly rooting for their opponents.

Before the start of each night's festivities, a rider paraded around the arena hoisting the American flag.

Besides the Saturday night events, Rick also hosted horsemanship clinics and Fun Days. Riders at any level were welcome at Fun Day, where beginners and up could test their skills navigating a cloverleaf pattern around barrels or weaving in and out of a poles course. The advanced classes were fast and highly competitive, but beginners and intermediates could walk or trot through the courses. As riders improved, they could work their way up.

Since the spring weather was so unpredictable and there was no indoor arena at Double Rock, Rick arranged to temporarily use Ed's barn to host a couple of Fun Days.

On the appointed Saturday morning, Wendy arrived to get Pork Chop ready to compete in a Fun Day trotting class. When she went to get him ready, however, she noticed a big gash over his right eye. It wasn't deep enough to require stitches, but we knew the big goober was probably suffering from one heck of a headache. Pork Chop is one of those accident-prone horses who could cut himself on a round corner.

"I'll bet he was playing with Metro last night," Wendy said.

Although Pork Chop and Metro were best friends, they loved to engage in bite fights. The two horses would stand facing each other, then each would try to nip at the other's head while attempting to avoid the return nip. They rarely made actual contact and seemed better at dodging bites than landing them. Pork Chop's injury probably had occurred when he raised his head too high, trying to avoid Metro's attack, and hit his head on the doorjamb. We gave Pork Chop some analgesic to relieve his headache and decided it was best to give him the day off from any physical exertion.

Wendy was pretty disappointed. She'd been looking forward to Fun Day for weeks.

Then I had an idea. "Why don't you ride Metro?" I could tell the thought of Metro being available for riding now had never occurred to her. But Metro had thirty days of training with Emily on his resumé and Wendy had taken her fair share of rides on him the past few weeks. Plus, Metro was looking healthy enough to participate. I knew from riding him he was still competitive and could out-trot any horse that tried to pass. I had visions of blue ribbons hanging from Metro's stall door. A little "Kiss Metro's Ass" to all his naysayers.

"I suppose I could ride him. Do you think he'll be a jerk?" she said thoughtfully, eyeing the unsuspecting Metro.

Metro, a jerk? Nah...

"He'll be fine." I grabbed his lead rope and slid open the stall door. "Go get your tack and I'll start getting him ready."

I cheerfully groomed him with all the confidence in the world that he'd be on his best behavior. Metro had made astounding progress from his pre-Emily days. When he was saddled and bridled and Wendy was ready, we walked him to the arena. But to my surprise, once Metro got a look at the scads of people around the perimeter and the twenty horses and riders warming up inside, something happened. The new, sedate version of Metro vanished and he suddenly became Metro Meteor, the champion racehorse and the jerk.

Lifting his head and tail high, he began to bounce around. We continued trying to work our way through the crowd to the arena gate, but as his excitement soared, it became obvious we needed to get him into the arena quickly, because I didn't know what he was working himself up to do. Would he take off running? Or kick out and hurt someone?

"Wendy, do you have your helmet?" I asked.

"Uh oh. I left it in the tack room."

"I'll go get it," I said. "Why don't you walk Metro around the arena and try to calm him down?" It was a great plan. Unfortunately, it didn't work. Walking Metro around the arena while twenty horses ran circles around him was not the best way to calm him down. His competitive instincts were beginning to awaken.

When I returned with the helmet, I found Wendy in the corner of the arena, wide-eyed, trying to hang on.

"I'm not riding him." There was fear in her eyes. "He's rearing up and kicking the walls."

I knew we'd better get him out of there fast. Metro had transformed back into that racehorse in the paddock at Saratoga who just wanted to go out and run like a category-three hurricane. I could picture what would happen if he got loose from Wendy, took off into the crowd of horses and started his own private match race.

Wendy and I had spent hours desensitizing our horses to scary moving objects and loud noises to make them bomb proof. But how do you desensitize a racehorse to large crowds and bunches of horses running around when we were the only boarders at Ed's barn? This was the first time in a long time that Metro had seen any other horse besides Pork Chop, Sunny or Poco.

Maybe instead of putting Metro in the competition, I could use this Fun Day event to begin to acclimate him to crowds of people and horses. I decided to lead Metro into an outdoor field where people were galloping their horses around and try to work him. *He's used to keeping his attention on me now. All I have to do is keep his feet moving.*

I tried out some groundwork, but all Metro wanted to do was watch what the other horses were doing while he danced around. I probably backed him up a quarter mile through that field in an effort to keep him focused on me. Nothing worked. I finally gave in, because there was no settling him down. A race call sounded in my head—*Metro Meteor, once one of the fastest turf sprinters on the East Coast, now scratched from trotting events at a local Fun Day.*

One month later, I decided to try again. After another month of riding Metro under my belt, we arrived early at the barn for the next Fun Day. This time, we planned to enter both Pork Chop and Metro in the trotting classes. While Wendy got Pork Chop ready, I groomed Metro. I had a new game plan this time and I took him outside to acclimate him to the day's upcoming activities by taking him on a walk down the gravel road. Already, he was doing better than last time, with his head relaxed and down. Last month, he'd kicked out at any other horse that came too close.

I walked him around the far end of the arena and through to the door to watch the other horses as they warmed up. So far, so good. We walked down the aisle and out the other side toward the outdoor arena. No fatalities...yet. This just might be the day.

When we entered the outdoor arena, the metamorphosis started once again. Metro began to transform as his mane stood on end, his tail went up in the air and his winter coat puffed out like I'd forgotten to throw in a dryer sheet. His neck and chest swelled to twice their normal size while he began the dance, jogging in place and not actually going anywhere. It was the dance only real racehorses know how to do.

This was the same horse that, only two seconds earlier, was dragging his nose on the ground a step behind me. Now he was twice his normal size and floating like a butterfly on the end of my lead line.

My hopes of riding him today were starting to slip away, but the spectacle was too much fun to watch. Metro was beautiful. I spotted Wendy on the other side of the fence and I couldn't stop myself from yelling, "Hey, Wendy. Look what I have!"

A couple of people in the arena, noting that I probably had a little too much horsepower on the end of my rope, reminded me about the round pen across the gravel drive. They obviously didn't know Metro actually lives here and we were regulars in the round pen. But it was a good idea, anyway. Maybe a few laps would knock some of the fresh off.

I led my dancing horse out of the arena into the round pen and pointed to the fence after I took his halter off. Pointing was his cue to move to the fence and await further instruction. On any other day, he would have done it. Next, I would have pointed the direction I wanted him to go and he would have done that, too. But not today.

Metro already knew what direction he wanted to go and what pace he wanted to go and that pace was *fast*. But first he threw in a couple of leaps, about, oh, four feet straight off the ground and took off like a bottle rocket.

I'd cantered him in the round pen before, but this was a whole new gear. Metro was running his own private Kentucky Derby, only in a sixty-foot circle with me in the middle. He was zooming so fast around the round pen and digging in so hard, I was afraid he'd lose his footing and go down, sliding into the fence like an Olympic speed skater after clipping a rival's skate.

What am I going to do? I thought about attempting to slow him down or change his direction, but that would mean stepping in front of this speeding train. By the time I moved forward to do what my brain was telling my feet to do, Metro had gone by in a blur. So I just let him run.

I glanced up at the other riders, who by this time had stopped what they were doing to watch this crazy horse set the short-track record at Bristol.

If I can't slow him down, maybe I can just stop him. I tilted my head and then looked at his hindquarters, the cue I'd learned to direct him into the middle to come to me. He came to me, all right. At full speed. My heart nearly stopped as he raced to a sliding stop right in front of me. I knew all eyes were on us and assumed my best *yeah-that's-how-we-roll* posture.

I nonchalantly scratched his head while the dust cleared and then looked up at the spectators. People were looking at us and talking. Even though I couldn't hear, I knew what they were saying.

"He's not planning on riding that horse, is he?"

Not today. He's a bit too much horse for me.

With Metro, I got a two-fer. One was a gentle, slow-moving, eight-year-old Thoroughbred with the body of a much older horse. His racing days were over and he bore the scars. He had bad knees and made grunting noises when I asked him to trot. He was retired, he knew it, and he only did what he had to do. Under protest. A beginner could ride him and I wouldn't have hesitated to put a five-year-old on his back, because he wouldn't go faster than a walk if he had anything to say about it.

My other horse was a lightning bolt. Only experienced riders dared mount him and they'd better be prepared to go fast. He was perfectly sound, could go from zero to forty miles per hour at the clang of a starting bell and he was full of himself. He was the greatest horse in the world. Just ask him. He'd tell you.

On most days, he was just Metro, in no hurry to get anywhere. When I asked him to get moving, he tossed his head, along with some equine four-letter words under his breath, at the fat guy on his back.

But there were days when he changed personalities. Once again, he was Metro Meteor, stakes horse, with $300,000 in his account and gunning for more. He could smell competition in the air and he wanted first place.

My dilemma? Both of my horses occupied the same body. And I never knew which one was going to show up.

Chapter 20

Airborne

"Horses lend us the wings we lack."

—*Unknown*

I glanced over at the lumpy saddlebags on Poco's back. They were stuffed full of something. *How odd.* As far as I knew we were out on a short trail ride, so I wasn't quite sure what Ed had up his sleeve. Had he brought along some medicine in case we needed to doctor up a horse? Or tools to pull a loose horseshoe?

This was my very first trail ride on Metro. I was beyond excited, but I also felt like I should've consulted *HFD*, because I had no clue what essentials I should have brought. I was sure that everyone else was also prepared, except for me.

I felt kind of foolish but kept staring at Ed's saddlebags, wondering. Ed finally caught my gaze, reached into one of the saddlebags and pulled out a frosty bottle.

"Wanna beer?" He pointed the bottle toward me.

I chuckled when I saw what constituted Ed's emergency supplies. "Any other time, Ed. My hands are full right now."

I'd been looking forward to this day for several months, even though I wasn't quite sure Metro would ever be healthy enough to actually go out on the trail. Wendy had smiled as I groomed and saddled Metro. She knew how excited I was.

Spring was just ending and the trails on Ed's property were muddy. To avoid the mud, we'd decided to trailer the horses to Gettysburg so we could enjoy the well-maintained trails, carpeted with pea gravel. We had already been on the Gettysburg Battlefield dozens of times on foot. We'd also ridden the trails there on horses from a local riding stable. But today I'd be riding my own horse. I was tacked up before anyone else and waiting on Metro's back, anxious to get started.

"Keep an eye on Metro and let me know if you see something that doesn't look right," I asked Kim, as she strapped a helmet over her red hair and rode Bart to where I was waiting.

Kim Brokaw had been our veterinarian since we moved the horses to Ed's barn. She had grown up on horseback and adopted a Thoroughbred off the track who became a talented jumper. She was a fearless and skilled rider. Kim was also a dedicated and talented vet who was known for hosting an annual chicken race, using cake for motivation, every year on Kentucky Derby Day.

We'd been happy with our last vet, but Kim lived across the street and rode her horse over to Ed's every day. With all of Metro's problems, I was delighted to have a vet onsite daily. I didn't realize for several months that Kim and Ed were dating. Ed was older than Kim, but they had a strong love of horses in common.

Kim's friend, Tara, would be joining us, so with Wendy that made five. When everyone had assembled, including Ed's dog, Betty, we headed toward the trailhead. As we moved out, I began to worry about the droves of joggers who used the battlefield trail. When Wendy and I had ridden the rental horses, the joggers always sped up and darted in between the horses, angering the trail guides. The rental horses were used to it, but Metro was not.

Early on, Metro let me know our first trail ride would not be the idyll I'd been dreaming of. From the first few steps, I had to pull back on the reins to slow him down. While the other horses seemed content to stroll in a line, Metro pursued a never-ending quest to get to the front.

"Looks like the racehorse showed up today," Ed said as I rode up next to him.

"Yes. It might be a long day," I said as I pulled back harder on the reins.

Betty trotted up the line of horses, happy as could be, trying to catch up with her master. When she came even with me, she looked up and recognized Metro. Her happy canine smile vanished and she immediately dropped back to the next horse. She had not forgotten about her last encounter with Metro.

While everyone else rode at a leisurely pace, my racehorse was jogging in place and pulling at the bit. My arms soon grew tired, but I was afraid if I gave Metro any rein at all, he might take off running. I'd ridden with Wendy and Pork Chop around the pasture before and Metro had remained calm and kept a slow pace. But five horses ignited his competitive fire and all he cared about was getting up to the front. Metro took four times as many steps as the other horses while covering the same exact distance. He was doing his little racehorse-tapdancing-in-place routine and I was growing tired of it.

"Why can't you be a normal horse?" I said under my breath.

He jigged from side to side, looking for a hole in the pack to squeeze through and pass the horse in front. If the trail widened enough for two horses to walk side-by-side, Metro was even more aggressive, pushing up right behind the horse in front and looking for a chance to shoot through.

"I'm sorry," I repeated, as Metro bumped and passed each horse.

Maybe I can turn this into a training opportunity. I can teach him some patience and get him used to riding in the back of the pack. I started holding him back with a stronger hand and forcing him to trot in place while the other riders passed. But ultimately, it didn't work. Metro just got angry and started nipping at the other horses when they got close. One time he reached over and bit Pork Chop on the butt, making him jump and almost causing Wendy to fall.

Wendy laughed. "Your horse is an ass." She said that every time Metro was being himself, which was often.

"I know he is." Finally, I gave in and let Metro have his head, allowing him to work his way to the front. I didn't really want to lead but, once he was in front, I hoped he'd lay off the racehorse antics.

We closed in on Tara, who was leading the pack on Jester. Metro crowded in on Jester's hindquarters.

"Jester likes to lead," Tara said as she looked back. "He won't let anyone pass him."

I chuckled quietly. Apparently she had no idea who was behind her. *This is Metro Meteor. If I let go of the reins, Jester would be nothing but a small, dusty black blur in the rearview mirror.* I was half-tempted to allow Metro the freedom to prove her wrong, but I also didn't want to spend the evening in the local hospital emergency room.

An hour and a half into our three-hour trail ride, Metro finally relaxed and calmed down enough to stop pulling on the reins. He wasn't choosing to relax; he just didn't have any juice left in the tank. He was a sprinter, not a long-distance runner. And with the extra dance steps he had covered about five times as much ground as the others. His head dropped and his body was covered in sweat. *I hope he has enough energy to get us back to the trailer.*

"You'll have to learn to pace yourself, buddy." He was a different horse now, content with a slow walk. He didn't even lift his head when a jogger passed us from behind. He did come alive at every rock, though. The battlefield was sprinkled with giant granite boulders and I don't know if it was the rocks themselves that frightened Metro or if he thought something dangerous lurked behind them.

Every time that we passed a boulder, Metro put an extra two feet of space between his body and the killer rock, watching it with a careful eye for any sudden moves. I'd worked hard and taken great pride in exposing Metro to a variety of scary objects to help diminish his fears, but granite looked like it might be his kryptonite.

Back at the barn that night, Metro didn't bother with his dinner dance. I always enjoy watching him put on a show by doing a little jig when he eats. He constantly lifts and moves and twirls a front foot. When one foot hits the ground, he immediately lifts the other. But now he just stood there with his head in the food bucket. When he finished his grain, he laid down in the stall with a groan and went to sleep.

I went over to Pork Chop's stall, slid open the door and crossed through in the shared paddock. I snuck in through the open back door of Metro's stall. His sleeping head was pointed toward me. I knelt down and rubbed his ears.

"Sweet dreams, buddy." I got up and closed the door so Pork Chop wouldn't come in and disturb him.

By the end of the summer, Metro had become a nice trail horse. Ed's property was a trail rider's paradise, covering sixty-five acres of fields, woods and creeks. Ed was good friends with his neighbors, so we routinely rode across the property lines on two-hour trail rides with Ed, Kim and Wendy.

Pork Chop loved the water and had a favorite creek crossing, where it formed a pool. Pork Chop was fascinated by the deeper water. He'd sink his head down, blow bubbles with his nose and paw furiously at the water with his giant hooves. Water flew everywhere and onto everybody within a few feet. Wendy always gave a little yank on the reins, because whenever Pork Chop started pawing, it usually meant he was getting ready to lie down. And he didn't care if it was in two feet of water. Next, Metro would follow Pork Chop's lead and start pawing at the water, too, flinging up water on anyone who still happened to have a few dry spots.

I was having the time of my life on these trail rides with Metro. Eventually, he learned not to use up all his energy trying to get to the front of the line. He relaxed and seemed content to stay back in the middle of the pack. We were never at the end. That spot was reserved for Pork Chop, who insisted on lagging behind.

Ed, Kim and Wendy enjoyed lively conversation on these rides, but I seldom joined in. My hearing was so bad, I rarely could grasp what the conversation was about. I was content just to enjoy the ride and watch Metro take it all in. Once he settled down, he developed this mesmerizing, windshield-wiper head movement. I don't know if he was scanning and keeping tabs on his surroundings, making sure nothing was about to pounce, or keeping an eye on Pork Chop in the rear.

We encountered plenty of deer on the trail, but our work with desensitization kept Metro and Pork Chop from panicking and running away every time one sprung out of the bushes. Betty always accompanied us and she'd crash through the bushes ahead and chase away most of the deer.

On days Ed and Kim were at work and unavailable for rides, Wendy and I didn't range too far afield, not wanting to take advantage of the neighbors' good will. But even when we stayed on Ed's property, there were plenty of trails to enjoy and we could get a good ride. We developed a little loop to take us down along the creek, up a few hills, through the woods and then out at the bottom of a hayfield. From there, the horses could see the barn and they knew they were on the homestretch. They always picked up the pace a little, heading home over the freshly-cut grass path.

I became more and more comfortable riding Metro. I trusted him and didn't think he would throw anything at me I couldn't handle. One day, on the path beside the hayfield, I gave Metro a little squeeze and took off at a brisk trot. I could hear Wendy mumbling and criticizing me from behind. She didn't enjoy it when I sped up on Metro without warning. Apparently, Pork Chop liked to adopt whatever gait his buddy Metro decided to use, without any warning to Wendy.

Metro could trot fast, especially when he was headed back to the barn. I had to pull back firmly on the reins a few times, because he wanted to go into a canter. I posted up and down in time with every step Metro took and we soon fell into an easy rhythm. I didn't look back to see if Wendy was close, although I could hear Pork Chop's hooves. I was pretty sure Metro wouldn't let them pass us.

Then it happened. Maybe I'd gotten a little cocky, but in the next instant I found myself flying through the air. It was disorienting; I'd just had a thousand pounds of horse underneath me, trotting briskly to the barn. But Metro had caught a glimpse of another horse through an opening in the trees and now he was gone. All four of his feet had left the ground as he jumped sideways, abandoning me to my own fate.

I don't believe he spooked out of fear, just surprise. Time slowed down and although my life didn't pass in front of my eyes, I did visualize several different possible scenarios for my future, some of them involving permanent disability.

While I was still airborne, my next thought was a fervent hope my foot would cleanly exit the stirrup. Somehow I was aware that although my left leg had already come up and over Metro's back as my butt left the saddle, my right foot was still lodged in the stirrup. I've seen enough movies where cowboys are bucked off and dragged through the desert upside down with one boot tangled in the stirrup. I knew this was not the way I wanted to leave this world. So I felt relief as I watched my right foot slide out in slow motion. One possible way of dying avoided.

My next thought was of Metro. *What will become of him? Will he keep going across the field without me? Will he run away and never return?* I had never fallen off a horse before, so I was uncertain of the procedure. I had seen a few people fall off in the arena but, since it was enclosed, the horses had nowhere to go. We were in an open field, with acres and acres for Metro to run to. Would I be spending the next hour limping around the fields trying to catch him?

I watched as the ground came closer. My final thought, just before I hit the ground, was, *this is going to hurt.*

Thud!

I was right. It did hurt. I felt pain like I hadn't felt in a long time. When you're a kid, there isn't a week that goes by that you don't find yourself hitting the ground at some point, playing tackle football or doing something crazy like imitating Mary Poppins and wondering if an open umbrella really will slow your fall when you jump off the roof. But it had been thirty-five years since I'd fallen down regularly and I wasn't a kid anymore. My fifty-year-old body wasn't going to shake it off. Whoever said you have to get right back on a horse after you fall off was an idiot.

After I hit the ground, I found myself sprawled out on my back, my body forming a perfect outline in the tall hay, like the chalk at a crime scene. Metro had spooked so far sideways that we'd left the mown path and I was now looking up through the stalks of hay.

I mentally reviewed my physiology to see if anything was broken and, once I determined everything seemed to be in the right place, I got up slowly. I wondered where Metro was. Then I saw him. He had stopped, returned and walked over to stand next to Wendy and Pork Chop. Metro nudged Pork Chop's flank, then put his head down and looked at me sheepishly out of the corner of his eye. I don't know if horses are capable of showing remorse, but Metro looked like he was saying, *I'm sorry.* There was a look of embarrassment on his face for spooking and sending me hurtling through the air.

"Are you okay?" Wendy asked.

"I'll live," I said.

I knew what was coming next.

First a giggle, then Wendy started laughing and before long, she couldn't stop. "Oh, my. That was the funniest thing I have ever seen."

I wasn't sure whether to laugh or cry.

"Stop it! You're gonna make me pee my pants!" Wendy chortled. "Look at that big patch of matted down hay. That's where you landed. It's like a big crater!"

At least she'd checked on me before she started laughing, I consoled myself. It was an unusual departure from Wendy's strict *Laugh now, ask questions later* policy.

"Come here, bud," I called to Metro. He came out from his hiding place behind Pork Chop and walked over to me. He put his head down in my chest and let me rub his ears. I couldn't be mad. He was just doing what horses do—react first and figure out what scared you later. I often wonder if horses feel stupid when they realize the candy wrapper that tumbled across their path in the wind and sent them reeling was actually just a piece of plastic, not a charging mountain lion.

This is the most dangerous part of riding a horse, any horse. Even the most seasoned riders occasionally fall off when their horses overreact. You have to expect the unexpected, because a horse has a mind of its own and can react in a split second by launching into space. It was the first time I'd fallen off Metro and it probably would not be the last.

I didn't get back on. Instead, I gathered up Metro's reins and we walked back to the barn with our heads down. All the while, we could hear Wendy cackling behind us. I was glad we could provide some amusement.

Chapter 21

Velocity

"I believe God made me for a purpose, but He also made me fast. And when I run I feel His pleasure."
—*Colin Welland, Chariots of Fire*

"I think I'm going to ride Metro next week at Fun Day." I was walking alongside Wendy and the horses back to the trailer after a horse show. Pork Chop had competed and I'd brought Metro along to get him more used to being around a bunch of other horses.

Wendy turned to me with a questioning look. "Do you really want to go through that again?" My first attempt at Fun Day had not been much fun for her.

"Look at him," I said hopefully. "I think he has it all out of his system now."

Wendy looked at Metro thoughtfully, then shook her head and rolled her eyes a bit. She'd been progressing quickly with her riding skills. She was now taking Western riding lessons from a young trainer named Brenda, who had talked her into competing in the horse show.

Brenda was just twenty-two, incredibly loud and always covered in dirt. A cloud of dust seemed to follow her around, like she was a comic strip character. "I've had a lot of short-term relationships, but guys just don't stick around," she had once told Wendy.

I had also been taking lessons from Brenda. Even *I* could hear Brenda's voice booming across the arena and, with her help, I was beginning to master the posting trot.

When Wendy and I had first arrived at the horse show, north of Gettysburg, we looked around and noticed dozens of kids dressed up in English attire. "I hope I'm not the only adult riding in this class," Wendy said. She quickly got Pork Chop saddled up and ready, then headed down to the arena to warm up with Brenda in tow.

Moments later, I heard Brenda calling my name. She must have been about 200 yards away, but I had no problem hearing her. I walked Metro down to the arena and saw Wendy by the gate.

"Can you work Metro down here? Pork Chop is going nuts, because he can't see him." I realized how attached they'd become. It dawned on me that this was probably the first time in a year they had been out of each other's sight.

Metro showed some excitement as he watched the horses moving around the arena, but I was relaxed and neither of us felt any pressure. We weren't showing today; all we had to do was stand, watch and behave ourselves. After a while, Metro began to graze while the horse show began just yards away. I was happy he was finally making progress on his manners. The next test would be strolling calmly through the crowd. He passed that one, too.

"This is just what Metro needed," I told Wendy as she waited for her class to be called.

"Just make sure you don't leave. Pork Chop needs to be able to see him when we're in the arena."

We heard the announcement for Wendy's class and she headed into the arena. As feared, she was the only adult in her class. It didn't help she was on the back of the world's tallest Thoroughbred. At the end, everyone lined up side-by-side for the presentation of the awards. Wendy and her horse looked out of scale, like Godzilla destroying a miniaturized model Tokyo, when compared to the kids on their cute little ponies.

"I'm never doing that again," she said, embarrassed, as we packed up to leave.

That's when I sprung it on her about riding Metro in the next Fun Day. It would be a much different crowd from Wendy's English show. Sure, there would be kids on ponies, but we would be riding in a separate class.

As soon as we could, we paid Rick our Fun Day entrance fees, registering for the Adult Walk/Trot class. I was pretty sure Metro was going to win every event in the class: Trail, Barrels, Poles and the Flag Race. The events were timed, not head-to-head competition, which lessened the chance that Metro would shift into high gear. And Metro was so fast even when he was trotting.

The only rule in the class was you had to keep it to a walk or a trot. If your horse cantered for more than five steps, you were disqualified from the event.

I really wanted to win a ribbon for Metro. He'd been written off by so many people as a horse with no future. I'd been told he'd never be ridden again. Winning a ribbon would be a validation for him. Metro had won $300,000 on the track and now all I wanted for him was a fifty-cent piece of blue satin.

The first event was the trail class. It didn't really look like the trails we had been riding at Ed's. The course was more of a series of obstacles or tasks. I watched carefully as the first two competitors navigated the course. I visualized my strategy.

Then it was time. "Whenever you are ready, Ron," said Rick over the loudspeaker. I turned Metro around and trotted him in a circle so we could get a running start at the line and be at full trotting speed when we tripped the timing beam.

The first task was to pick up a small flag from the fence and place it in a holder thirty feet away. *Done.* We performed it perfectly. The next task was to open a gate from horseback. Metro stopped right in front of the gate as I reached forward and pulled it open without losing my balance. We made it through, dodged a barrel and headed toward a short wooden bridge about a foot off the ground. Metro trotted right over the bridge without slowing to a walk. *All of the scary objects I exposed Metro to really worked!*

The last obstacle was the keyhole, a chalk outline on the ground in the shape of an old fashioned keyhole. You had to enter through the narrow end, rotate 180 degrees and then head back to the finish line. Once inside, Metro spun around quickly and headed back. *I think we have a chance at this.* I gave him a squeeze with my legs and a *tch!* with my mouth to encourage a fast trot. Metro knew about finish lines. He realized we were in the homestretch and bolted out of the keyhole.

"One, two..." I heard Rick say over the loudspeaker. *Shoot! He's counting Metro's steps.* Metro had gone into a canter and I had to slow him back to a trot before we hit five steps. I pulled on the reins, but Metro's head rose even higher and he showed no signs of slowing down.

"Three, four, five...sorry, Ron. Disqualified."

Metro didn't slow down until he crossed the finish line. I heard some clapping and murmurs of excitement from the spectators. On our way out of the gate, we passed Wendy and Pork Chop waiting to compete.

"You guys looked good, until the end." She wore a slight smile. I knew she was laughing inside. My battles with Metro had turned into comic relief for Wendy and for me, too. Pork Chop had been the perfect horse since the day we got him. He was always well behaved, always a perfect gentleman. Metro, on the other hand, had been such a train wreck that sometimes all we could do was laugh. Every time I felt like I was making headway, he offered up a new challenge. I was happy to be riding him, but I also wanted to be able to control him.

The barrel race went about the same. Metro ran the barrel pattern perfectly but then took off sprinting for the finish. *Disqualified.*

Pole race: *disqualified.*

Flag race: *disqualified.*

When it was over, I hopped off Metro, put on his halter and tied him to the horse trailer so he could get some water and a bite of hay. We stood there facing each other and I looked in Metro's eyes. "You just can't help yourself, can you?"

You can take the horse out of the race, but you can't take the race out of the horse.

Metro lowered his head and I rubbed his ears with both hands, then kissed him on the forehead. I couldn't help it. I loved this horse. Even though we didn't earn a ribbon, I wouldn't have changed anything about Fun Day. In fact, I wasn't even that disappointed. I actually preferred disqualification. I would have hated to lose to another horse via the timing clock, especially Pork Chop with his sloth-like speed. I knew Metro had given it his all—he just didn't understand the rules. But we had successfully competed, which was a big step.

We did get to celebrate with Wendy and Pork Chop, who earned a small handful of second and third place ribbons. When we got home, Wendy proudly displayed them on Pork Chop's stall door.

"You see this?" I told Metro. "You were beaten by the world's slowest racehorse."

Over time, Metro seemed to grow more and more comfortable with his second chance career on the trail. Gone were the white-knuckle rides where I had to hang onto the reins, thwarting his efforts to get to the front of the line. He seemed content to ride in the middle of the pack and displayed a surprising amount of patience, given his past approach.

He was always great at the walk. The trot and the canter still gave him problems, though. He had good days and bad days. Sometimes he came up with a limp and we had to lighten up on the riding. But if he didn't limp, it was a good day and I could ask him to work a little harder. We also continued a daily dose of supplements with his breakfast, the monthly shots of Adequan in his neck muscle for joint health and the special wedge horseshoes with pads to support his ailing knees. All of these things seemed to help, but Metro still had bad days when he wasn't up for a trail ride.

Metro's vet, Kim, suggested knee injections. She told me later she did not harbor much hope for Metro's long-term rehabilitation. She thought, *It's not going to be a happy ending for this horse.* But for now, at least, she offered a chemical cocktail of steroids and fluid to help keep his knees lubricated and operating smoothly, like motor oil in an engine. I'd researched knee injections but had always avoided them as a temporary fix. I wanted long-term health for Metro. When the bad days became more frequent, I decided it was time to let Kim give it a try. I didn't want Metro to be in pain. He'd had enough of that in his life.

Kim injected Metro's knees and prescribed two days of rest. There is always some soreness involved when a giant needle is inserted into your knee. Luckily, the two-day rest ended on a Sunday, when Wendy and I usually did a big group trail ride with Kim and Ed, bulging saddlebags and all.

When I climbed up on Metro's back and started toward the trailhead, I immediately knew I had a different horse under me. It felt like I had just switched from a Buick to a Maserati. The newly patient Metro was no longer so patient. He wasn't content in the middle anymore, but he wasn't trying to get to the front, either. This time, he acted like someone had shifted him into turbo and he wanted to open up and gallop at full speed across every field and run up every hill. The injections had worked and Metro was feeling really, really good.

Then I had a realization. The only thing that had kept me from getting killed riding Metro was the ailing condition of his knees. Because if this was normal operating procedure when he was feeling good, he was way too much horse for me. I did not have the skills.

Whenever the group came to a stop, Metro would start to spin in circles. I was trying to hold him back, but he couldn't seem to stop moving his feet.

"You look like you're in a cowboy movie!" shouted Ed.

"I'm so happy for you," said Kim, giddy with excitement at the success of the knee injections.

"But I don't want to die!" I gasped, trying to stay balanced on my dancing rocket horse.

It would prove to be a long, stressful trail ride, as I spent the whole two hours trying to contain Metro and postpone my death-by-horse. When Metro would cut me a break now and again, I took the time to think about my secret dream—I had always wanted to ride Metro at a full gallop. Just once, I wanted to feel what it was like to fly across the grass at thirty-five or forty miles an hour on the back of a great racehorse. I imagined myself on the scene at one of his greatest days, galloping into the sunset down the homestretch of the turf course at Belmont.

Since I had first decided Metro would be mine, I'd dreamed that Metro's knees would heal and he'd be able to run and it would coincide with my progress from novice rider to advanced. But Metro got there before me. He was ready to run like the wind and I wasn't.

The trail ride had exhausted me and I was ready to get back to the barn and off Metro's back. Even after two hours, Metro was still full of energy and prancing around like it was time for the Derby.

When we finally arrived, the sun was beginning to set and I saw Brenda on Ed's porch, resting after a day of working with the horses. Then I had an idea. I knew she was fearless when it came to riding horses. "Brenda, I have a question for you. Metro wants to run. Do you want to take him for a spin?"

"Sure," she said, stepping down from the porch. She hopped up on Metro's back and off they went at a canter toward the hayfield. Ed grows his own hay and keeps a fifteen-foot wide path of grass mowed around the edge of each field. It's like a natural grass track, with about 200 yards to the first turn, another 200 yards to the second turn and then a long quarter-mile straightaway, before dropping down a gentle slope toward the woods.

I watched, almost holding my breath, as they went around the first turn. Brenda was relaxed, not asking Metro for speed as they headed across the short side of the field to the second turn. The reins were loose and she was letting him set the pace. He continued to canter as he approached the second turn. I could almost read Brenda's mind. *This old racehorse just doesn't have it in him anymore.*

But I knew better. Metro was a turf sprinter and a come-from-behind horse. His races were never run in a full circle. They usually started on the backstretch, made a sweeping turn to the homestretch and then on to the finish. His racing strategy had been to conserve energy to the final stretch, then kick it into high gear and pass the rest of the pack for the win.

So when Metro rounded that second turn and saw the quarter-mile of freshly mowed grass that lay before him, he must have flashed back to the homestretch at Belmont, because he kicked it into a gear I had never seen before. Correction: I *had* seen it in his old racing films, but never in person.

Brenda and Metro were now galloping at full speed heading west, toward the setting sun. The burnished light shone on Metro's face and his mane rippled in the wind. *What a beautiful animal.*

I could hear his thundering hoofbeats from 200 yards away. I could feel them in my chest. My dream was finally coming true. The two years of knee issues and attitude problems sloughed away, along with the aggravation, the struggles, the good days and the bad days, too. This was the moment I'd been waiting for. It was all here. The tightly mowed grass, the setting sun and my beautiful racehorse in all his glory.

The only thing missing from my dream was me. A profound sadness flowed through me as I realized a twenty-two-year-old girl was living my dream and I was relegated, once again, to watching from the grandstands.

It should be me up there, not her.

But as I watched Metro gallop away, my disappointment faded with the sunlight. I was happy. Going fast is what Metro was born and bred to do.

Today is not about me. It's about Metro. Today he is living his *dream.*

Chapter 22

Into the Black

"Walking with a friend in the dark is better than walking alone in the light."

—Helen Keller

No one had thought to bring a light. We had stopped at the entrance to an abandoned tunnel. Built with a slight upward curve to allow water to drain out, I could tell after a few hundred yards that the entrance would disappear under the horizon, leaving us inside in total darkness. Since I always count the horses too, there were eight of us, with Ed on Poco, Kim on Bart, Wendy on Pork Chop and me on Metro.

With winter done and the ground thawing, the trails at Ed's were still too soft and muddy for trail rides. Itching to get out on the trail after a long winter, Ed had discovered the old, abandoned Pennsylvania Turnpike.

When the two-lane turnpike opened up back in 1940, it was known as Tunnel Highway, because it traversed seven tunnels from east to west: Blue Mountain, Kittatinny Mountain, Tuscarora Mountain, Sideling Hill, Rays Hill, Allegheny Mountain and Laurel Hill. Each mountain had a tunnel through it, originally built for the South Pennsylvania Railroad.

A new six-lane turnpike was built and the old, outdated one retired in 1968. Even though the tunnels are not maintained, they're still considered structurally sound. The old Pennsylvania Turnpike is now a tourist destination for hikers, bikers and riders. Somehow, though, we missed the "helmets and lights are recommended" advice as we planned for a long trail ride. The paved road meant we didn't have to worry about soft ground and mudholes, and the thought of riding the horses through an abandoned tunnel sounded like a great adventure.

We loaded the horses into the trailer and made the two-hour drive. After we unloaded them and tacked up, the horses were anxious to get going and the half-mile ride to the entrance of the tunnel went by very quickly. I don't remember who took the lead, but Metro and I brought up the rear.

The tunnel entrance had an eerie feel. Water was dripping down into the tunnel and freezing, creating six-foot-high stalagmites made of ice. We headed into the tunnel and, once we lost sight of the entrance, it quickly grew gloomy. Immediately, one of the horses at the front spooked, backing up into the other horses and creating a chain reaction of scared horses backing frantically away from some undetermined danger ahead. I couldn't hear or see anything and had no idea what it was.

Horses are born to live afraid, because in the wild they are food for wolves and big cats. Any noise or moving object can send a horse running or jumping away. It's an instinct buried deep in their DNA and this flight behavior is the reason we have horses around today. Otherwise they'd be long gone after serving as satisfying meals for the top of the food chain. The horses with strong flight instincts survived to graze another day, so it has nothing to do with emotional instability or a lack of intelligence.

Although the science community has been studying dolphin, ape and dog intelligence for decades, scientists are just now starting to study horse intelligence. That's pretty shocking, considering how important horses have been to humans for thousands of years. In the wild, horses face tremendous challenges, like finding food and water, dealing with other horses inside or outside the herd and avoiding predators.

Horses don't see, hear or smell the way we do, so it's been difficult to study them. We do know, like other intelligent mammals, their brain-to-body ratio is fairly large. But one thing scientists *have* been able to prove is that horses have extraordinary long-term memories, which help them survive. They also have keen perception which we don't completely understand—that's why you'll sometimes hear an experienced horse handler say that a horse can read your mind.

But at the end of the day, a horse's biggest fear is a mountain lion jumping on his back and bringing him down, so allowing a rider on his back contradicts a horse's deepest drive for survival. It's all fun and games until a lion, imaginary or otherwise, jumps on your back. Then, all bets are off. To make it even worse, humans ask (or demand) that horses wear saddles made out of the hide of other, less fortunate animals. That's why there is such a thing as a bucking bronc; the cowboy is trying to stay on the horse for eight seconds so he can get his score from the judges and the horse wants whatever creature is on his back to get the heck off.

Learning about Metro's fears taught me I had to earn his trust. I had to teach him that not every moving object or abrupt noise was a danger to his life. The last thing anyone wants in a trail horse is a startled reaction every time a twig breaks or a plastic garbage bag rustles by in the breeze.

I'd continued to expose Metro to everything possible that could scare him and my repertoire had expanded to walking him over tarps while under a tarp or even dragging a tarp. We'd also dragged bags full of cans and walked through walls of streamers blowing in the wind. I'd even fired off cap guns nearby. I wanted Metro to trust me even when he wanted to flee what he thought might be a dangerous situation. But teaching Metro to trust me taught me also to trust in Metro. I was feeling more and more confident he wasn't going to spook unnecessarily and do something stupid while I was on his back.

In the tunnel, as the horses all started backing into each other, I just held on and tried to stay calm. Pretty soon the three horses ahead ran out of room and backed into Metro, who in turn backed himself up onto a one-and-a-half-foot-high concrete sidewalk on the side of the tunnel. Once upon a time, maintenance workers had used it to walk the tunnel, but now Metro and I were perched up on the narrow, two-foot wide ledge. Never having been in this particular position before, I was unsure how to proceed.

Should I give him a little nudge with my heels and ask him to step down? Probably not a good idea, because Metro, the drama queen, usually overreacted. If I asked him to take a step, most likely he would take five frantic steps.

What if I try to slide off Metro's back? I wasn't sure that would work either. If I could even get myself safely to the ground below the ledge, I'd be a couple feet below Metro, who was still perched on the sidewalk, and he could potentially step off or fall off on top of me.

I quickly realized the only option was to trust Metro. *I'm going to have to give him a loose rein and let* him *work out how to get down.* I slid my hands forward so he had plenty of slack in the reins and said with my most calm and confident voice, "Come on, buddy. Get us down from here."

Metro paused for a few seconds, looked down, surveyed the situation and then stepped down nice and easy. *Whew.* There could have been several other less successful and much more painful endings to that little scenario.

The four of us talked and decided that since the horses weren't comfortable in the tunnel, it would be best for everyone else to dismount so we could walk them through to the other side. All except for Kim. She was the best rider among us and I was quickly finding out she was fearless on a horse.

Any remaining glimmers of light quickly vanished as we moved forward into the darkest dark I have ever experienced. I could not see anything of Metro, even though he was just a foot or so to my right. I could hear his feet *clip clop* on the pavement, though, and I could hear him breathe. Every once in a while, I reached out and touched the warmth of his neck just to make sure he was still there. I could hear the other horses' footsteps, but I had no idea where anyone else was.

About halfway through the tunnel, my heart seized when Metro suddenly stopped. The reins tugged as he turned his head to the right, looking at something in the dark and listening intently. *What was out there?*

Then I noticed the other hoofbeats had ceased. Dead silence.

"Did everyone else's horse stop?" I said, wanting confirmation.

A chorus of yeses.

"Do they see something in the dark?"

Yeses again.

"Do you want to keep moving?"

"Yes!"

It gave me comfort to know Metro could see in the dark better than me.

We trudged on through the blackness, all the time wondering what the horses had seen in the dark. It could have been an empty can rolling away from a hoof, but then again it could have been some nasty verminous underground dweller lurking in the darkness. Maybe it (or they?!) were just hiding and waiting for some unsuspecting hiker to serve as the next meal. My mind flashed to the stereotypical old codger character in horror movies, who always gave out warnings no one ever listened to. "Aye, riding on the old turnpike, are ye? Well, steer clear of the tunnel. Riders go in...but they never come out." Cue scary music.

Finally, we started to see a hint of light as we started down the slight incline to the end of the tunnel. Ed had told us the tunnel was a mile and a half long, and I estimated we had walked at least a mile in utter darkness.

When we finally exited the tunnel, our time was already growing short and we decided we needed to turn around and start heading back immediately. No surprise, but no one was overly excited about going back through the tunnel.

"Why don't we try and find a path *over* the tunnel?" someone suggested. "We can stay in the sunshine, where it's safe."

We decided to try and we bushwhacked with the horses up and over the tunnel, looking for any signs of a trail. Nothing. The going was tough and a little slippery. We suggested Kim pull out her cell phone to try and map where we were and how we could possibly get back to the horse trailer.

After studying the map on her phone, Kim determined the new turnpike was in between the trailer and us. Kim suggested we ride the horses across the six lanes of buzzing traffic which constituted the new Turnpike, jumping them over any concrete barriers we might encounter along the way. We quickly responded with a chorus of no's and a couple of hell no's. Kim might have been the smartest one in the group, but common sense did not appear to have been a core requirement for her college degree.

Once Kim accepted that we would not be crossing the freeway with our horses, we turned around and picked our way back down the hill, trying to find the tunnel entrance again for the long and perilous journey back. It was one thing to go through the tunnel when we didn't know what to expect but, now that we knew, it was much harder to contemplate a trip back into the dark.

On the way down the hill, we came across a fallen log. Kim and Bart got a running start and jumped it with ease. The log wasn't big enough to require jumping, so Ed and Wendy had no problem walking their horses up to it and asking them to step over. Metro and I, still bringing up the rear, approached the log. When we got close, Metro stopped. I gave him a little nudge with my heels and all he did was turn his head around to see what the problem was. *Don't you know my knees can't lift high enough to get over that log?* his eyes seemed to be saying.

"Sorry, buddy. I forgot. We'll find a way around." And we did.

We rode up to the back entrance to the tunnel and stopped to discuss the options. Should we walk the horses again? Should we ride? In what order? And tell me again why no one brought a light?

I knew I was not going to walk it again, leading Metro. If we were forced to do this tunnel again, we were going to do it like a real horse and rider should. But I sure as heck didn't want to be at the end of the line and dependent on what the other horses were going to do (or be the easiest to pick off, becoming the next meal for whatever lurked in the dark. That was Pork Chop's job). I was confident Metro would do well if he was in the lead, with no horses in front to spook and back into him. I did not want to end up stranded on the elevated sidewalk again.

I didn't ask anyone if we could lead; I just knew we had to and I gave Metro a squeeze. With a deep, collective breath, my horse and I headed back into the tunnel. The light seemed to dissolve faster this time. But we seemed to make better time riding, rather than walking. Very soon the darkness enveloped us, but this time I was on top of Metro instead of walking beside him.

The scene from *Seabiscuit,* where the famous racehorse was being secretly trained at night, came to mind. Trainer Tom Smith told jockey Red Pollard to take Seabiscuit around the track in the dark.

"But I can't see out there," protested Red.

"That's alright," said the crusty old trainer. "He can."

Metro can see, I kept reminding myself as the darkness closed in like a thick blanket. I couldn't see the tunnel walls. I couldn't even see Metro's ears right in front of me. I had to let the reins go slack, ceding total control to Metro. There was no sense in steering him if I couldn't see where I was going.

Trust Metro.

There was no other choice. There was nothing else I could do. My safety was in Metro's hooves. I thought again of the time and energy I'd spent exposing Metro to what could scare him and, in the process, building trust and confidence between the two of us. I'd always wanted him to know that nothing would hurt him when he was with me. Now, I had to trust in him to get us safely to the other side.

I listened to the hoofbeats of the other horses behind us but, with the echo of the tunnel, I couldn't tell how close they were. They could have been six feet or sixty feet or six hundred feet behind.

Metro kept moving forward at a steady pace. I didn't have to urge him or steer him. He seemed to know where he was going and I felt like a passenger along for the ride. I began to talk to him softly, not to comfort him, but to remind him I was still on his back. That he was responsible for me. "Hey, buddy. You're doing a good job. We're almost there."

Then I sang the old Popeye song to him, with a slight modification. "He's first to the finish 'cause he eats his spinach, he's Metro the Wonderhorse."

Next came the race calls, like I did those first few days together.

"Here comes Metro Meteor, on the outside."

"He just inhaled the field!"

"Oh, he just blew them away."

Then, drawing out the syllables, like the great announcers do. "Me-tro Me-te-or wins it!"

Ignoring my nonsense or maybe amused by it, Metro just kept striding forward. Solid. Steady. Soon I caught a glimpse of light and, as the tunnel curved slightly back down, I could feel Metro quicken his steps. Together we had made it through the darkness, monsters and all.

Chapter 23

A Short Walk in the Woods

"It's always been and always will be the same in the world:
The horse does the work and the coachman is tipped."

—*Unknown*

Am I doing the right thing? Whenever Metro's limp suddenly reappeared, I always started my personal cross-examination. *Should I be riding Metro or are those days over? Should I put him out to pasture? Does he need a different treatment?*

Overall, Metro's good days were growing fewer and his bad days beginning to be more of the norm. The trot was the giveaway. Some days he had no limp, some days he'd have a very slight limp that loosened up as he worked through it and some days he had a limp that wouldn't go away.

Sometimes, when he went for months without a limp, I had high hopes that Metro's knees were improving. Then I descended into disappointment when the limp returned and lingered for a month or so. Strangely enough, the limp never did slow him down out in the pasture, where he continued to run and play and prove to the other horses that he was still Metro Meteor, the fastest horse around. And I didn't mind, because it was his choice to frolic around. I wasn't asking him to do it. But if I brought him into the arena or the round pen and asked him to trot, I felt guilty when the limp reappeared. It was always an inner struggle and I wondered if I was doing the right thing or if I was hurting my horse.

Deep down I knew Metro was declining. I had been waiting for it to happen. I wished that I could talk to him and ask, *How much pain are you in? Is it a constant pain or just now and again?* But I couldn't, so I just had to watch him and guess. All I knew was I didn't want to be the source of it, causing him pain just for my own enjoyment of riding him.

More often than not, I found myself passing on the trail rides with Wendy, Kim and Ed. "Go on without me," I said, while I drank a beer on Ed's porch and watched Metro graze in the front yard. Sometimes I'd think about retiring him to a leisurely life in the pasture. But I also knew how much he loved heading into the woods with the other horses. I saw how his body language changed, his ears pointing forward as he swung his head side to side, taking it all in. The trail put a bounce in his step and I didn't want to take that away from him.

I noticed how he watched other horses as they passed by with their riders. When Wendy and Pork Chop headed out, Metro followed along on the other side of the fence until he ran out of pasture. Then he stood and watched his friends disappear into the woods. That's when I couldn't stand it anymore and I took him out and set him loose to graze on Ed's lawn.

I started thinking more seriously about his future and one day I surprised Wendy. "What do you think about getting another horse?"

"I think it's a good idea," she said. "You won't be able to ride Metro forever."

We asked Brenda to find us another horse. She had a better eye and, with our past history of horse shopping, we figured it best to let a professional do it. She started looking around and found a sweet young quarter horse named Hotshot. He was young and kind of small compared to Metro and Pork Chop, but he was still growing.

Hotshot was Bay Roan in color, a little darker red than Metro, with flecks of gray that would become more prominent as he matured. He came from a good Western pleasure bloodline. I thought Brenda was more interested in finding a horse she could train for Western pleasure shows, when we were just looking for a reliable trail horse. We wanted one who was a little older and already had some trail miles on him. But he was a good, sweet, willing horse. I just hoped he'd grow a few more inches.

I started teaching Hotshot the Clinton Anderson groundwork that had worked so well with the other horses. He surprised me, learning the steps much quicker than Metro. I don't know if I was a better teacher after so much practice or if Metro was just more difficult to coach. Probably both.

Meanwhile, Metro and Pork Chop were now known as the calmest, most well-behaved horses in the barn. We weren't the lone boarders anymore. Ed had begun taking in more horses and trying to make an income from his barn. Metro still had attitude and could unleash a nip or kick at any time, but his behavior was more predictable. Everyone learned what he didn't like and how to avoid retaliation. "It's just Metro being Metro," was the standard phrase, now that he was no longer considered a dangerous horse.

The other horse owners even started asking me to teach them and their horses the same groundwork Metro knew. "I wish my horse could be more like yours," they said. They hadn't seen Metro when he was at his worst. Now, instead of being the black sheep of the barn, he had risen to become teacher's pet.

Metro loved Hotshot. Even though Metro was older than Pork Chop, he was younger in spirit and liked to play and have fun. Pork Chop wasn't rowdy and he preferred not to run or play or have bite fights with Metro. He avoided any activities that burned calories.

Metro and Hotshot, on the other hand, galloped around and engaged in lots of play-kicking and biting. Hotshot was like the playmate Metro had been missing. A bonus was that Metro was finally above another horse in the pecking order. Hotshot was the first horse Metro could boss around and he finally had a protégé he could instruct in the ways of the field. That is, until Pork Chop came over and schooled them both.

For some reason, though, I didn't connect with Hotshot like I had with Metro. Working with Hotshot made me feel like I was cheating on Metro. He was my first love and it's not like he was out of the picture, either, because he was still there watching my every move. So I rarely rode Hotshot. Once in a while, I'd take the younger horse out on a trail ride, but it broke my heart to ride past Metro, looking forlorn on the other side of the fence. He seemed to know we were heading into the woods without him.

As a work-around, I paid Brenda to ride and train Hotshot. Even though he already had been in training and I'd gone through the horsemanship exercises with him, I told myself Hotshot wasn't quite ready yet. Brenda rode him for the first three months and it was almost like he was her horse, even though we owned him and paid his bills. Eventually, I figured out I wasn't ready for another horse, because I wasn't ready to give up and retire Metro yet. I still did groundwork with him and some light riding, but we avoided the woods, the creek crossing where he and Pork Chop used to splash around and the hills he liked to conquer. Instead, we stayed on the safe, grassy paths around the hayfields.

There were times Metro turned toward the woods, where the trailhead started. "Not today, buddy," I said as I pulled his head back around to keep him in the hayfield. "I wish we could."

As summer's heat and humidity faded away and the trees began to unleash their fall colors, I got the itch to take Metro out in the woods again. One day, Wendy was riding Pork Chop and I was riding Metro in the outdoor arena. I decided to ask Metro to trot. *Maybe today is a good day.*

Metro responded quickly. I listened with my whole body to see if I felt any hitch in his movement. *Nothing. No limp!*

"Wendy, how about a short walk through the woods?"

"Really? Do you think we should?"

"I trotted him a few laps and he seems fine. This might be the last chance we have for a trail ride until spring."

"Okay, but don't push him." Wendy frowned. "Don't take off cantering up that last hill."

Wendy knew I wouldn't do that. I cared more about not pushing Metro too hard than anyone, but Wendy still told me what to avoid.

Anticipating the ride ahead, I allowed myself a small smile as we headed out of the arena and down the side of the upper hayfield toward the trailhead. Metro and I went first, because we always led when it was just Wendy and me. Pork Chop seemed to prefer being the last horse. Maybe it was because he was the slowest or maybe he liked some space, because he'd often kick out if another horse got right up on his hindquarters.

Taking a short ride and staying on Ed's property meant an easy ride for Metro, mostly flat with a couple of gentle inclines in the woods. The one steeper hill at the end of the ride, a short climb of about a hundred yards, was the hill Metro always wanted to run. I usually let him, although I vowed to say no today. It wouldn't be good for his knees, plus Wendy had forbidden it.

It had been too long since our last trail ride. I could tell Metro was enjoying himself even though we'd ridden this same trail many times before. I felt his step pick up.

He always gathered energy in the woods and I could feel the power of Metro Meteor underneath me. I paid attention to the pressure of my legs, mindful not to inadvertently give him a squeeze and send him into an instant, turbocharged gallop. I was on a powerful animal born and bred to run and it was like sealing lightning inside a bottle, just waiting to be uncorked.

We passed by deer stands in the trees, unoccupied and waiting for hunting season. The leaves were just starting to fall, although many were still green. Metro took the slight inclines with no problem. It was a good day and he loved every moment, with his eyes and ears drinking in the aliveness all around us. We headed down to the creek, passing by the stream. At the end of the forest path, the trail opened up into Ed's pastures. I spotted Hotshot ahead on the other side of the fence and he followed along as we walked.

Now we were on the homestretch, following the grassy path to the barn. I felt Metro's step quicken beneath me as he anticipated that last hill. It gave him great joy to end a trail ride with a final run up the hill. *But not today.*

I pulled back gently on the reins to let him know that he couldn't shift into a faster gait. I knew if I made a kissing sound with my mouth, his cue to go, he would have bounded joyfully up the hill toward the barn. But I held him back and made him walk. He obeyed, bobbing his head up and down in protest, the reins flopping.

"I know. I know. You want to run." I felt a little sad but knew it was for the best. Then, I felt Metro's step change. He bobbed his head again, but this time not in protest.

Is he in pain?

I heard Wendy yell behind me. I couldn't make out her words. All I heard was, "Ron...Ron!" and then, "Metro!"

Did he step on something? Did a snake bite him? What is going on?

Immediately I pulled back on the reins until he stopped, grabbed the saddle horn, swung my right leg over the back of the saddle, slid my left foot out of the stirrup and let myself down. After a quick check, I didn't see anything wrong. That meant it was probably his knees. "I'm sorry. I'm so sorry," I said to Metro, kissing him on the forehead.

"He really looked like he was struggling," Wendy said as she rode up on Pork Chop.

"I know. I could feel it. Go ahead and go on without us."

"I'll wait for you," Wendy protested. "You can just walk him the rest of the way."

"No. Go ahead and go. Please."

I wanted to be alone with Metro. I was feeling incredible guilt and I was afraid I might cry. I didn't want to do that in front of Wendy.

"I am so sorry, buddy." I stroked Metro's neck as we walked up the rest of the hill. Metro wasn't limping, but he had other ways of telling me when he was in pain. He'd nip at my hand holding his lead line or take the lead line and hold it in his mouth, almost like he was trying to keep himself from nipping at me.

"Go ahead and bite me if you want to," I said as we walked. "I deserve it today."

I remembered Kim's prognosis, back when she first started taking care of Metro. The news had been grim. Because of the pre-existing injuries to his knees, irregular bone growth would eventually close up the gaps in the joints that allowed him to bend his knees. Flexibility would slowly erode and one day, he would lie down and not be able to get back up. When that happened, he could either die in the struggle to get back up or someone would discover him there, waiting to be put out of his misery. Kim can be incredibly clinical. There was no riding off into the sunset, no rainbow bridge in her description. The day Metro's knees locked up, he would most likely have to be euthanized. Kim's words drilled down into my heart.

I'd always known my days with Metro were numbered and that he would probably not die of old age. His damaged knees meant a shortened life. I had been forced to come to terms with the fact that Metro was not going to live twenty-five or thirty years or even longer, as a horse should.

That's why I have a love/hate relationship with horse racing. I hate that the sport caused Metro to go lame, ended his athletic career and cut years off his life. He had been a gifted racehorse, but his speed and his heart made him profitable and he had been asked to race too long. His gift had turned into a curse.

I would have given anything to see him in his prime, prancing around the paddock and tearing up the track.

I wish I could have experienced firsthand that trademark burst of speed as Metro kicked it into gear in the homestretch, digging deep into the turf and blowing past every other horse in the field. I would have loved to stand beside him in the winner's circle, proud of what he had accomplished.

But that part of his life was over and done. Since Wendy and I had bought him, he'd been held together by pharmaceuticals and duct tape. And it seemed like those weren't working anymore.

After we slowly made our way back to the barn, I tracked down Kim and asked her to take some new x-rays. "I want to see what's going on with those knees."

I needed hard proof, but I already had a hunch that Metro's riding days were over. I'd been anticipating this day for a long time.

Kim's veterinary clinic still hadn't upgraded to digital x-rays yet, so it would be days before we found out the news. When the results came back, she made an appointment to meet us on Ed's porch for a beer.

When we arrived, I watched Kim's face and I could tell this wasn't easy for her. Vets see life and death every day and are used to giving bad news, but Kim had become attached to Metro, too, and she knew how important he was to me. Kim had received the x-rays days earlier, but had been avoiding us until she could offer some hope.

Kim held the x-rays up to the sun and delivered the news to Wendy and me. "Since the last set of x-rays, Metro has experienced significant bone growth in his knees. Most likely, they will lock up in two to three years."

She wasn't at all unkind, just straightforward. There was really no way to sugarcoat the news.

With her words still hanging in the air, I felt like someone had slapped me hard in the face. I'd always hoped Metro would make it to his fifteenth birthday, but now I wasn't sure. The time frame hit me hard. *What kind of life will he have?* I wondered.

Kim continued, not quite ready to hand down a death sentence yet. "He may still be able to function in the next year or two. We just don't know yet."

Kim's words rang in my ears, over and over. I knew there was no hope and that Kim was just trying to be nice. She wanted to give me some optimism that, even with partially locked knees, Metro might be able to live for a while yet.

But how can he function if he isn't able to move? That's no kind of life for a horse like Metro.

Further, Kim recommended that we stop the regular knee injections and the monthly shots of Adequan, because she wasn't seeing any benefit in terms of halting the bone growth. We also stopped putting wedge shoes on him. The discomfort Metro's knees had to go through with the shoeing process now outweighed any benefit he would get from them. It felt like we were pulling the plug on Metro's life support and waiting for the line on the monitor to go flat.

We had lots of questions and Kim answered them all. No, surgery was not an option. During his racing career, Metro had already undergone two surgeries to remove bone chips. Now there wasn't enough bone left in his knees to remove any more. The remaining bone chips were going to be with him the rest of his life.

Yes, there were some experimental treatments we could attempt. She mentioned one drug we could try, not yet approved by the FDA, that could be imported. The experimental treatments would run into the thousands of dollars, however. And there was no guarantee of success.

I felt another wave of anger, silently cursing the sport of horse racing for letting him race so long. Surely his owners had known about his bad knees. Why did they send him for two surgeries? And why did they continue to race him? But I knew the answer—as long as Metro Meteor made money, they would continue to run him. *Metro, why did you have to be so fast?*

I sat in silence, pondering this new information, wondering what to do. *Maybe we should just put him down now, so he won't ever have to suffer.* I didn't think I could watch him slowly freeze up, every step agonizing. But I couldn't really even think about telling Kim to put him down, either.

That left the experimental drugs. Would the medication work? Could it possibly help save Metro? Or at least slow down the bone growth so he could have a longer, more comfortable life?

I took a deep breath and made a vow to myself. *I'm not going to let you go without a fight, Metro. We're going to try this.* But I had no idea where we were going to get the kind of money necessary to purchase the drugs.

Chapter 24

Studio Six

"Life and death matters, yes. And the question of how to behave in this world, how to go in the face of everything. Time is short and the water is rising."

—*Raymond Carver*

Am I doing the right thing? I found myself agonizing over that same question again, as I had so often over the three years Metro had been with us. When the x-rays showed destructive new bone growth in Metro's scarred and battered knees, Kim had made it clear that she believed Metro would have no more than two years or so before his knees completely locked up.

The only lifeline Kim could offer, an experimental drug called Tildren, was not available in the United States. It would have to be imported from Europe, where studies had shown some success using it to treat navicular disease in horses. Navicular disease is a common disease that degrades a small bone in the horse's hoof, causing lameness. No one, to our knowledge, had used Tildren for local injections to a horse's knees.

There were all kinds of reasons not to use Tildren. Not only was there significant potential for dangerous side effects, but it was extremely expensive, had never been used for knees before and Kim could not guarantee it would actually fix Metro's knees. In fact, Kim couldn't guarantee that Tildren would do anything at all and she was thinking, *It's experimental, but if we do nothing, Metro's future is death.* She felt badly, because she knew the reality. Racehorses are typically done racing at three or four but, if taken care of, they can have lots of years to live.

I was in agony, haunted by the idea that I was giving up on Metro—something I'd vowed I would never do. We had been through so much together and so many people had given up on Metro in his short lifetime. Plus, I was beginning to understand Metro's desperate situation. If Wendy and I had not adopted him, it's likely he would have ended up in a slaughterhouse. I once heard a shocking story from Kim about a chestnut colt named Ferdinand who won the Kentucky Derby in 1980. He had been retired to Japan, then killed and eaten in Japan at the age of nineteen.[3] It was sinking in that Metro had faced extreme risk due to his lameness, his specialized training, his attitude and his behavior.

The reality was that Wendy and I didn't have thousands of dollars to spend on a Hail Mary treatment with absolutely no guarantees. We had nearly exhausted our savings account with Metro's vet bills and were fighting a losing battle with his health. So I decided against the Tildren. And it wasn't just the money. It was the potential side effects. Would this unproven treatment, that no one had ever used for a horse's knees before, actually do more damage to Metro? Would it speed up his untimely end? Or even possibly kill him outright? I just could not take that chance. A part of me wanted to try it, would have mortgaged my house to try it, but without more evidence for its safety, I just couldn't take the chance. I would never knowingly do anything to hurt my horse. I would not be able to live with that guilt.

Millions of thoughts and feelings and regrets and worries were flashing through my mind. But the same haunting thought kept rising to the surface, circling back around again and again. *Am I doing the right thing?* I didn't know. Maybe I would never know.

As my mind and heart struggled with the decision and the possible outcomes, I kept thinking about a future without Metro. What would that be like? Metro was such a big part of my life. At first he had almost been like a project. In the early days, I'd liked and admired him and I'd wanted to help him, almost like you'd want to help an aging athlete back to his feet to regain some of his former glory. Who wouldn't have wanted to give someone like Babe Ruth a hand up, then sit and watch him launch a few out over the fence again?

But as Metro nudged and nipped and whinnied his way deep into my heart, my relationship to this ailing racehorse became so much more. Metro had tested me in every way possible, especially when he had bitten Wendy. I wasn't sure if he'd ever accept me as his master, much less eventually allow me to saddle him up and ride him. And when I finally rode him on trail rides in the woods, through the creek and even into the tunnel, I'd begun to love and trust him more than I'd ever loved and trusted anyone or anything, besides Wendy. Metro's crankiness and attitude were part of him, so I loved that, too. I loved him for who he was, not for what I wanted him to be. He wasn't just an extension of me or a pet or a servant animal. Metro was my buddy and knowing him had made me a better man.

Was I doing the right thing? I wasn't going to put Metro through an expensive treatment that might or might not work. I just couldn't do it. Along with this nagging worry, another idea had been swirling around in the chaos inside my head. Maybe there was a way for Metro to live out the rest of his life, even if it was only two more years, doing something that I loved to do. I'd been thinking about it for a while, but I hadn't told anyone. I decided that now was the time, as the words popped into my head and out of my mouth. It was a question Kim wasn't expecting. It was a question probably no other veterinarian had ever been asked before.

"Kim, can he paint?"

"What? Paint?" Kim had seen it all and done it all in her work with animals, but I had caught her off guard.

I took a deep breath. "Yes. Stand in front of a canvas and hold a paintbrush in his mouth."

Kim took a second or two to think, then stammered out, "I imagine so."

For a while I'd been nursing this dream deep inside. I had always known my days riding Metro were limited. I had known our rides in the woods would come to an end. I'm not sure exactly when the idea had first occurred to me but, from the very first day in the stall at Karen's barn,

I'd watched Metro hang his head out of the stall door and throw it up and down, trying to get someone's attention. Metro is a habitual head bobber. Some horses do it from boredom and some from nerves. But when Metro bobs his head, he is trying to tell you something. I'd studied his body language in the thousands of hours I'd spent at the barn. When he bobbed his head, Metro either wanted attention or was protesting about something.

One day, a thought suddenly surfaced. *If I could get you to hold a paintbrush in that mouth, you could probably paint a house.* That image had made me laugh. I could picture Metro in tattered overalls, painting a white fence like Tom Sawyer and his pals.

But when I thought about the day Spencer the cat had decided to track red paint around my studio at home, something clicked. Maybe I could teach Metro how to paint; not a fence, but on canvas. Maybe it could be something we could do together, a way I could spend some time with my best friend. Just two buddies throwing paint around and having fun. So I made a second decision that day. I was going to teach Metro how to paint.

Early the next morning, I woke up energized. A small part of me was still processing and mourning the news, but it also seemed like a fresh start. The sorry condition of Metro's knees had not been a surprise. The increase in his bad days had prepared us. But seeing the worsening condition in black and white on the x-ray films and hearing the two-year prognosis from Kim's mouth had spurred me to action. I had no more time to waste. It was time for Metro and I to move on to other things. He was still around, at least for the moment. And we were going to live life to the fullest, for as long as we could.

I quickly gathered up some old paintbrushes, paints and a canvas. I threw in a white cotton smock I used to cover my clothes when I painted animal portraits in my studio and drove to the barn. I felt a sense of joy in this new undertaking. It was different from when I'd first tried to learn how to groom and train Metro, when I'd been nervous and insecure, unsure about how to proceed and not getting much support or encouragement from Karen. This time, I knew what I was doing. I knew how to paint. I just didn't know how to paint with a horse. But I had a feeling my idea was going to work. I don't know why; I just did.

As I drove, I planned my approach. Metro loved horse treats and we had spoiled our horses with the best treats at the tack shop, so he was used to brown sugar and molasses horse cookies. Pork Chop especially loved red licorice bites. Metro also loved to nibble on things. He was always touching things with his lips, using them almost like a hand to feel and taste parts of his stall or my arm or shoulder. Occasionally he'd still bite when he was staking his claim on his stall or expressing displeasure at a certain touch on his body.

I was pretty sure if I could get Metro to nibble at a paintbrush and hold it in his teeth, combined with the head bobbing and a treat afterward, I could show him how to touch a brush to canvas. But would he make strokes? I had no idea how to teach him to move his big head a certain way and stroke paint onto the canvas. He might drop the paintbrush when it touched the canvas or throw it or even chew it apart. He might just touch the brush once, smell it and taste it, then drop it and be done. That could be the end right there. My dream of making paintings with my horse would be over and there was no back-up plan.

When I got to the barn, tied a canvas to an easel and set it up in Metro's stall, it went better than I'd hoped. Metro learns things incredibly fast. Getting him to do it twice, without protest, is the difficult part.

When I teach him to do something, he will do it perfectly the first time. Ask him to do it a second time and he will bob his head up and down in protest, as if he is telling you, "Hey, I already know this one. Let's move on, already!"

Repetition annoys Metro. So, in the course of ten minutes a day for about a week, Metro learned to hold a dry paintbrush in his mouth and touch it to the canvas.

Now came the time to introduce paint into the equation.

I set up one of Ed's empty stalls with canvas on the walls and floor and an easel from home, squeezed out some non-toxic acrylic paint and brought Metro into what would now be his art studio. Ed named it Studio Six.

When I handed him the brush full of paint for the first time, he turned to the canvas just like we had been practicing and began stroking paint across it. I couldn't breathe. *My horse is amazing. Does he know this is his destiny? That he is done being just a horse, doing the normal things horses do? Does he know I'm seeking a new career path for him and he is embracing it?*

It was all coming together so quickly, this painting horse thing. Usually everything with Metro involved drama. Nothing with my boy had ever come easily, but somehow teaching him to paint was effortless. He just did it. He seemed to almost know what was going on.

I wondered how much of the white canvas he could see. Since horses are prey animals, they are built with eyes on the sides of their heads to give them a 360-degree view. That makes it easier to spot oncoming danger from the sides or the rear, but they do have a blind spot directly in front. Metro would be able to easily spot a mountain lion approaching from either side, but he can't see two feet directly in front of him. So I wasn't sure how much of the canvas he could actually view. But I knew he could feel it. With his first dozen or so strokes on the canvas, he dragged his nose through the wet paint and picked up a lot of paint on his nose and lips. He quickly learned the boundaries and, within an hour, he could judge the distance so he could use only the brush to make contact with the canvas.

We spent the next three days working on that first painting. I learned quickly that if you had too many colors going on the canvas at the same time, Metro tended to smear them together. While some colors look good combined, when you have many wet colors you can start to get a muddy brown mess. I realized we had to build the painting up in layers, working with one or two colors a day, then let it dry overnight and start with a different color the next day.

I also learned how to work with Metro's preferred movements. Metro had certain patterns when he painted and, if I handed him the brush at different angles, I could sometimes predict what kind of stroke he was going to make. Not always, but sometimes. He wasn't a robot or some kind of machine. It was up to him how much movement he was going to make, what kind of pressure he would apply and for how long. I couldn't control any of those things.

He got impatient if I took too long to mix the paint or load the paintbrush. Metro wanted the paintbrush in his mouth at all times and didn't like waiting for me to give it to him. If I took too long, he began to paw at the ground or yank on my shirt as I bent over to mix the paint.

After about three days, the first painting was done and I was proud. What made me the happiest was that Metro really seemed to enjoy painting. I wasn't sure what he liked—maybe the sensation of the brush strokes or the feel of the brush in his mouth. But he liked it.

That first painting was strokes of reds, oranges and yellows on a black background. I brought the painting outside and took photos of Metro standing next to it. Was he admiring it?

It was a nice abstract painting, but if someone told you it was painted by a horse, you'd probably say, "Yes, it looks like it was." Metro's second painting, however, was something completely different.

Chapter 25

Caramel Sundae

"The purpose of art is washing the dust of daily life off our souls."

—Pablo Picasso

Metro's second piece, *Caramel Sundae,* took three days to paint as we built it up in layers. The canvas was covered in heavy, textured swaths of paint in rich browns and caramels, with streaks of white and spots of red that reminded me of whipped cream and cherries. When we completed the painting, I wiped the paint off Metro's nose and put him out in the pasture with his buddies.

I picked up the canvas and moved it into better light, so I could get a good look. This painting had rich textures and deep colors. The composition worked, with streaks of white pointing to a focal point in the Golden Third. *Maybe we have something here!*

But as excited as I was about what I was looking at, I was also conflicted about whether I could call the painting art or not. Metro wasn't the first animal to ever paint a picture. There was a Chimpanzee named Congo, supposedly the first animal artist to be discovered, in the 1950s. Congo started by drawing with a pencil and seemed to show some ability. Later, he began to make paintings, usually a radiating fan design. Zoologist (and surrealist painter) Desmond Morris worked with him and believed the chimp displayed a sense of composition, as well as a passion for his work that caused him to scream if someone took away a painting prematurely before it was finished.

Elephants at a camp in Thailand were trained to draw or paint simple images, such as a flower, using their trunks to hold a brush. Other elephants created paintings by smudging paint on a canvas with their feet. Elephant art has become popular and can now be found at zoos, museums and galleries around the world.

Then there are *Moneighs,* paintings created by racehorses like the recent Triple Crown winner, American Pharoah. The horse is nudged to dip his nose into non-toxic, washable paint and then snort, lick or smudge the paint onto an artist's pad. The finished paintings are a combination of light, colorful, wispy swirls and streaks.

An animal painting a picture is nothing new or earth-shattering. What was different, however, was the texture we produced, created by several days of layering on heavy brush strokes. Also, most of the other painting animals worked on their own. We had a partnership—Metro and I painted together in collaboration.

Since I'm an artist by trade, I make a plan regarding what the colors should be. I squeeze the paint out of the tubes, load up the paintbrushes and hand them to Metro to apply the strokes. Metro has a mind of his own and applies the paint any way he wants.

I have asked myself, is a Metro painting truly art? The textures and colors are pretty, but they are applied to canvas by a horse. If another artist can throw a bucket of paint into the air behind a jet engine and call it art or if someone can flick paint on a wall and call it art, why can't I call it art when Metro applies paint to a canvas?

One of my favorite painters, Robert Burridge, says the idea of deciding what is and what is not art is never for artists to worry about. "Who gets to call art, art?" he said. "This whole art thing is for other people to worry about. We just go do our work. I keep going to my studio and I don't worry about this." Burridge doesn't waste any thought on art critics. "It's their job to be dramatic," he said. "I really don't pay attention to those people."

I knew there would be critics, mostly other artists, pompous individuals who claim their brushes are guided by a higher power. It was possible they would take great offense to this horse holding a brush in his teeth and making strokes on the sacred canvas. But I am the artist and the paintings are my vision. The only difference between what I was doing and what they were doing was that my paintbrush had an attitude and would occasionally bite me. And *his* name goes on the painting.

Early on, when Metro was still new to painting, I decided we'd be painting for the love of it. I wasn't going to worry about receiving validation from others. To me, Metro's paintings were art. It was the art of teamwork, working together with Metro to create something. It was the art of communication, a man and a horse speaking without saying a word. It was the art of dance, anticipating each other's every move.

As I stood back and admired *Caramel Sundae*, I was thinking back to the recent and very painful meeting with Kim. The news had been terrible, but my hunch about Metro had been correct and he had quickly learned how to paint. Metro and I were on our way to a new adventure that wouldn't put any pressure on his ailing knees. I looked forward to partnering with Metro on many more paintings and he seemed to really enjoy it. But if we began to paint every day or almost every day like I hoped, we'd be producing dozens and dozens of paintings. What were we going to do with them all? Would people possibly want to buy them?

I'd never been successful trying to sell my own abstracts, but Metro's were much better and freer. He had no inhibitions about applying paint and his strokes were bold and intense. I had a feeling they just might sell.

Then it hit me. If Metro sold paintings and made some money, we could use the proceeds to try a course of Tildren. I wanted to jump and high-five Metro, although that probably would have broken my hand. It was time to contact Gallery 30.

I'd sold my own paintings at Gallery 30 in Gettysburg a few years back and had pretty good success. Gallery 30's usual fare included landscape paintings in oil, so my colorful acrylic dog paintings were pushing the envelope. Before long, rows of my whimsical dog and cat paintings hung in the gallery. I enjoyed painting in watercolor, but they were a pain to present as they needed to be matted and framed behind glass. So for my gallery paintings, I used acrylic. Very easy to frame, with no mat or glass. All I had to do was varnish the painting and pop it into a frame.

However, I'm my own worst critic and I didn't think my acrylic work was as good as my watercolors, so after a couple of years I stopped painting and selling acrylics at the gallery. Now it was time to get back in contact with the owner of Gallery 30, Linda, and her manager, Peggy. I wondered if abstract paintings by a horse would be a tough sell.

I emailed Linda and Peggy to let them know what Metro and I had been up to. I made it a point not to brag about how cool the paintings were, but instead about how we could probably generate some good publicity for the gallery. Maybe we'd even get a write up in the local newspaper. Linda thought for a moment, then said, "Bring them on down."

Metro's last owner, Bob Oliva, was excited about Metro's new venture when I emailed him a video of Metro working on a painting. "I'm telling you, Metro is going to be famous." I could sense his excitement over the phone. "I'm going to start working on getting him a day to come back to the track and paint. We'll call it Metro Meteor Day."

Bring Metro back to Penn National? To paint a picture? I wasn't quite sure how Metro would feel about that. Then Bob asked about the financials, wondering what I was going to charge. He gave me one piece of advice: "Whatever you are planning to charge for the paintings, double the price and donate half to New Vocations Racehorse Adoption."

I wasn't sure about the famous part, but I liked the cause. If Metro's paintings actually did sell, I wanted to use part of the money for Tildren treatment and give the rest to a charity, something to do with horses. There were plenty of local horse rescues to support, but Bob gave me the answer I needed. Financially supporting retired racehorses who needed a second chance would be a perfect fit for Metro.

When they are done racing, these horses need homes. Many are injured and need rehabilitation for their injuries. Many need training for second careers. Metro had been lucky that his path crossed ours, but many horses aren't as lucky. New Vocations sounded like just what we were looking for. I learned that founder Dot Morgan and her family had raised horses for generations and, through New Vocations, she has rescued and adopted out over 5,000 racehorses. Each rescued horse costs several thousand dollars to rehabilitate as it recovers from stress and injuries. They always need funding and Metro would be helping his own.

After I found the contact information for Sandy Seabrook, the marketing director for New Vocations, I sent her an email that went something like this:

> Hi. I have this retired racehorse that paints. We have a couple of paintings for sale and we would like to give half of the proceeds to New Vocations. Here is a video of him painting.

It was a very unassuming email. I didn't know Metro's fame would soon go worldwide. At the time, I thought *all* horses could potentially paint. Sandy responded and seemed very interested. She also included information on how to set up my donations.

Within a week of putting a couple of Metro's abstract paintings on display over at Gallery 30, Metro and I landed on the front page of the *Gettysburg Times*. The story started with this: "A retired racehorse, once considered one of the best turf sprinters in the East, is now an artist." When the article appeared on December 9, 2012, Metro had already completed three paintings and sold one at the gallery.

Two days later, Susan Salk's Off-Track Thoroughbreds blog featured Metro. Susan, who has written about many of the big names in the equestrian world, is passionate about making sure that retiring racehorses get the care and the new life they deserve. She is making a difference and Metro's burgeoning new career got her stamp of approval. This one horse was going to make it possible, through art, for other horses to survive and thrive.

Before long, news of Metro made it to the desk of Jason Bristol, Sports Director of WHPTV in Harrisburg. When I emailed Jason, he asked if he could come out the next day and film a story on Metro. That caused a dilemma. Being married to a flight attendant meant having your wife out of town three days a week. But even though she was gone a lot, I felt it was bad form to do anything fun like this when she was away. Occasionally, she tortured me by sending a photo of her enjoying a Piña Colada on the beach as she overnighted in Fort Lauderdale; she maintains it's just part of her job. But if I were to have to leave town and do something fun in her absence, I would have some explaining to do. If Metro was going to be on TV while Wendy was out of town, I was going to have a big problem. Wendy was just as much a part of Metro's life as I was and she needed to be there when the TV crew arrived.

"I can't do it tomorrow, Jason. I could do it on Friday instead."

"Tomorrow is the only day I have free," said Jason. "Then I'm going on vacation."

"I'm going to have to decline."

I couldn't believe I'd just said that. I felt like it was Metro's only shot at getting his story out and I was just sick about it. Wendy was on an airplane up in the skies and there was no way I could ask her. And without her being there, I just couldn't commit to it. *But there is a chance. Maybe if I call her and explain, she'll be okay with the idea.*

"Fine; do what you need to do," Wendy said on the phone. I think she had just given me permission, right? Anyone who's been married for more than a day knows that *Fine-do-what-you-need-to-do* is not a blessing, but in my euphoria at the thought of seeing Metro on TV, all I heard was, "That sounds like a great idea. Go for it." So I called Jason back, told him about the change in plans and set things up for the next day.

I couldn't sleep that night. The realization that it wasn't just Metro on TV scared the hell out of me. *I am going to be on TV, too.* I was now Metro's spokesperson and I would be the one doing all his interviews. *Metro, why can't you learn to talk?* I went over and over every possible question and every possible answer. I thought about canceling, but didn't. *This is for Metro.*

The next morning, I watched as the TV crew set up. That was the day Metro began his habit of painting camera operators. When the camera came in close to get footage of the paintbrush on canvas, Metro turned with brush in mouth and painted a big, yellow streak across the camera and the cameraman's face. Jason happened to be filming Metro with his camera phone and that footage made the broadcast. Metro kept his streak alive and just about every cameraman who came after went home covered in paint. I began to wonder if Metro was doing it on purpose.

When Metro made the very first brushstroke, I heard an audible gasp from Jason, along with the other reporters and news crews who followed him that winter. Media members know they are there to do a story on a painting horse, but I don't think they believe it until they see it. Or maybe they're expecting more coaxing and participation by me. They don't seem to believe Metro actually paints all on his own. Soon they pull out their camera phones and grab their own personal footage, to show their kids they saw a painting horse at work.

The camera operators, although they have to dodge the paintbrush, always love Metro. As they pack up to head back to the studio, more than one has said, "I swear that horse knows when the camera is on." Metro did seem to be a different horse when the camera crews were around. He's a showman and he never failed to give them the footage they wanted. He loved the attention. Metro's hungry ego was getting fed.

Jason's story aired that night but it was bittersweet, because Wendy wasn't there to enjoy it with me. I had hurt her by not waiting and I felt badly about it. Luckily, it was just days before another film crew came out and this time Wendy was there to participate. After that first TV spot, Metro got famous quickly and everyone wanted to do a story.

Gallery 30 sold ten paintings that first month and sales grew from there. Two gallery employees named Shelly and Sarah called themselves "Metro's Secretaries," because they spent so much time answering calls about Metro. Paintings began to sell before they ever hit the gallery walls and the waiting list for Metro's paintings grew to over a hundred people. One of my worries came true when an artist who had been represented by the gallery for many years left, because she didn't want to be associated with a gallery whose best-selling artist was a horse.

Metro was soon seen on television programs all over the country and articles about him started showing up in newspapers around the world. I couldn't believe it. My favorite part of the day was when I typed "Metro Meteor" into the search bar on my Internet browser and clicked on the most recent Metro stories. I saw articles in Russian, Spanish, Chinese and other languages I'd never heard of. At the top of each article was a picture of Metro's handsome face.

Orb had just won the Kentucky Derby, but I knew in my heart that Metro was the most famous horse in the world. Then, *The Today Show* came calling.

Chapter 26

The Dance

"Art is not a thing—it is a way."

—*Elbert Hubbard*

The *Today Show* camera was rolling at the barn, big boom microphone waving overhead, when Kim grabbed Metro's right foot, squeezed his knee, then picked it up and flexed it at a 90 degree angle. The producer, Sarah, had asked for Kim to do a routine exam of Metro's knees for some B-roll footage.

When Kim bent his leg, Metro didn't bite, but he did turn his head around for a quick glare at Kim to show his discomfort. Next, she walked around his hindquarters and over to his left side. All business for the camera, she repeated the squeeze and the flex. This time, Metro didn't turn his head and glare. Instead, he seemed relaxed and stood looking straight ahead. It was an almost entirely unnoticeable event. But it was also one of the most exhilarating moments of my life.

At first I felt a brief surge of excitement, then Kim, Wendy and I shared quick, surprised looks. The fuzzy boom mic was looming over our heads so we couldn't say anything unless we wanted our voices to end up on tape. But I felt like I was about to burst. I couldn't wait for the crew to leave so I could ask Kim to confirm what I thought I might have just seen.

Jill Rappaport, an award-winning animal advocate and reporter for *The Today Show,* was in town to do a segment on Metro. He now had about a dozen television interviews on his equine resumé, including an appearance on the Fox morning show in Baltimore. That one was a live, five-hour event with the show cutting to Metro every half hour, including several painting demonstrations. Toward the end of the show, Metro got tired of the hoopla and grew more and more sour when the other horses got turned out into the pasture and he was stuck under the lights in the studio. He was like the kid who has to do every bit of homework before his mom lets him out to play with his friends. The last couple of segments, we had to coax him back into his studio with peppermints just seconds before the cameras went live again.

Metro had also been featured in newspapers across the country, along with his appearances on the Discovery Channel, *TIME* Magazine's web page and the home page of MSN's website. That one delighted my father-in-law, who was quick to mention that Metro's photo was twice as big as President Obama's that day. It also meant that, for one day, when millions of people turned on their computers Metro's handsome mug was smiling back at them.

The *Today Show* crew was the biggest we'd yet seen. It included Jill along with her cameraman, a producer and a sound guy with a big mic. Dozens of spectators lined the arena, murmuring in excitement. Everyone from the barn had shown up to watch and enjoy the big day. I found it all pretty nervewracking. For a guy who wasn't even comfortable answering the door when a Girl Scout rang the bell, this kind of attention was a very, very big stretch. But I made myself do it for Metro.

Metro himself, however, had no problem with the attention. He seemed to soak it in and put on a show. While I tried to answer Jill's questions about Metro on camera, he was behind me bobbing his head up and down, making faces and shoving me aside out of the shot. He seemed to know this was all about him. And he was like the Chevy Chase of the horse world—always ready with a sly expression, a snarky eye roll or a dash of physical comedy.

Metro was a natural in front of the camera, but I was not. I knew I was Metro's voice and he needed a spokesperson, but it would have been easier for me if I didn't have to be on camera. When I had to give an interview to tell Metro's story, I always asked for him to be in the shot. I felt as if Metro could somehow sense my fear of talking on camera, so he always came alive when the camera rolled, taking the pressure off me. I knew he couldn't possibly know what a camera was or how it worked, but it made him a different horse. He was a natural.

Once Jill's interview with me was out of the way, it was time to get footage of Metro painting. You can't do a story about a painting racehorse without showing the painting process. By now, Metro and I had the routine down cold, since we'd done it a dozen times before.

Usually it was just one camera operator and one reporter. Metro always painted and then ended with his new signature move, swiping paint across the camera. Sometimes he even flicked his big head and threw a loaded paintbrush at a crewmember.

Sarah signaled and I knew it was go time. Metro and I took our places in front of the easel. With the cameras rolling and Sarah nodding at me with a smile, I dipped Metro's brush into the paint and turned to hand it to him. And for the first time ever, he refused to take it.

It wasn't a purse-your-lips-and-shake-your-head type of refusal. Instead, Metro stared off into space like I didn't even exist. I had never seen this reaction since the start of our painting adventure. Metro had never refused the brush before.

I've learned you can get a horse to do a lot of things against his will, but painting isn't one of them. I knew Metro, though, and I knew he was going to paint. I don't claim to be a horse expert, but I had become an expert when it came to Metro. I knew exactly what he liked and what he didn't like. I knew just how to push Metro's buttons and piss him off and he knew mine. We were in each other's heads and we were much more alike than I cared to admit.

I knew this cantankerous attitude well but I'd learned to deal with it, even how to capitalize on it. I believed Metro was eventually going to paint. He just had to do it on his schedule, on Metro time. He wasn't used to this many people and expending this much energy. I was feeling the strain, too. I just had to be patient and let Metro take it all in, then paint when he was ready.

After a few quiet minutes where he seemed to just be looking and listening, soaking it all in, Metro seemed to wake up. He turned and walked casually away from the easel toward the sound technician. He stopped to sniff the boom mic, then moved on to the camera operator. He paused at the camera, as if telling the cameraman which side was his good side or maybe warning him of the blob of paint that would soon be coming his way. Once he and his equipment got the sniff treatment, it was Jill's turn. Then Sarah. No one moved. No one tried to coax him back to the easel. We just stood and waited.

Metro continued to waltz around the arena and stop every few moments to take it all in. He stopped and looked at all the people hanging over the arena wall, intently looking back at him like spectators at a golf tournament. I knew they were all thinking the same thing. *Oh, no, not today, Metro. This is* The Today Show*!*

No one said a word. They just watched Metro and hoped he would paint. Soon, Metro had made a full circle, slowly and carefully walking around the entire crew and all of the equipment, seeing all there was to see, sniffing all there was to sniff. Finally he strode purposefully back to the easel in the center of the arena. He didn't need to be confined in order to paint; he would paint wherever I placed his easel. There was no rope or any walls keeping him there. He could have wandered off again at any point, but he wanted to paint.

I gave him a little cluck with my mouth, my cue for him to come closer, and handed him the brush loaded with paint. This time he was ready and he took it and began stroking away on the canvas like he had a thousand times before. “What a good boy,” I said, getting his next brush ready.

Metro and I had developed a rhythm when we painted. He knew how I worked and I knew how he liked things done. We were a team and we operated smoothly together. I understood that Metro liked to be handed the brush a certain way and that he would throw a fit if things weren’t done the way he preferred. He had very little patience when he was in his painting mode. He wanted the brush and he wanted it now. If I took too long mixing paint, he’d begin pawing at the ground with his hooves or biting at my shirt to tell me to move it along. He was a painting diva.

Over the past few months, as the story spread in the media and Metro’s paintings sold at Gallery 30, a lot of people continued to debate whether Metro’s paintings can be considered art. I just think they haven’t seen us work together, because Metro’s paintings *are* art, as we anticipate each other’s every move and work together to create something new and beautiful. Thomas Merton said, “Art enables us to find ourselves and lose ourselves at the same time.” If that is true, Metro and I find ourselves a little more with each stroke of the brush.

After the *Today Show* crew got all the footage they needed, we said goodbye to Jill, Sarah and the others as they packed up and headed back to New York. We turned

Metro out into the pasture and as soon as the halter was off, he trotted around a bit, then sniffed the ground in preparation for a good roll. Time to scrape off the stardom and go back to being a horse.

I hurried back into the barn. I couldn't wait any longer and I needed to know. The excitement of Metro appearing on *The Today Show* had faded away in the face of something a million times more exciting. Had Metro reacted the way I thought he did when Kim did the knee flex test on camera? I'd wanted to shout for joy when I saw it but couldn't. Metro standing there calmly, not reacting, had to mean one thing and one thing only—the treatments were working.

Back in November, not long after Metro started painting, I'd decided to begin the Tildren treatments on his left leg. Tildren was not yet approved by the FDA, so Kim got a special license to import the medication from Canada and prescribe it for Metro.

Since the treatment was experimental, we decided to do one leg only to see if the bone-remodeling drug would work. When it had been used in Europe for navicular disease, the standard method of dispensing it was through an IV in the jugular vein over a course of ten treatments. But Kim wanted to try injecting the drug directly into the bloodstream of Metro's lower leg, one treatment every month for three months. Her plan was to use a blood pressure cuff as a tourniquet during the injection, thereby keeping the medication localized to the knee area for a full thirty minutes. The hope was that the Tildren would be concentrated in the problem area and would act by eating away the new, unhealthy bone growth while leaving the old bone growth intact.

After Metro had starting painting and selling pictures, I felt more confident that we could afford to try the drug, so I'd given Kim free rein to do what she could, no matter the cost. My plan was to keep painting with Metro to raise the necessary money. At this point, I didn't care if I ever got to ride him again. My concern was giving Metro more time on this earth. If Tildren could prolong his life, it was worth a try. And Metro's art was helping us to do it.

Kim and Wendy were as excited as I was at what had just happened during the filming. Metro's left leg seemed as if it was no longer hurting. But ever the clinician, Kim wanted cold, hard proof. She showed up the next week with brand new digital x-ray equipment. Her office had just invested in the state-of-the-art equipment and I was excited, because we didn't have to wait a week anymore to get the films back from the lab. Now we could look at them right away on her laptop.

Although Metro was a charmer in front of the camera, he never stood still for x-rays. He was always lifting his leg or shucking and jiving to the side. He was so impatient that asking him to stand still for something like this was pretty much a guarantee he wouldn't. It was funny, because he was happy to stand for a long time when he was painting.

Kim finally got the shots she needed and uploaded them to the computer. As she scrolled through the images, I waited anxiously. After a few moments, she began to point at the screen and explain to me what she was observing.

"You see these gaps between the bones here? They weren't there three months ago." I could hear the excitement in her voice.

Could it be true?

"See how translucent the bone chips in his knee have become? Those were opaque white on his last x-ray. Not only does the Tildren seem to be fighting the new bone growth that was threatening Metro's mobility, but it looks like it is also dissolving the floating bone chips in his knee." Kim stopped to let the good news sink in.

I was still trying to process the news. "So this new procedure could also turn into a nonsurgical alternative for bone chip removal?" It seemed almost too good to be true, but I trusted Kim. She was a realist and she didn't mince words when it came to Metro's health. She always gave me the facts and I appreciated that.

"Yes," Kim nodded, smiling.

"Why hasn't anyone tried this procedure before?" I asked.

"Because no one is willing to invest this kind of money in a lame horse."

I thought back to what the spectator on the rail at Metro's last race had said as Metro limped off the track, exhausted. *Looks like that one is done being a horse.* Another saying I'd heard around the barns and tracks came back to me. *No feet, no horse.* Because horse ownership requires such a large investment of time, energy and money, most people won't keep a horse around who can't move. No one has yet invented walkers or wheelchairs for lame horses. To live in our world, a horse has to be able to move.

Suddenly, I realized that Metro might just have a chance at a future. Not only had he learned to paint, but the money he was earning by selling his paintings was helping other retired racehorses. He was also making the money to pay for his own Tildren treatments. Was it possible Metro might have a second chance at moving and trotting and jumping and kicking and everything else involved in being a horse? And not just for the next two years, but for a lifetime?

I shook my head. I couldn't quite believe what I'd seen and heard just a few moments before. "So, could you and Metro end up in the medical journals?" I asked Kim. Not only were Metro's paintings raising money for himself and for other horses, but now they were also going to fund medical research on Tildren.

"I'm going to write it up and submit it." Kim chuckled.

"And you'll call it the Metro Meteor procedure, right?"

Her chuckle became a full-on laugh.

"Well, let's get started on the right knee," I said.

Chapter 27

The Girl with the Painting Horse

"Beware: I ride horses.
I know how to use a pitchfork. I have the strength to haul hay.
I've got the guts to yell at a half-ton animal
after being kicked, bit, shoved, or stepped on.
You will not be a problem."
—*Unknown*

Metro had been on television over a dozen times by now and Wendy was there for almost all of his appearances. It had become so common an occurrence, she didn't even mind anymore if Metro and I went on TV when she was out of town. Her only requirement was that she wanted to be present if Ellen or Oprah invited us to appear. The reporters often interviewed her, but since news stories are typically edited down to a three-minute segment from an hour's worth of footage, Wendy's interview usually ended up on the cutting room floor. If you watched carefully, you might see a passing shot of her walking Metro or standing nearby while we painted, but that was about it.

Wendy didn't say a word about the size of the parts she was allotted in the news broadcasts, but I knew it must have bothered her on some level. She was just as big a part of Metro's life as I was. Wendy groomed and bathed him, put up with his antics and dodged his bites and kicks, too. So I was happy when Southwest Airlines (SWA) showed some interest in Metro.

Back when Metro was beginning to attract significant television coverage, Wendy thought it would be a good idea to ask SWA if it was okay to mention her employer on camera. Just to play it safe, she decided to get official approval. When Wendy went to her supervisor to ask the question, she also had to explain how she co-owned a famous painting horse who was raising money for charity.

While Wendy's supervisor believed the story, not everyone else did. Some people who heard about Metro assumed Wendy was telling a big whopper of a lie. Once I was picking up art supplies at the hobby store. As the checkout clerk scanned and bagged the $200 worth of acrylic paint, she asked, "Are you the artist?"

"No, it's for my horse," I said. "He paints by holding a paintbrush in his mouth."

She looked up, eyes narrowing as she wondered if I was some kind of smartass. Then she just handed me the receipt with an abrupt, "You have a nice day."

So it wasn't a slam dunk for Wendy's supervisor to buy into the story, because it seemed like a fantasy, but she did. After listening carefully, she picked up the phone and said, "I have to call headquarters in Dallas and let them know about this."

The next day, company officials were on the phone with Wendy, asking permission to send a SWA film crew out to film Wendy painting with Metro. The problem was, Wendy hadn't ever actually done it. Painting with Metro had always been my thing, but I was more than happy to let Wendy take all the credit for this one. Besides, I was tired of being on TV. I was happy to have the news crews visiting, stirring up good publicity for Metro and New Vocations, but I hated talking to the cameras. I was starting to get a little better, feeling more comfortable with each new interview. Being Metro's spokesperson had evicted me from my comfort zone; I was ready to let Wendy have some of the fun.

As the film date approached, I kept reminding Wendy that she needed to learn how to paint with Metro. "Get some practice in," I urged her.

"I know. I will," she always answered. But she kept putting it off. Maybe she wasn't quite ready to pry open this whole new can of whup-ass Metro drama.

I was hoping the first time would go smoothly, but I had a feeling it wouldn't. Metro and I had developed a rhythm when we painted. We had become a team and operated smoothly together. I knew that when Wendy went into the studio with Metro and unknowingly upset his flow of work, he wouldn't like it. Wendy knew it, too.

Finally, when the film crew was due to arrive in four days, Wendy realized she could put off P-Day (Painting Day) no longer. For better or for worse, it was time for her to face off with Metro in his art studio.

Day one went about as well as could be expected. I tried to stay out of the way, but I heard Wendy keep screaming, "Stop it!" and I saw a lot of Metro tossing his head in frustration, protesting the disruption of his usual routine. After about a half hour of chaos, both Wendy and Metro emerged from the studio. Metro had paint all over his face and Wendy had paint all over her clothes. Without cracking a smile, Wendy thrust the lead rope out to me and said, “Here. You can have your horse back.”

On day two, Wendy decided to give it another go. This time, the painting session went better. Either Wendy figured out how Metro liked things done or Metro was a little more tolerant. They began to work in sync and Wendy complimented Metro on every brush stroke.

When I talked to him in the studio, it was usually something generic, like “Atta’ boy, Metro. Good horse.” But Wendy supplied commentary with each brush stroke. “Ooh, a swirly stroke! Look at the big, swirly stroke you just made, Metro.” He loved it, feeding off her excitement. All was well.

Two days later, the crew arrived and filming went off without a hitch. The short video featuring Metro and Wendy was posted to SWA’s Nuts About Southwest blog (you can still see it on YouTube). It was a beautiful piece, simple, with no voiceover. It was just a nicely filmed segment of a girl painting with her horse. The two looked like they’d been painting together for years.

After the video aired, Wendy took off to work her usual SWA shift. One of the flight attendants scheduled for Wendy’s crew saw her and said excitedly, “Hey! You’re the girl with the painting horse.” Wendy was becoming famous, too. But neither of us minded the notoriety. It meant the message was getting out about the need for giving racehorses a hoof up. By the time Wendy’s SWA video was released, Metro’s paintings had already helped about twenty retired racehorses receive training for second careers, become healthy and find new homes. Retiring racehorses needed help and Metro was using his paintbrush to make a difference.

Two months after *The Today Show* visited us, once Metro had finished the Tildren treatment on his right leg, Kim rechecked him. She verified that the right leg was improving along with the left leg and she suggested we start riding him again.

I was shocked. I knew he was improving and he was starting to have more good days. But I couldn't quite wrap my mind around the idea that we might be able to ride Metro again. Ever since he'd been diagnosed and given a two-year expiration date, I had resigned myself to the reality that I would never ride him again. I missed riding him, but I had moved on to Hotshot. Riding the young quarter horse did not compare to the joy I'd experienced on Metro's back. We'd been through so much together that riding Metro was special. Every time I'd ridden Metro, I was thinking, *This could be the last time.* I cherished every ride, because every ride was like his last.

Kim's voice cut through the fog in my brain, giving us instructions. "...just light walks on flat ground, once or twice a week. Metro will probably enjoy riding again, especially outside."

Wendy and I discussed the good news and decided she was the one who needed to ride him. She weighed a hundred pounds less than me and a lighter rider would be easier on his still-compromised knees. It was the logical decision. But deep down, I was also hesitant to start riding him again, because I was afraid of falling in love with it, only to have to give it up if his knees began to fail. Wendy would be his jockey for now. We headed into the barn to get the horses ready for a ride around the pastures.

I saddled up Hotshot, the perfect gentleman, and he stood like a rock as I groomed him and prepared to ride. Metro, on the other hand, was down the aisle filing a protest by bobbing his head up and down while Wendy tried to saddle him. Frustrated that she couldn't get him to stand still, she yelled over to me, "Your horse is an ass!"

Yes, he is. But he's my *ass.*

Some things never change.

As we circled the pastures on the tightly clipped grass path, Hotshot and I lagged back so I could watch Metro under saddle again. His head swiveled back and forth, the old windshield-wiper motion that I had loved. He looked like a Midwestern tourist in the middle of Times Square, soaking up the sights. His ears were standing at attention and he was enjoying every minute.

I nudged Hotshot to catch up and he responded, speeding up and acting like he wanted to pass up the old racehorse. As we trotted by, I looked over to see how Metro would take it. His ears went back and the happy look melted away. Metro hated being passed by any other horse. He glared at Hotshot, showing the whites of his eyes. Then he reached over and bit Hotshot on the butt.

Metro Meteor was back.

Chapter 28

Back at the Track

"A horse is the projection of people's dreams about themselves—strong, powerful, beautiful—and it has the capability of giving us escape from our mundane existence."

—*Pam Brown*

Metro was heading back to the racetrack. But this time he wouldn't be tearing up Penn National with his trademark come-from-behind burst of speed. Instead, he was going to be the star of Equine Aftercare Awareness Day, an event originated by Bob Oliva.

It wasn't exactly Metro Meteor Day, but it was close. Penn National was preparing for the biggest day in the Pennsylvania racetrack's history, along with the biggest purses ever offered and the biggest crowds. New Vocations would be setting up a booth right next to Metro, along with two other organizations who worked with training and rehoming retired racehorses.

Wendy and I felt really good about being there and Penn National had promised to donate $10,000 to each of the three organizations. Just by showing up, Metro helped raised $30,000 for the cause. We did our best, though, to help promote the event with TV interviews and ads. Metro and I worked hard to produce lots of Metro Minis, the smaller paintings people loved. New Vocations would have a stack of them available at their booth for a donation. Pork Chop would also be making the trip. He was more of a groupie than a star, but we thought it might be good for Metro to have his buddy there to keep him calm.

We groomed the horses, packed up Metro's mobile studio and paintings and loaded everyone and everything into the trailer. The second we turned into the Penn National driveway, Metro erupted into a gut-blowing whinny from the trailer. He knew where he was. He remembered the track and he was announcing his return.

Wendy called ahead to Dan Silver, Penn National's Director of Racing and the man who had put all of this together, to let him know that Metro was close. We pulled up in front of the temporary stalls that had been set up for Metro and Pork Chop and found ourselves in the middle of a greeting party of about ten people. I saw security officers, men with shovels waiting to clean out the horse trailer after we unloaded the horses, and Dan hovering with camera in hand.

Metro backed out of the trailer first and immediately transformed back into a mighty racehorse. He puffed up to twice his normal size and dusted off a little trot just like he used to do when he was being walked in the paddock before a race. He looked beautiful. Dan snapped a couple of photos and posted one to the track's Facebook page, with the caption, "Metro Meteor Has Arrived."

The horses were ushered into two side-by-side stalls, both ten by ten feet. Each stall had a stall guard, a half-door made of rubber netting that spanned the doorway of each stall. I had requested the stall guards so people could get up close and meet Metro or even touch him if they wanted to.

In front of the stalls stretched a velvet rope, the same kind of rope museums employ to keep people from touching the priceless treasures. A security guard was posted next to Metro's stall to keep the horses safe and to make sure people stayed behind the rope. We'd come a long way from Karen's barn, where Metro was an outcast and was treated like a pariah. Now his equine star was rising and for all the right reasons. This time, he was at the track to inspire and encourage people to help racehorses have a second chance.

I walked Metro around a bit. He wasn't ready for his stall yet, since he was still a little excited and breaking out the racehorse dance at the end of the lead rope. While he pranced around, his head kept turning toward the track. Just on the other side of the waist-high fence was Metro's old workplace and the turf track was like a magnet for his eyes. I walked him around in a circle, but the track hypnotized him and he couldn't summon the willpower to turn away.

After about ten minutes, I decided to get Metro settled in his stall before the crowds arrived. But Metro had other ideas. He walked up to the stall but wouldn't go in. *Hmmm. I'll try backing him in.* Backing up made him concentrate and it worked. Once both horses were in their portable stalls, I began to unload Metro's painting gear. I put his brushes and tubes of paint in a five-gallon bucket. I set up his easel in front of the stall and put a few partially finished paintings on display. Metro would be doing some demonstrations later in the evening.

Both horses stood motionless, leaning against their stall guards and staring at the track just fifty yards away. I imagine Metro and Pork Chop had different memories. Pork Chop hated to run. He hated any activity that didn't involve eating hay or Twizzlers, sleeping or socializing with the barn cat.

Pork Chop had failed, running just six races and finishing close to last each time. He'd retired quickly, when it became clear he wasn't going much of anywhere. He spent the next eight months as a pony horse, assisting racehorses to the starting gate. So for Pork Chop, the track meant work. And work is what he did not like to do.

Metro, however, loved to run and had succeeded at horse racing, amassing that $300,000 war chest.

I was pretty sure if I let both horses out, Metro would blast down toward the track, ready to hop the fence and join the race. Any race. Pork Chop, however, would probably scamper back to the trailer, climb in, put on his sweats, pop open a cold one and wait for his ride home. But since he couldn't get out of his stall, Pork Chop spent the next two hours standing as still as a statue. He never moved a muscle or shifted a leg, as far as I could see. I could almost read his mind. *Maybe if I stand perfectly still, no one will notice me and put me to work.*

About an hour before the first race, people mostly stayed inside to take advantage of the air conditioning and the slots. I looked up at the sun, willing it to hurry up and dip behind the grandstand to give us a break from the 90-degree heat. We had brought box fans to keep the horses cool and I was tempted to go into Metro's stall and share his fan with him.

First I had to set up for the demonstrations. This stall was smaller than his studio back home and I wasn't sure how many people would be able to watch him paint if he was inside. I decided to set up his easel outside the stall so Metro could paint while standing in the doorway, with the stall guard holding him back. *Maybe we'd better try a dry run, to see if this works.*

I offered Metro a dry brush. Nothing. Metro wasn't having any of it. I wiggled it. Still nothing. I waved a horse treat under his nose. But all he could see was the track and he could not take his eyes off it. Painting a picture was currently at the bottom of his to-do list.

"Metro, my man!" yelled a voice. Bob. He hadn't seen Metro since he'd given him to us four years ago and there was a little bounce in his step as he crossed the pavement. On any other day, Bob's greeting would have elicited a friendly nicker. But this time Metro just gazed off into the distance, staring at the track. Bob ducked under the velvet rope and entered Metro's stall to rub and scratch all over him. The Olivas had set up an informational table, hoping to solicit new partners for their racing stable. Bob's wife, Val, taped up a banner on Metro's stall that read, "Retired Renpher Stables Horse, Metro Meteor" in the colors of the Renpher silks.

People began to filter down out of the casino and into the stands. Dozens and then hundreds of race fans wandered by to get their glimpse of Metro, my priceless treasure behind the velvet rope. And then it started to happen—something I'd never seen before and didn't at all expect. People already knew Metro. They'd seen him on TV or read about him in the racing blogs or in the newspapers and they were giddy with excitement.

I was surprised, no, make that shocked, as people stood next to Metro to have their photo taken or reached out to touch his nose. Metro must have had his picture taken a thousand times that day. No one asked who he was or why he was there and he needed no introduction. I knew he was popular. I knew how fast his paintings sold and I had politely turned down hundreds of requests from people who wanted to drive out to Metro's stable and meet him face-to-face. But everyone there seemed to know his story. I understood that Metro was famous, but now I actually got to see how famous he was.

People asked about Pork Chop, too. "This is Metro's bodyguard," Wendy told everyone. He looked the part, standing tall and not moving a muscle. If Pork Chop had been sporting a pair of reflective sunglasses and an ear-piece, he could have easily passed for Secret Service.

Metro stood still, too, providing the perfect photo opp. He stood like a Leonardo da Vinci horse statue, oblivious to everything going on around him. At least statues won't bite their admirers.

I posted a sign on Metro's stall: *Next painting session 5:30*. I'd have an hour and a half to get Metro settled and into a painting mood. But I was beginning to lose hope that he was going to do any painting at all. I remembered Kim's recommendation. She had sent along a vial of sedative to inject into Metro's neck muscle, if needed. The medicine wouldn't put him to sleep, but it would help calm him down. By the time Kim arrived, I'd already given him a couple of doses.

Then it was post time for the first race. In the distance, we could hear the starting gate clang open and the horses pounding down the track toward us. We turned in unison to look at Metro and gauge his reaction as the horses thundered by, heading for the first turn. Metro's eyes followed the pack, his body straining against the stall guard. I could see his body begin to tremble. If Metro could have escaped his stall, I know he would have run across the pavement, jumped the fence and joined the race. I could see it in his eyes and feel it in his bones.

Kim did, too. She quickly grabbed the sedative vial, filled a syringe and injected it straight into Metro's jugular vein. I knew how to give Metro an injection in his neck muscle, but luckily Kim was there to put the medicine straight into his bloodstream so it would take effect faster. It helped and Metro stayed calm the rest of the night, but I was grateful I got to see first-hand how much of a racehorse he still was. It was so exciting for him to be at the track and to see, hear and feel the races once again. His instincts to run and to win were still there, still intact. How much he would have loved to be a part of it again, bad knees and all. Metro was watching other horses do what he no longer could, what he had once done with such strength and power. Then I felt a tinge of regret. Had I done the right thing? *Maybe it wasn't the best idea to bring him back to this place.*

I looked up and saw a crowd of people behind the ropes, cameras and phones in hand, ready to watch Metro paint. I checked my watch. It was time. But I was terrified he wasn't going to paint. Metro was still watching the races and was not at all interested in putting on a show.

I knew I was about to face my biggest fear—standing in front of a crowd of people and giving a speech, just me, with no help from my buddy, Metro. He was the one with the charm, but he wasn't giving any of it away tonight. Feeling like I was on my way to the gallows, with no chance of reprieve, I set up the easel in front of Metro's stall again. The crowd stood, waiting. I could feel their eyes on me. I looked over at Wendy sitting in her lawn chair, hoping for support. She had happily found a stand that sold Margaritas in a juice box and she sat there, straw in mouth, waiting for the show to begin. I was on my own.

"Metro is probably not going to paint tonight, but I will give it a try," I announced to the crowd. Then I handed Metro a dry brush, not even bothering to load the brush with paint, because I knew he wasn't going to take it in his mouth, let alone stroke it on the canvas. And I was right. He didn't. Metro was going to leave me alone to face my fears. Maybe he knew I needed to.

Already drenched in sweat from the heat, I felt myself beginning to sweat more than I thought humanly possible, like a sponge being wrung out. I looked out at the expectant faces, searching for something, anything, to say. I was tongue-tied. Most of them had already heard Metro's story, so what was there left to say? They didn't want to hear about me. I wasn't even sure if they wanted to hear about rehabilitating racehorses. I swallowed hard and tried to breathe. I looked over at Metro, still focused on the track, and then at the easel. *Of course! They want to hear about art. Metro's art. I know something about that. I can talk about that.*

Relief rushed through me as I picked up one of Metro's paintings and began to stammer through a description of how Metro and I painted together. How we built up the painting in layers. How it took several days to complete a painting. As I talked, I noticed people's eyes beginning to turn toward Metro, behind me. I turned too and saw him starting to come back to life. The horse statue that had been standing so still, staring off into space for two hours, now woke up and started to ham it up for the crowd. Maybe he sensed I needed him or maybe he just couldn't resist showing off for people, but I was grateful. I had been going down and Metro had suddenly thrown me a lifeline.

People laughed and snapped photos as Metro stood there, bobbing his head up and down. I explained to the crowd how his head bob had inspired me to think about teaching Metro how to paint. Suddenly, it all clicked. I could talk about Metro and training horses and painting and art. I could do this, because Metro wasn't going to make me do it alone. He was with me and I felt comfortable talking to the crowd, because we were doing this together, just like we made it through Fun Day, the tunnel and the knee problems.

The rest of the night went off without a hitch. Metro greeted his fans energetically and I met and talked to many people. Holding a one-on-one conversation with a stranger was something I had always struggled with. I could never figure out what to say and by the time I did, the opportunity was gone. But now I was finding it easy, because I was talking about Metro.

When it was finally time to go home, we packed up our stuff and pulled the trailer around. Pork Chop went in without any hesitation, but Metro stopped in his tracks at the top of the ramp. He rarely refused to load, but tonight he was different. I backed him down off the ramp and walked him in a large circle. The whole time, his head was turned for one last, long look at the track. I walked him quickly up the ramp again and this time he went right in. Maybe Metro had just needed one last bittersweet moment with his memories.

On the drive home, Wendy and I talked about how stressful the track visit had been for Metro. We agreed this would be his last time at the track. It was too hard on him not to be able to run with the pack as he had in his glory days. He still had his memories, though. No one could take that away from him.

After the appearance at Penn National, news spread about the biggest day in the track's history. I turned down requests for Metro to make appearances at Churchill Downs, Pimlico and Belmont Park, the three tracks that host the races which make up the Triple Crown. Somehow Metro had gone from being a damaged, unwanted, biting and kicking brat to one of the world's most famous horses and an ambassador for racehorse rehabilitation. And all along the way, when I thought I'd been teaching him, he'd actually been teaching me.

Chapter 29

Fields and Woods

"Earth and sky, woods and fields, lakes and rivers,
the mountain and the sea, are excellent schoolmasters
and teach some of us more than we can ever learn from books."

—*John Lubbock*

One day, I took my camera out to the pasture where Metro and Hotshot were playing and snapped away as they jumped, kicked and ran. It was like trying to capture flashes of summer lightning. Hotshot made Metro feel young again and, since Metro was a troublemaker and liked to stir the pot, trouble usually ensued when those two were put out together.

Pork Chop, an aficionado of the quiet, uneventful life, rarely went along with Metro's antics. But Hotshot was born ready to cavort. The two usually started out with a bite fight. Next, Metro spun around and threatened to kick Hotshot, who wheeled around and cantered away with Metro on his heels. The two horses ran and played for the next twenty minutes as they trotted, cantered and galloped around the field, throwing in a few joyous leaps for good measure. Every once in a while, all four of

Metro's feet left the ground as he gleefully kicked out with his hind legs.

Hotshot was young, strong and a hard act to follow. Quarter horses are known for being able to turn on a dime, a crucial skill when separating cattle out from a herd. Playing chicken with a fleeing cow requires a ranch horse to instantly change direction, so he can thwart the cow's escape plan. As he and Metro played tag, Hotshot threw in plenty of sharp turns to try to shake the racehorse on his tail, but Metro answered every quick turn with one of his own.

I reveled in their athleticism and high spirits. The whole time I watched I never saw a hint of a limp or any kind of discomfort on Metro's part. He had usually displayed a slight limp at any gait faster than a walk, but now it was absent.

Ever since Kim gave us the go-ahead to ride Metro again, Wendy had been saddling him up and taking him out for a trail ride a couple of times a week. I envied her being on Metro's back, but I still couldn't bring myself to get on him again. I had mixed feelings; I badly wanted a replay of those earlier, idyllic trail rides with Metro, but I was afraid his newfound health was just a blip and it would soon come to an end again. I couldn't bear having to give up riding him a second time, so I just watched as Wendy rode or Metro played.

One day, Ed pulled up to us on his tractor, taking a break from mowing the track around the edge of the hayfields. He sat and watched the Metro and Hotshot show. "There is nothing wrong with that horse," he said.

"I know."

Ed nodded, then fired up the tractor and went back to mowing.

I stood in the sun, pondering. It had to be true. If I believed my own eyes, I was looking at a horse with four legs that actually worked well enough to dash around with a feisty young quarter horse.

Later that afternoon, I went home and downloaded the photos I'd taken. As I sorted through them, I was amazed. My lens had captured two horses having the time of their lives, but some of the photos of Metro made him look like a different horse from the one I knew. He was electric with life. One photo caught him launching into a midair leap. He must have been three feet above the ground.

I emailed a selection of the photos to Kim and asked her to come out and do a soundness evaluation on Metro as soon as possible. I'd seen him moving and my camera had captured that movement, but I wanted Kim's expert opinion. Maybe it was all just a big mistake. Kim responded quickly that she would come out to the barn the next day. She also mentioned that she had winced when she saw the photos, worrying about the stress on Metro's knees.

During the examination, Wendy rode Metro so Kim could watch him under saddle as he sped up, then slowed down. I watched too, almost positive I would see a limp after his activities of the day before. In the past, those kinds of shenanigans would have made Metro sore for a couple of days. But he still looked perfect.

"How much Bute have you given him today?" Kim asked. Bute is short for *Phenylbutazone,* an aspirin-like medication for horses.

"None." I hadn't given him any Bute for a month. Metro had taken no medications except Tildren since he was diagnosed with the abnormal bone growth ten months prior. If Metro had taken a drug test, he would have come up clean, probably for the first time since his early racing days.

"This is amazing," said Kim. She rated him a 2 on the lameness scale, on a scale of 1 to 5, with 5 being broke-leg lame. During his diagnosis ten months ago, he had been rated a 4, just one grade better than a horse with a broken leg. A 2 was a huge improvement and about as good as it gets for a horse with arthritis and bone chips.

Kim decided to take another set of x-rays, then loaded the new x-ray images side-by-side on her computer with the images taken three months earlier. The results were remarkable. The gaps—the spaces in his joints that allowed him to bend his knees—were back. The old x-rays showed solid white, where bone growth had filled in the gaps. Now we saw big black lines, meaning healthy space right where it was supposed to be. Even the bone chips looked better. I knew them from memory from studying the many previous sets of knee x-rays. Where once they looked jagged and painful, they now looked rounded and translucent. *Are the chips starting to disappear?*

One thing I knew for sure: Metro's knees looked better on the computer screen than they ever had. What I'd been fearing as temporary was starting to look more permanent. Metro was on the road to recovery and I could no longer talk myself out of acknowledging it. Maybe Metro's rediscovered health was here to stay. *Maybe it* is *time for me to get on his back again.*

That night, I had a hard time sleeping. Metro's hold on me was so strong that good news or bad news affected me equally. Good news, like we'd heard that day, opened up a whole new can of worries. *Maybe what we saw was wishful thinking. Maybe Kim was wrong. Or maybe this is just a one-time deal and tomorrow he'll turn up lame again.* I was hopeful but very, very cautious. Where I'm from, miracles are pretty hard to come by.

The next day I went down to the barn, opened Metro's stall door and stood, turned partially away from him. Metro understood this as his cue to walk up beside me, put down his head and allow me to gently strap his halter around his head so we could walk over to the art studio.

But today was different. We were going to get tacked up and go for a ride for the first time in almost a year. As we strolled across the gravel path between the barns, I turned to look at him, hypersensitive to the smallest hint of lameness. My expectation was so strong it would have almost been a relief to see his familiar limp. But I saw nothing, not even a hitch in his step. I took a deep breath. All systems were go.

We stopped at the spot outside Metro's studio where I usually groomed him and I hooked a cross tie onto each side of his halter. As I brushed him down, he threatened to kick me when I brushed too close to his flank. He turned to try to bite me when I placed the saddle on his back and again when I tightened the cinch around his chest. At the mounting block, he stepped sideways just as I reached the top and extended my foot toward the stirrup. I was forced to climb down, reposition him closer to the block and start the mounting procedure all over again. Nothing had changed from our old routine. This was the Metro I remembered, acting like a jerk.

I loved every minute of it.

Metro and I started off slow, just an easy walk around the pastures. He moved smoothly. No limp. When I felt like he'd warmed up, I asked for a trot. I watched for any hint of a head bob, indicating pain. Nothing. I did see Metro tuck his head down into his chest, then fling it high into the air. It wasn't the rhythmic head bob of a horse in pain, but a *damn-this-feels-good* type of head bob.

I could sense the harnessed energy below me and I knew if I gave him the slightest encouragement, he'd take off and run across the field. This was a different Metro from the horse I'd ridden a year ago and I thought about how far he'd come. Just before we left on our trail ride, Kim approached me. "A year ago, if I'd have been forced to guess whether you'd be trail riding him or burying him today, I would not have picked the trail ride," she said.

A deep happiness descended over me, like a column of sunlight across my back. Metro and I had come so far. We trotted to the end of the field and reached the trail-head. I leaned down and rubbed Metro's neck. "Are you ready for some trail?"

He didn't respond and I didn't expect him to. But I knew where he wanted to go. His ears turned forward and his head lifted as his nostrils flared, drinking in the wild and dark beauty before us. Then we stepped out of the field and into the woods.

Chapter 30

Almost Perfect

"Sometimes the heart sees what is invisible to the eye."

—H. Jackson Brown, Jr.

Cody, Foster and Pork Chop reached the end of the pasture, wheeled around and were running back past Metro, who stood watching them. In his excitement, Metro did a little hippity-hop, raising his front legs off the ground and bringing them back down, then kicking out with his hind legs. But he didn't join the others.

I hadn't seen Metro complete one of these mock races in quite a while. Maybe he didn't feel the need to prove he was the fastest horse in the pasture anymore. Or maybe he knew he couldn't.

For the first four years we had Metro, I never saw him lose one of these pasture races. He was the king of the Pasture Derby and usually appointed himself the official starter, recruiter and instigator. He'd trot around, weaving through the herd while snorting and holding his tail high. Soon another horse's tail would lift like a battle flag, then another. After he had two recruits, it was just a matter of time before the entire herd followed Metro, flags waving.

To start the race, Metro would dig in and sprint off with the other horses following. Metro would relax to a canter and let the others pass. Not that his knees hurt—I don't think he felt any pain during these runs—he was just taking up his usual strategic position.

When the time was right, Metro would kick it into high gear and rocket his way through the pack. This is when Metro was at his best and he always looked happiest when he was passing the other horses. The race was over at this point and I'm sure he gave a little *See ya later, chump,* in horse-speak as he passed each one. His competitors would change gears and try to catch Metro, but never could. He was long gone.

Pork Chop and the others continued to circle as Metro watched from his own victory circle in the center of the pasture. Soon they tired out and trotted over to where Metro stood. The four of them lowered their heads in sync and began nibbling grass.

Everything we had done with Metro over the last six years—the trail rides, the groundwork, the grooming—always reminded me there was a mighty racehorse inside his broken body. I could feel the energy and speed radiate out from his fiery core, even when he was standing still. Although we knew Metro's racing days were done and understood his body couldn't take it anymore, Metro didn't. He never accepted it. I felt that, in his mind, he was forever plotting his comeback.

That had finally changed and I believe he knew his racing days were over. The fierce, competitive racing spirit had left his mind and body and he was now a kinder, gentler Metro. Nowhere was this more evident than when he painted with his new part-time assistant, Hailey. Foster, Hailey's pony, was boarded at the same farm and Hailey took a special interest in Metro. Even though she didn't weigh much more than one of his legs, Metro showed a tenderness around Hailey that I hadn't seen before.

Hailey stood in front of his stall and waited while Metro pushed his chest against his stall guard and stretched his neck as far out as it would go, trying to touch his lips to Hailey's face. She tilted her head from side to side as Metro tilted his, mirroring Hailey's movements.

Whenever I asked her, Hailey was always up for painting with Metro and he showed more patience with her than he had with me. He was content to work at her pace, when he would usually be pawing the ground or nipping at my shirt trying to speed me up. Once in a while he nudged her ten-year-old frame with his giant head, sending her reeling to the side. But it was all meant in good fun. Just Metro playing with his new buddy.

We had moved the horses to another barn last winter. A new dressage trainer had moved into Ed's place with her students and high-dollar horses, and she had taken over the day-to-day operations. The manicured trails became overgrown and we saw less and less of Ed, because he was spending more time at his house in Colorado.

Hotshot stayed behind. One of the other boarders had fallen in love with him and offered to purchase him.

We were comfortable that he would be in good hands with her. I never felt right about having another horse, even though Hotshot was perfect. He was everything I had hoped Metro would be. But he wasn't Metro. My horsemanship career would begin and end with Metro and that was as it should be.

Our new barn owner, Kate, was great with horses and she made it her personal mission to put some weight back on our boys. She got them looking healthy and happy pretty quickly. She gave Metro a stall with a space right outside his door that we could set up as his studio. It was the perfect place for a painting horse.

After watching the Metro-less pasture race, I left my spot on the fence and headed to the barn, stopping at the truck to grab an empty duffle bag and the shopping bag full of art supplies from the back seat. Once in the barn, I opened the padded lid to Metro's tack box. There at the bottom, under the bags of peppermints and licorice twists, was Metro's riding tack.

Last week, Kim made it official when she visited and took new x-rays of Metro's knees. Even though I hadn't ridden him in over a year, I knew what she was going to say. I could see it in the way Metro moved. The racehorse was gone. Tildren had given him a respite for a time, but I knew there would be no more comebacks, no more come-from-behind victories.

Kim said Metro's x-rays looked good. We were still keeping the bone growth from coming back and locking up his knees. But this time Metro's arthritis was the problem. It was getting worse.

Kim asked me to run beside Metro in the arena, then trot him on a line. All she said was, "You're right. Don't ride him."

There was no sadness now as I reached down into the tack box, scuffed up from years of use, and removed Metro's bit-less bridle, a helmet and riding gloves. I pulled out the shopping bag and filled the newly empty tack box with tubes of paint and paintbrushes. Metro wasn't done with life; he was just done with *this* part of his life.

I opened the tack room door for only the second time since we had moved the boys to their new home. There on the rack was Metro's saddle, in the same position I had left it eight months ago. A Phillips-head screw stuck out from one side like a sore thumb. It once had held a faux-silver concho, lost on the trail somewhere.

I picked up the lightweight saddle with one hand and walked outside to the truck. Metro was still standing in the field and for a brief second, I thought about climbing on his back and taking one last spin around the arena. *What could it hurt? Just a slow walk around the arena for old times' sake.*

But I knew it wouldn't be the same. Metro would be like any other horse. I'd miss the experience of living on the edge, knowing an accidental squeeze could give Metro the excuse he needed to go racing across the field. Better to leave memories alone than to try and replace them with new ones.

I placed the saddle and duffle bag in the back of the truck and closed the tailgate. Metro's tack would be going in a dark corner of our basement next to his first easel, caked with layers of multi-colored paint from Metro's first year of brushstrokes. Perhaps after Wendy and I leave this earth, whoever cleans out our basement will find these treasures. If they know the story of the painting racehorse from Gettysburg, maybe they will understand their significance. That is all I ever wanted for Metro—for him to be remembered.

I walked down the hill to Metro's pasture and called his name as I reached the gate. "Metro!" He lifted his head in my direction and began trotting toward me. I detected a slight limp just before he slowed to a walk, his bare feet crossing the rocky bottom of the creek that split his pasture in two. He reached the other side and picked up the pace. He always came when I called him. He was never one to make me chase him across the field.

Metro has taken great pride in making our interactions difficult at times, but he also has his own way of making me feel special. From the way he nickers when I enter the barn, to the way he runs across the pasture when I call his name, it's his way of saying, "Yeah, I know I can be an ass, but I still love you. You're my guy."

I buckled the halter over his head and closed the gate behind us. Thankfully, none of his pasture buddies followed Metro, which would have made getting him out more difficult. Metro walked beside me, his legs making a snapping sound caused by the degraded cartilage around his arthritic joints. I asked him about his day but he gave me no answer as I led him into his stall. As I hung Metro's halter and lead rope on the hook by the door, I glanced at the information sheet on the wall. It was a computer printout encased in plastic. Metro's data was filled in with a dry erase marker.

Name: Metro Meteor
Age: 12 *Sex:* G
Color: Bay

Underneath was a section with my phone number. Kim was listed as the veterinary contact. At the bottom was a section titled *Notes* with several lines underneath. In the notes section, written in marker, was the warning:

MAY BITE

Metro is not the perfect horse. If it weren't for the fact that he could paint and had some fame, no one would give him a second glance. No one would want him.

But to me he is perfect. Well, almost perfect. *And that is going to change today.*

Metro has come so far and changed my life in so many ways. His fame has forced me to deal with my own social issues. I can somewhat carry on a conversation with a stranger and I'm comfortable in front of a television camera or talking to a group of people. But as much as Metro has prompted me to deal with my social inadequacies, we still haven't dealt with his. Namely, the biting.

You still can't spend more than thirty seconds near him before he tries to lay his mouth on you. You can't walk in front of his stall without him reaching out and flashing you his pearly whites. Metro does it to everyone, not just me. At the barn, everyone says, "We just love Pork Chop." But no one ever says "We just love Metro." No one labels him as dangerous anymore, but people only tolerate him. He's still "Just Metro being Metro," but I know it's a nice way of saying, "Your horse is an ass."

Metro doesn't bite to be mean and he is not trying to hurt anyone. He just doesn't know that a 1,200-pound horse can break an arm with his teeth. To him, it's just play. But after six years of always keeping one eye on his mouth, I don't want to be his chew toy anymore.

Groundwork was supposed to take care of all this. It cured every other issue and Metro is the most obedient horse in the barn. He'll do anything you ask of him in the arena or on a lead line. When I wiggle my finger slightly, he'll back up twenty feet.

But the training didn't fix this issue and I'm done with this little game. I still have reservations about visitors or taking him out in public, because eventually he will bite someone. Taking care of the biting is the final piece in the puzzle.

Little did I know that the answer was sitting on his painting table, where I'd been staring at it for the last three years. We were in the middle of one particular painting session when Metro impatiently took a nip out of my arm while I was spraying water on his acrylic paints to keep them from drying out. Shocked that he bit me, I turned quickly and sprayed his lips. Metro snapped his head back and stared at me wide-eyed. He didn't look scared; it was more the look of realizing that maybe it wasn't such a good idea to bite me.

I stared at the ugly green spray bottle in my hand and realized that the answer to my final issue with Metro, the biting issue I could never resolve, was nestled in my palm. A ninety-nine cent spray bottle was the last piece of the Metro Meteor puzzle.

Today, my newly discovered key to the universe (also known as my spray bottle) was going to help me erase the **MAY BITE** warning off Metro's stall once and for all.

For the next hour, I put Metro into every situation where he usually tried to take a chunk out of me. I groomed him and every time he turned and showed me his teeth, they got sprayed with a stream of water. I went into his stall and touched him in every spot that usually prompted a reaction. Every time he turned, his lips got misted.

I walked back and forth in front of his stall and when he stretched his neck out and tried to intimidate me, I shot him with a stream of water. I even pretended I was blasting away at Jaws, the infamous villain with the mouthful of metal braces, by doing my best James Bond pose, raising my left arm and shooting from underneath it.

Within an hour, the biting ceased and Metro transformed into a loving horse. Metro had never been a loving horse. He tolerated humans but he always wanted to dominate, to show you he was the boss. Sure, he would let you stroke his head a couple of times, but any more and the teeth would bare. However, after an hour of Spray Bottle Training, Metro was hanging his head out of his stall, letting me rub his face. For ten minutes, I stroked his long nose and ran my hands over his eyes and ears. Metro closed his eyes and soaked it in, enjoying every moment. Not once did he pull away or try to bite.

"See what happens when you let someone love you?" I looked into those white-rimmed eyes.

Now you are perfect.

Appendix

How We Gave Comfort to an Unhappy Ex-Racehorse Who Paints For a Living

The Effects of Regional Limb Perfusion of the Bisphosphonate Tiludronate Disodium On Osteoarthritis in the Equine Carpus

by Kimberly Brokaw, DVM

I first met Metro Meteor and his owners, Ron and Wendy, several years ago. They had just moved to a new boarding facility and wanted me to evaluate Metro's bad knees. Metro is a former racehorse, with many miles of running in his past. Metro had two knee surgeries during his racing days, but his owners now needed other options to keep him comfortable. While Ron and Wendy had no desire for Metro to race, they wanted him to be comfortable for light trail riding.

We discussed several options including oral medications, IV and IM injections and the alphabet soup of joint injection choices (IRAP, PRP, HA, PSGAG, etc.). As Metro was already receiving injectable Adequan and oral Cosequin to help with his arthritis, joint injections were the next option. Soon after our conversation, Metro was sedated, his knees were shaved and cleaned and I injected his knee joints with a steroid, a combination chondroitin/HA (hyluronic acid) product and antibiotic. His owners were instructed to give Metro an anti-inflammatory (Bute) for the next couple of days and then they could take him for a trail ride by the weekend.

I was fortunate enough to be riding with Ron and Wendy the weekend after Metro's injections. Metro was feeling great. He was trying to run, jigging up hills and acting very full of himself. As we were riding through the fields, with Metro chomping at the bit, I was wondering if the joint injections had worked almost too well. I remember another client who banned me from injecting his horse's joints when, after the procedure, the horse felt so good, he ran off with his rider and bucked him off in a field. Luckily, Ron was so pleased to have Metro feeling good that he was willing to put up with the exuberance and added challenge to the ride.

Unfortunately for Metro, the positive effects of the joint injections were short-lived and six months later we were repeating them. Again, after the procedure,

Metro was back to being an energetic former racehorse. Another six months passed and we were repeating the injections again. I took x-rays of Metro's knees to see how much bone change and arthritis was present. It didn't look good for Metro. As expected, his arthritis was worsening. The joint spaces were collapsing and filling with bone. A horse's body doesn't always respond to injury in the most helpful manner and, unfortunately, Metro's knees were not getting better.

Metro had damaged and fractured a couple of the bones in his knees while racing. Although the chips had been surgically removed, the trauma had made him more prone to developing abnormal bone deposits and osteoarthritis. Metro's joint pain, tenderness, stiffness, locking and swelling were due to the degradation of the cartilage and subchondral bone, as well as the growth of bone in abnormal locations of the joints. Metro Meteor's lameness and flexibility were going to worsen as, unlike for people, knee replacements are not currently a feasible option for horses.

Over the next year, the joint injections became less effective. I took a new set of x-rays of Metro's knees. I found myself in the unfortunate position of telling Ron and Wendy that Metro wasn't going to be rideable on most days. His condition had deteriorated and except for when he was having "good days," Metro couldn't even be taken on light trail rides.

Ron asked me if there was anything we could do to help. He'd done enough research on the subject to realize that if Metro's knees continued to deteriorate, we would be looking at having to euthanize him. While most people think that horses can sleep standing up, they can only nap that way. For a good deep sleep, they have to lie down. This means they have to be able to stand up. I have euthanized several horses that have lain down to sleep and then were unable to get back up due to arthritis.

Unfortunately, we had exhausted our options of FDA-approved medications. However, there was a relatively new medication that was being used in Europe. While it was not FDA-approved at that time, I could apply for an import license to acquire the medication and use it for Metro. I explained to Ron that I could find no documentation that it had been used to treat knees. While it had been shown effective for navicular disease and other vets were starting to use it for hock arthritis and ringbone, I couldn't guarantee that it would work. Ron agreed to try the experimental therapy.

Tiludronate disodium (Tildren) can be administered in several manners. It was originally labeled in Europe for IV use for ten days in a row. It came in a box with ten individual vials of 50 mg each that could be individually mixed up and administered as needed. Some veterinarians tried giving all ten vials as a single IV dose. When given as a single large IV dose, there is risk of renal toxicity or acute renal failure as well as colic (severe abdominal pain). In fact, 41 percent of horses in one clinical trial and 44 percent of horses in another trial given a single Tildren dose did show signs of colic. If a horse colics following Tildren, you do not want to give the usual colic medication, Banamine. While Banamine is usually the medication of choice, giving it in this situation can increase the chances of causing kidney failure. Because of these reasons we decided to treat Metro using regional limb perfusions. This would allow us to achieve high concentrations of Tildren around the knee without giving a high total body dose.

Metro was sedated with a combination of detomidine, xylazine and butorphanol medications, so he would not be uncomfortable and resistant during the treatment. A sphygmomanometer was applied just proximally to the carpus and adjusted to 120mm Hg. A single vial of Tildren (50mg) was then mixed with saline and given IV distal to the carpus in the medial palmar vein. The sphygmomanometer was left in place for thirty minutes. We repeated this procedure monthly for three months, taking radiographs before initiating treatment and again following the three-treatment series. The three-treatment protocol was done on one leg at a time. In addition to a physical exam, Metro was also evaluated for lameness using the AAEP scale, as well as having radiographs taken before and after treatment.

At the start of treatment, Metro was a grade 4/5 lame on the AAEP scale on both front legs. Even just standing and flexing his knee for hoof picking or farrier work caused some discomfort. His knees were tender and he resisted palpation, demonstrating his dislike by trying to bite anyone who was near him. Synovitis and capsulitis were present. The radiographs showed exophytic growth at the margins of the articular surfaces, osteophyte formation with protuberances into the joint space and margins and sclerosis in the subchondral area, in addition to large chips and fragments.

Following treatment, Metro showed tremendous improvement. I first noticed Metro was doing better just walking out of his stall. Prior to treatment, you could see soreness at a walk, and he now seemed much more comfortable just walking down the aisle. I prepared to dodge Metro's teeth as I flexed his knee. The teeth didn't come. I continued to palpate his knees, pressing firmly on the joint. Still no teeth. I was starting to think that perhaps this treatment had worked better than I had hoped. While I was hopeful it would be successful, since I couldn't reference any peer-reviewed journals to confirm that the treatment would work, I had my doubts. I had Ron trot Metro down the aisle. He looked good. Metro was led into the indoor arena and put on the lunge-line. At a trot on a circle there was still the occasional head-bob, but overall there was a tremendous improvement. Metro was now a grade 2 on the AAEP scale. I didn't need the x-rays to tell me that this treatment was working. However, we still took them. The subchondral sclerosis had decreased and the osteophytes seemed smoother and less dense.

Prior to the treatments, Metro had been resigned to the easy life. Painting only. No riding. Now I told Ron he could do light riding. No crazy trail rides like the old days, but leisurely walks in the grass or indoors were fine. Since we were getting such good results with the treatment plan, the next step was to come up with a maintenance schedule. We decided to treat each leg on a six-month rotation. There were whisperings that Tildren was going to be approved by the FDA and soon it would be easier to get. While I had been able to import the Tildren from Europe, I still had to jump through a few hoops to get it.

Unfortunately, Tildren's eventual FDA approval turned out not to be the blessing we had hoped for. While the price had come down, it was no longer being packaged in the box of ten 50mg vials. Instead it came in one large 500mg vial. Once the vial was mixed it had to be used immediately. While previously the treatment had cost just under $200 per leg per injection, now one vial was going to cost Ron around $800. Currently we are weighing our options. Due to the risk of colic and renal disease, Ron is reluctant to give the entire vial as an IV dose and I concur with his reluctance to use the higher medication dose.

One option is to use one-tenth of the vial and throw the rest out. While wasteful and costly, this may be the only option if we want to continue using Tildren in the manner that has been successful and safe for Metro in the past. While having a compounding pharmacy mix the Tildren individually has been suggested, the FDA won't allow compounding in this scenario, in that there is an FDA-approved product available at the correct concentration and mode of administration. Cost isn't a legally acceptable reason to compound an animal medication. Either way, we will come up with a solution that continues to keep Metro happily painting and playing in the fields with his friends for as long as possible.

Kimberly Brokaw graduated from the University of Maryland, College Park, in 2004, with a degree in Animal Science. She received her Doctorate of Veterinary Medicine from the Virginia-Maryland Regional College of Veterinary Medicine in 2008. She has worked at the Walkersville Veterinary Clinic since 2008. When not working, Kim enjoys playing with her Chesapeake Bay retrievers and riding her horses, Bart and Ace.

METRO METEOR (USA) b. G. 2003 {4-m} DP = 11-4-5-0-0 (20) DI = 7.00 CD = 1.30 - 27 Starts, 8 Wins, 3 Places, 3 Shows **Career Earnings:** $299,420

Owner: Ron Krajewski
Breeder: Gus Schoenborn Jr.
State Bred: NY
Winnings: 27 Starts: 8 - 3 - 3, $299,420

At 2: 2nd With Anticipation S. (R,Sar,8.5fT)
At 5: 3rd Pebo's Guy S. (Bel,6fT)

Foaled March 13, 2003
Updated (last raced): 11Jun09

CITY ZIP (USA) ch. 1998	CARSON CITY (USA) ch. 1987 [8I]	MR. PROSPECTOR (USA) b. 1970 [8C]	RAISE A NATIVE (USA) ch. 1961 [8]	NATIVE DANCER (USA)	gr. 1950 [IC]
				RAISE YOU (USA)	ch. 1946 *
			GOLD DIGGER (USA)* b. 1962	NASHUA (USA)	b. 1952 [IC]
				SEQUENCE (USA)	b. 1946
		BLUSHING PROMISE (USA) b. 1982	BLUSHING GROOM (FR) ch. 1974 [8C]	RED GOD (USA)	ch. 1954
				RUNAWAY BRIDE (GB)	b. 1962
			SUMMERTIME PROMISE (USA) b. 1972	NIJINSKY (CAN)	b. 1967 [CS]
				PRIDES PROMISE (USA)	b. 1966
	BABY ZIP (USA) b. 1991	RELAUNCH (USA) gr. 1976	IN REALITY (USA) b. 1964 [8C]	INTENTIONALLY (USA)	blk. 1956 [8I]
				MY DEAR GIRL (USA)	ch. 1957 *
			FOGGY NOTE (USA)* gr. 1965	THE AXE (USA)	gr. 1958
				SILVER SONG (USA)	gr. 1957
		THIRTY ZIP (USA) dkb/br. 1983	TRI JET (USA) blk/br. 1969	JESTER (USA)	b. 1955
				HAZE (USA)	b. 1953 *
			SAILAWAY (USA)* b. 1976	HAWAII (USA)	b. 1964
				QUICK WIT (USA)	ch. 1956
HERE COMES NIKKI (USA) b. 1997	THE PRIME MINISTER (USA) b. 1987	DEPUTY MINISTER (CAN) b. 1979	VICE REGENT (CAN) ch. 1967	NORTHERN DANCER (CAN)	b. 1961 [8C]
				VICTORIA REGINA (CAN)	ch. 1958
			MINT COPY (CAN) dkb/br. 1970	BUNTY'S FLIGHT (CAN)	b. 1953
				SHAKNEY (USA)	dkb/br. 1964
		STICK TO BEAUTY (USA)* br. 1973	ILLUSTRIOUS (USA) br. 1965	ROUND TABLE (USA)	b. 1954 [S]
				POSTER GIRL (USA)	b. 1960 *
			HAIL TO BEAUTY (USA) br. 1969	HAIL TO REASON (USA)	br. 1958 [C]
				LIPSTICK (USA)	br. 1961 *
	MISS REPRESENTED (USA) b. 1992	SOVEREIGN DANCER (USA) b. 1975	NORTHERN DANCER (CAN) b. 1961 [8C]	NEARCTIC (CAN)	br. 1954
				NATALMA (USA)	b. 1957 *
			BOLD PRINCESS (USA)* b. 1960	BOLD RULER (USA)	dkb/br. 1954 [8I]
				GREY FLIGHT (USA)	gr. 1945 *
		RIVER GUIDE (USA) ch. 1971	DRONE (USA) gr. 1966	SIR GAYLORD (USA)	br. 1959 [IC]
				CAP AND BELLS (USA)	gr. 1958
			BLUE CANOE (USA) b. 1958	JET PILOT (USA)	ch. 1944
				PORTAGE (USA)	b. 1952 *

Metro's Pedigree. Source: PedigreeQuery.com. © 2015 Select Web Ventures, LLC. All rights reserved.

Lifetime Past Performance for Metro Meteor

Powered By EQUIBASE COMPANY

Owner: Renpher Stable
Trainer: David C Lupo
Owner & trainer as of 06/11/09

Year	Age	Starts	1st	2nd	3rd	Earnings (USA$)
2005	2	5	1	2	0	$51,868
2006	3	7	4	0	0	$112,406
2007	4	7	3	1	2	$117,450
2008	5	6	0	0	1	$16,070
2009	6	2	0	0	0	$1,626
Totals		27	8	3	3	$299,420

Metro Meteor

Bay Gelding by City Zip (98) -- Here Comes Nikki (97) by The Prime Minister (87) -- Bred in NY by Gus Schoenborn Jr. (Mar 13, 2003) (SPR=85; CPI=3.8)

Date #Track		Dist	Run Up	Temp Rail	Splits	Type/Value/Clm	E	Points of Call	Jockey	W		First Three Finishers	Comments	Earned (USA$)
061109 1PEN	gd	5f	40		22^{05} 45^{37} 58^{14}	CLM23.3k/8k	75	2 6 6^{8} 6^{10} $5^{10\frac{1}{2}}$ $5^{8\frac{1}{4}}$	QuinonesAR	116 L	5.70	Lucky Frolic$^{2\frac{1}{2}}$,H F Manix^{nk},Chickn Surprise^{2}	no threat	$660
020609 1PEN	ft	6f	40		22^{34} 45^{79} $1{:}11^{55}$	CLM16.1k/7.5k	79	7 6 $5^{4\frac{3}{4}}$ $5^{3\frac{1}{4}}$ 3^{2} $4^{5\frac{1}{4}}$	RodriguezE	116 L	*3.20	Graded by Results$^{2\frac{1}{4}}$,Riggins$^{1\frac{1}{4}}$,Tormento de Oro$^{1\frac{3}{4}}$	evenly	$966
092108 8BEL	fm	6f		T18	22^{12} 44^{85} $1{:}08^{32}$	(S)AOC51k/50k	94	1 11 $11^{17\frac{1}{2}}$ 11^{12} 9^{8} $9^{5\frac{3}{4}}$	SantiagoV	113 L	9.80	Redefined$^{\frac{3}{4}}$,Of All Times$^{\frac{3}{4}}$,Silver Timber$^{\frac{3}{4}}$	svd ground throughout	$170
081808 6SAR	fm	5½f		T12	22^{85} 45^{39} $1{:}02^{72}$	(S)Mechncvll	91	8 8 8^{6} 8^{6} $8^{6\frac{3}{4}}$ 8^{5}	CoaE	120 L	7.60	Ahvees Destiny^{hd},Canadian Ballet$^{\frac{1}{2}}$,Silver Timber$^{\frac{3}{4}}$	never in contention	$416
071108 8BEL	fm	6f		T18	21^{91} 44^{40} $1{:}08^{21}$	(S)AOC51k/50k	93	1 6 9^{7} 6^{6} $6^{3\frac{1}{4}}$ 4^{3}	PradoES	121 L	*2.35	Five Towns$^{1\frac{3}{4}}$,Elusive Fox^{nk},Inside Info^{1}	willingly	$2,550
... Claimed (by Charlton Baker for Kenneth L. Ramsey, $50000) from Schwartz, Herbert T. and Carol A., trainer: Scott M. Schwartz														
061508 9BEL	yl	6f		T0	21^{93} 44^{84} $1{:}09^{48}$	JaipurG3	102	6 3 $8^{6\frac{1}{2}}$ 8^{7} $8^{10\frac{1}{2}}$ 5^{6}	LuzziMJ	118 L	18.50	First Defence^{hd},Salute the Count$^{\frac{1}{2}}$,Mohegan Sky^{no}	3 wide, by tired ones	$4,899
053108 6BEL	gd	6f		T18	22^{33} 44^{99} $1{:}08^{94}$	(S)PeboGuy	100	4 9 $9^{8\frac{1}{4}}$ 8^{5} $6^{3\frac{1}{2}}$ $3^{1\frac{1}{4}}$	CoaE	122 L	12.00	Cannonball^{no},Redefined$^{1\frac{1}{4}}$,Metro Meteor^{nk}	broke in air, wide	$7,725
050308 7BEL	gd	6f		T0	21^{66} 44^{60} $1{:}09^{66}$	(S)MusicPrnce	91	5 10 $9^{5\frac{3}{4}}$ $9^{6\frac{3}{4}}$ 8^{8} 7^{6}	ElliottS	121 L	4.90	Mohegan Sky^{hd},Silver Timber$^{\frac{1}{2}}$,Southern Prince$^{\frac{1}{2}}$	no factor	$310
092807 8BEL	fm	7f		T18	22^{85} 45^{73} $1{:}20^{96}$	(S)AOC51k/50k	98	3 6 $7^{3\frac{3}{4}}$ $6^{5\frac{1}{2}}$ 2^{hd} $1^{3\frac{1}{2}}$	BejaranoR	122 L	*1.95	Metro Meteor$^{3\frac{1}{2}}$,Theconfidenceman$^{1\frac{3}{4}}$,Shaky Town$^{\frac{3}{4}}$	came wide, drew away	$30,600
091507 5BEL	fm	6f		T0	21^{69} 44^{58} $1{:}08^{18}$	CLM45k/35k	83	6 6 $9^{7\frac{3}{4}}$ $8^{6\frac{1}{4}}$ $6^{2\frac{3}{4}}$ 2^{4}	BejaranoR	120 L	*1.40	Ive Got Speed^{4},Metro Meteor^{1},Lord Louis$^{\frac{1}{2}}$	steadied stretch	$9,000
082307 7SAR	fm	5½f		T18	22^{45} 45^{22} $1{:}02^{56}$	(S)AOC63k/50k	97	7 6 $7^{3\frac{3}{4}}$ $5^{3\frac{1}{4}}$ $3^{\frac{1}{2}}$ 1^{nk}	BejaranoR	121 L	3.35	Metro Meteor^{nk},Citifest$^{\frac{1}{2}}$,Storm N Lightning$^{1\frac{1}{2}}$	gamely on rail	$37,800
080207 9SAR	fm	5½f		T12	22^{75} 44^{42} $1{:}01^{60}$	(S)AOC63k/50k	96	3 3 3^{7} 3^{8} 3^{7} $3^{3\frac{3}{4}}$	BejaranoR	123 L	*2.00	Southern Prince$^{3\frac{1}{4}}$,Storm N Lightning$^{\frac{1}{2}}$,Metro Meteor^{hd}	chased inside, no bid	$6,300
063007 5BEL	gd	6f		T9	22^{39} 45^{15} $1{:}09^{29}$	(S)AOC45k/50k	91	3 5 $5^{8\frac{1}{2}}$ 3^{7} $3^{7\frac{1}{2}}$ 3^{3}	CoaE	123 L	*0.85	Southern Prince$^{\frac{1}{2}}$,Redefined$^{2\frac{1}{2}}$,Metro Meteor^{hd}	inside trip, no rally	$4,500
... Claimed (by Scott M. Schwartz for California Dreamin' Stables, $50000) from Winning Move Stable, trainer: Kim Laudati														
060607 8BEL	gd	6f		T18	21^{83} 45^{30} $1{:}08^{98}$	(S)AOC45k/50k	105	9 2 $7^{10\frac{3}{4}}$ $4^{2\frac{1}{4}}$ 1^{hd} 1^{3}	CoaE	121 L	*1.95	Metro Meteor^{3},Redefined^{4},Southern Prince^{no}	quick outside move	$27,000
050507 7BEL	fm	6f		T0	21^{46} 44^{08} $1{:}08^{87}$	(S)AOC45k/50k	97	4 8 $7^{13\frac{1}{2}}$ $7^{11\frac{1}{2}}$ $6^{9\frac{1}{4}}$ 4^{2}	GarciaA	121 L	*1.10	Southern Prince^{nk},Theconfidenceman^{nk},Prince of Peace$^{1\frac{1}{2}}$	going well late	$2,250
... Claimed (by Gary C. Contessa for Winning Move Stable, $50000) from Obviously NY Stable, trainer: Linda Rice														
110506 8AQU	gd	1⅛m		T0	48^{44} $1{:}13^{88}$ $1{:}43^{94}$	NYSCrmrnt	82	9 7 $4^{5\frac{1}{2}}$ $5^{2\frac{1}{4}}$ $6^{8\frac{1}{4}}$ $7^{11\frac{1}{4}}$	VelasquezCH	118 L	5.00	Red Zipper$^{\frac{3}{4}}$,Pa Pa Da^{3},Classic Pack$^{4\frac{1}{4}}$	no response	$300
102206 9WO	sf	6f		T0	22^{84} 46^{68} $1{:}12^{41}$	NearctcG2	75	6 8 $8^{5\frac{3}{4}}$ $10^{9\frac{1}{4}}$ $8^{12\frac{1}{2}}$ $7^{9\frac{1}{4}}$	VelasquezCH	116 L	10.70	Fast Parade$^{\frac{3}{4}}$,In Summation$^{1\frac{3}{4}}$,Old Dodge^{1}	lacked rally between	$356
092106 9BEL	fm	6f		T9	22^{68} 45^{84} $1{:}09^{16}$	AOC 47k	100	8 6 $7^{6\frac{1}{2}}$ $7^{6\frac{1}{4}}$ $4^{3\frac{1}{2}}$ $1^{1\frac{1}{2}}$	VelasquezCH	120 L	4.80	Metro Meteor$^{1\frac{1}{2}}$,Paskettty^{nk},Bold Decision^{nk}	came wide, clear late	$28,200
082806 1SAR	fm	5½f		T18	21^{39} 44^{52} $1{:}01^{80}$	ALW 50k	100	9 5 $5^{5\frac{3}{4}}$ $5^{1\frac{1}{4}}$ 2^{hd} $1^{4\frac{1}{4}}$	VelasquezCH	119 L	4.00	Metro Meteor$^{4\frac{1}{4}}$,Bogota Bill$^{\frac{3}{4}}$,Payment in Kind^{no}	4 wide move, drew off	$30,000
080606 8SAR	fm	1⅛m		T12	46^{58} $1{:}11^{30}$ $1{:}47^{65}$	NYStallion	78	5 4 $3^{5\frac{1}{2}}$ $4^{1\frac{3}{4}}$ $4^{5\frac{1}{2}}$ 6^{6}	VelasquezCH	121 L	2.50	Classic Pack$^{\frac{3}{4}}$,Oedipus ONeal$^{1\frac{1}{2}}$,One Goodknight^{1}	rated outside, tired	$750
070106 7BEL	fm	7f		T9	22^{42} 44^{84} $1{:}21^{98}$	(S)AOC 45k	92	10 4 $5^{3\frac{1}{2}}$ $3^{5\frac{1}{2}}$ $1^{1\frac{1}{2}}$ $1^{\frac{3}{4}}$	VelasquezCH	118 L	*2.25	Metro Meteor$^{\frac{3}{4}}$,Drinkwater$^{1\frac{3}{4}}$,Buff Naked^{1}	4 wide move, gamely	$27,000
052906 9BEL	fm	6f		T18	21^{64} 44^{73} $1{:}08^{95}$	(S)ALW 43k	87	12 3 2^{1} $2^{\frac{1}{2}}$ 1^{3} $1^{1\frac{1}{2}}$	VelasquezCH	116 L	*2.80	Metro Meteor$^{1\frac{1}{2}}$,Im a Yankee$^{\frac{3}{4}}$,King Glacken$^{2\frac{1}{4}}$	drew clear when roused	$25,800
092505 7BEL	ft	7f			22^{77} 46^{47} $1{:}24^{20}$	(S)BFBongard	42	6 5 $4^{2\frac{1}{2}}$ 6^{3} $6^{21\frac{1}{2}}$ $6^{29\frac{3}{4}}$	VelasquezCH	117 L	6.80	Sharp Humor$^{\frac{3}{4}}$,Trading Pro$^{1\frac{1}{4}}$,Parkhimonbroadway$^{8\frac{3}{4}}$	wide throughout, tired	$2,154
090305 9SAR	gd	1⅛m		T12	50^{41} $1{:}16^{01}$ $1{:}45^{20}$	WAnticpatn	79	10 5 1^{1} 1^{hd} $1^{1\frac{1}{2}}$ $2^{1\frac{1}{2}}$	VelasquezCH	116 L	29.50	Stream Cat$^{1\frac{1}{2}}$,Metro Meteor$^{\frac{3}{4}}$,Immersed in Gold$^{1\frac{1}{4}}$	dug in gamely inside	$13,440
081405 2SAR	ft	5½f			23^{27} 47^{25} $1{:}06^{10}$	(S)MSW 45k	84	7 1 2^{hd} $1^{1\frac{1}{2}}$ 1^{3} $1^{3\frac{1}{2}}$	VelasquezCH	118 L	*0.70	Metro Meteor$^{3\frac{1}{2}}$,King Glacken^{2},Remorse$^{4\frac{1}{2}}$	soon clear, kept busy	$27,000
080105 4SAR	ft	5½f			22^{49} 46^{00} $1{:}05^{89}$	(S)MSW 45k	86	4 3 1^{hd} $2^{\frac{1}{2}}$ $2^{\frac{1}{2}}$ 2^{1}	BejaranoR	118 L	5.90	Whats Your Edge^{1},Metro Meteor^{no},Strummer$^{6\frac{1}{4}}$	dug in gamely on rail	$9,000
070305 2BEL	ft	5f			22^{06} 45^{48} 57^{52}	(S)MSW 41k	42	1 1 $6^{13\frac{1}{2}}$ $7^{10\frac{1}{4}}$ $5^{15\frac{1}{2}}$ 6^{17}	LuzziMJ	118	7.20	One Way Flight^{4},Couth$^{1\frac{1}{4}}$,Trading Pro$^{7\frac{1}{2}}$	bumped backstretch	$274

Workouts: \| Jun-03-09, PEN, 3F, Fast, 0:35.80, H, 1/10 \| May-16-09, PEN, 3F, Fast, 0:36.00, H, 5/66 \| Apr-25-09, PEN, 3F, Fast, 0:36.40, H, 3/49 \| Apr-17-09, PEN, 3F, Fast, 0:38.40, B, 17/28

Minimum Winning Distance: 5 1/2 furlongs
Maximum Winning Distance: 7 furlongs
Average Winning Distance: 6.06 furlongs

equineline.com

In Canada, United States

Horse Racing Facts

From HorseFund.org, a non-profit which educates the public on horse welfare issues

Bred to death: Thousands of Thoroughbreds are bred for racing every year. Depending on the country, only 5 to 10 percent ever see a racecourse. What happens to the others? Unless they are lucky enough to find another career, they are disposed of, typically at a slaughterhouse.

Dying to race: Horses begin training or are already racing when their skeletal systems are still growing and unprepared to handle the pressures of running on a hard track at high speeds. Strained tendons or hairline fractures can be tough for veterinarians to diagnose and the damage may go from minor to irreversible at the next race or workout. Horses do not always handle surgery well and may fight casts or slings, possibly causing further injury. Instead, seriously injured horses are often put down in order to save their owners escalating veterinary fees. In a count by the Associated Press, state racing jurisdictions reported more than 1,200 horse deaths at Thoroughbred racetracks in 2008, some involving breeds other than Thoroughbreds.

Drugged: A variety of legal drugs are used to treat medical issues, as well as enhance performance. Restrictions vary from state to state, as the racing industry prefers to police itself. Common drugs include Lasix (which controls exercise-induced pulmonary bleeding), corticosteroids (for pain and inflammation), phenylbutazone ("Bute," an anti-inflammatory) and morphine. But there are many more out there and drug testing labs cannot keep up with the vast number of illegal drugs trainers use on horses.

Ron's Favorite Resources

DVDS

Clinton Anderson's *Fundamentals* and *Intermediate* Series
Clinton Anderson's *Correcting Problems on the Trail*

BOOKS

Beyond the Track: Retraining the Thoroughbred from Racehorse to Riding Horse by Anna Morgan Ford

How to Think Like a Horse: The Essential Handbook for Understanding Why Horses Do What They Do by Cherry Hill

A fascinating read on equine intelligence is *The Mind of the Horse: An Introduction to Equine Cognition* (by Michel-Antoine Leblanc)

A helpful resource on racing was Glenn Thompson, who wrote *The Tradition of Cheating at the Sport of Kings*

OTHER

Ron's favorite artist is Robert Burridge: www.robertburridge.com

Visit Off Track Thoroughbreds, the first blog to report on Metro's paintings: www.offtrackthoroughbreds.com

Gallery 30 in Gettysburg represents Metro's paintings: www.gallery30.com

Metro's vet is Dr. Kim Brokaw at Walkersville Veterinary, Walkersville, MD

Metro's farrier is Sandy Zeigler: www.shoemyhorse.com

Metro's website is www.paintedbymetro.com

Ron's artwork can be found at www.ronkrajewski.com

About the Authors

Ron Krajewski is a self-taught artist who grew up in the suburbs of Seattle, Washington. Born into a fishing family, Ron spent his teenage summers working and enjoying the beauty of Alaska. A veteran of the first Gulf War, he spent ten years in the Air Force before leaving and pursuing a career in art. Ron specializes in pet portraits, but his favorite paintings are the ones he creates with his horse, Metro. Ron lives in Gettysburg, Pennsylvania, with his wife, Wendy.

* * *

Susy Flory is the bestselling author or coauthor of ten books, including the *New York Times* bestseller *Thunder Dog*. A breast cancer survivor, Susy celebrates life by riding a crazy ex-racehorse named Stetson, hiking in the High Sierras with her husband and adult kids and skiing black diamond runs whenever she can.

Endnotes

1. Pavia, Audrey and Janice Posnikoff, DVM. *Horses For Dummies, Second Edition.* Hoboken, New Jersey: Wiley Publishing, 2005.
2. "Horse Racing — The Chemical Horse," The Horsefund Special Report, http://www.horsefund.org/the-chemical-horse-part-9.php.
3. "No, Not Again!," ESPN Horse Racing, http://espn.go.com/horse/columns/misc/1589423.html.